II1046848

Also by Morgan Spurlock

Don't Eat This Book:
Fast Food and the Supersizing of America

WHERE IN THE WORLD IS OSAMA BIN LADEN?

MORGAN SPURLOCK

RANDOM HOUSE
NEW YORK

Published in the United States by Random House, an imprint of
The Random House Publishing Group, a division of
Random House, Inc., New York.

RANDOM HOUSE and colophon are registered trademarks of
Random House, Inc.

ISBN 978-1-4000-6652-0

Printed in the United States of America on acid-free paper

www.atrandom.com

2 4 6 8 9 7 5 3 1

FIRST EDITION

Book design by Simon M. Sullivan

For Sasha

For always supporting me
For always understanding me
For always being there when I come home
And for not changing the locks.

CONTENTS

WHERE IN THE WORLD
IS OSAMA BIN LADEN?

TERRORIZE ME

Ever since I was a kid, seems like every time I turn on the TV it tells me that I'm supposed to be afraid of something. Growing up in the waning years of the Cold War, it was the Russkies with their great big bombs and funny marching and their hatred of the American way. By the time I was old enough to notice, nobody seriously worried anymore about "nucular combat toe to toe with the Rooskies," as Major "King" Kong put it in *Dr. Strangelove*. Still, when the Soviet Union fell apart in 1990, I thought we were in the clear.

But it wasn't just the crazy freedom-hating Russians that we were told to be afraid of. They topped the hit parade for years, but in my life-time we've been told to panic about all kinds of things. Here are some of them, in no particular order:

Soviet nukes, North Korean nukes, suitcase nukes, nuclear power plants, dirty bombs, shoe bombs, guns, assault rifles, semiautomatic weapons, sarin, anthrax, Ebola, E. coli, Lyme disease, Legionnaires' disease, smallpox, salmonella, dengue fever, Asian flu, bird flu, swine flu, yuppie flu, West Nile virus, the pesticides sprayed on the mosqui-toes that spread West Nile virus, breast implants, AIDS, SARS, SIDS, ADD, ADHD, PTSD, TB, Y2K, EMP, WMD, illegal aliens, drunk drivers, road rage, asbestos, mercury, lead, oil shortages, the national debt, inflation, stagflation, hurricanes, twisters, tsunamis, asteroids, earthquakes, killer bees, killer canines, mad cows, global warming, the hole in the ozone, flesh-eating bacteria, stem-cell research, Franken-food, Halloween, poisoned Tylenol, sex addiction, identity theft, sec-ondhand smoke, Crips, Bloods, neo-Nazis, Satanists, pagans, cults, serial killers, postal workers, Catholic priests, heroin, cocaine, crack co-caine, methamphetamines, club drugs, ecstasy, Special K, day-care centers, retirement homes, hospitals, an epidemic of obesity, an epidemic of teen drug abuse, an epidemic of teen murders, an epidemic of teen suicides, an epidemic of teen gambling, an epidemic of teens having sex, an epidemic of teens having babies, an epidemic of child pornography, missing children, workplace violence, violence against seniors, violence on TV, violence in movies, violent video games, rap videos, rap music, heavy-metal music, Dungeons & Dragons, snuff films, Internet porn, high-voltage power lines, cell phones that explode, cell phones that cause brain cancer, drivers on cell phones, pedophiles on MySpace, the air, water, soil, eggs, ham, fish, peanuts, spinach, and dog food.

And in 2001 fear got a new mascot—a glorious rebranding featuring the godfather of fear, the hardest-working man in terrorism: Osama bin Laden. The attacks of September 11 ramped us up to levels of fear and paranoia I'd never felt in my life. Some of it was justified; I mean, it was the first time since Pearl Harbor that outside aggressors had attacked us on our own soil. But all the media-fanned panics that followed were even scarier than the actual event.

The odd thing is that when you look past the terror of the headlines Americans actually live longer, healthier, safer lives than ever before. Our average life expectancy is 60 percent greater than it was at the start of the twentieth century. Medical science has conquered all sorts of diseases that were once common killers. Violent crime has plummeted in every major city. We're safer in our homes, in our cars, on planes, trains, and bicycles than ever before. And globally, since the end of the Cold War no great military power has really threatened us. As shocking as 9/11 was, it wasn't nuclear war.

But we don't feel safer, do we? In poll after poll, we express our belief that times are more frightening now than they used to be, that people are more dangerous and the world is more violent, that we're so close to the apocalypse that you can smell the brimstone. We're afraid of strangers, we're afraid of our own teenagers, we're afraid of insects, we're afraid of the food we eat and the water we drink and the air we breathe, we're afraid of TV and movies and the Internet, we're afraid of the weather, and we're afraid the earth itself is dying.

Fear is a biological survival mechanism. But there's rational, useful fear, and then there are phobias—illogical, unwarranted fears of imagined or highly exaggerated threats. Take the fear of flying. Flying is a much, much safer form of transportation than, say, driving. In 2004, a representative year, almost 43,000 Americans died in car accidents. That same year, only 600 Americans died in aircraft crashes. Your chances of dying in an aircraft are around one in 10 million, versus one in 7,000 in a car. Statistically, you're far safer during your flight than you are driving to and from the airport. (Your luggage, however, is another story.)

Now, take terrorism. Since 9/11 we've been kept on a constant state of alert—i.e., anxiety—about terrorists. Depending on who's doing the math, the average American civilian's chances of being a victim of a terrorist attack are minuscule—about one in 9 million, according to one estimate. According to the National Safety Council, you have an equal, if not greater, chance of being struck and killed by lightning (6,188,298 to 1) or of being bitten to death by a dog (9,089,063 to 1). Yet the National Weather Service doesn't make you leave your golf clubs at the door when it starts raining, and the NSPCA doesn't have color-coded threat levels for German shepherds.

Let me put it another way: From the Oklahoma City bombing in 1995 through 2005, about 3,200 American civilians died in terrorist attacks, 2,973 of them on the single day of September 11, 2001. In that same period, in round numbers:

- about 700,000 Americans died of heart disease
- roughly 600,000 Americans died of cancer
- nearly 500,000 Americans died in car accidents
- about 200,000 died in homicides
- nearly 150,000 died after falls
- almost 40,000 people drowned
- and more Americans were killed by *police officers*—almost 4,000— than by terrorists.

Despite the infinitesimal chance that the average American will be the victim of a terrorist attack, Osama bin Laden, "the terrorist threat," and the Global War on Terror have turned our entire society upside down and inside out. We've started two wars that we can't seem to end, in which thousands and thousands of people are dying. The United States has committed what many see as war crimes and human rights abuses. We've made a lot more enemies around the world than friends, and by the fall of 2006 more Americans had died fighting the War on Terror in Afghanistan and Iraq than were killed by terrorists from 1995 to 2005.

So why, if the threat is so exaggerated, do we feel so much dread?

Partly because we're told to, over and over and over. We live in what sociologists call a "culture of fear," in which the media, the government, and various special-interest groups keep us in a constant state of anxiety about wave after wave of supposed new threats to our health and well-being. Since Machiavelli's time politicians have known how to use fear to keep people distracted, cowed, and obedient. Bureaucrats use it to justify their budgets and their jobs, TV newspeople use fear as a way to keep our eyes glued to the screen, and special-interest groups use it to keep our donations pouring in.

But since September 11, the government hasn't just kept *us* in a panic; the government *itself* has been in a panic. In 2002, the Bush administration created the Department of Homeland Security, whose very name invokes insecurity, not to mention the odd sound of that word "Homeland." Maybe it should have been called the Department of We Hate You, Osama, and You'll Never Catch Us with Our Pants Down Again! Because the DHS is nothing but a massive restructuring of the same old federal bureaucracy. It's an interdepartmental Frankenstein stitched together from existing agencies, including Customs, the Immigration and Naturalization Service, FEMA, and various parts of the FBI, the Coast Guard, the Secret Service, and the departments of Defense, Transportation, Energy, and Agriculture.

With an annual budget upward of $40 billion, the DHS defends us from terrorists, illegal aliens, drug smugglers, hurricanes, earthquakes, and epidemics. It guards our seaports and coastlines, our farms and reservoirs, and protects us in cyberspace. See, it really is the Department of Disaster Movie Plotlines. It's the DHS that issues those color-coded threat-level advisories and makes us take our shoes off at the airport.

And the DHS is charged with ladling out hundreds of millions of dollars every year in antiterrorism grants to the states. Having few legitimate terrorist targets in their districts but knowing pork when they smell it, many local bureaucrats have gotten very creative. On the list of 77,069 potential terrorism sites nationwide were "1,305 casinos, 163 water parks, 159 cruise ships, 244 jails, 3,773 malls, 718 mortuaries and 571 nursing homes." Specific targets included "the Old MacDonald's Petting Zoo near Huntsville, Ala., a bourbon festival, a bean festival and the Kangaroo Conservation Center in Dawsonville, Ga. . . . the Amish Country Popcorn factory, the Mule Day Parade, the Sweetwater Flea Market and an unspecified 'Beach at End of a Street.' " Ice-cream parlors, check-cashing joints, and tackle shops also made the list.

Meanwhile, the DHS spends about $5 billion a year screening us at airports. But the reality, as *The Atlantic Monthly* noted, is that it's "largely for show. . . . 'The inspection process is mostly security theater, to make people feel safe about flying,' says John Mueller, a political scientist at Ohio State."

Only it doesn't make us feel safer, does it? Take off your shoes! Empty that baby bottle! At Dulles Airport, security personnel ordered a woman to peel her banana. Banana bombs! When fruit and baby formula become potential WMDs, what's next? And who really feels safe? That nursing mother and her child in the seat next to you could be terrorists. She could be carrying liquid explosives in her breasts. How do you know she isn't? Don't rough her up when you arrest her—she might explode.

You think I'm joking? I met a woman who was ordered by an inspector at Newark International Airport to remove the gel inserts from her push-up bra! Just because she's a member of the IBTC (that's the Itty Bitty Titty Committee, for those of you who aren't or don't act like you're twelve), she's a terrorist threat. You'd never see Pamela Anderson getting stopped. Why? Because Pamela Anderson *loves freedom*, 36D times more than that other girl.

These were the thoughts that were running through my head as I sat in front of the TV in January 2006. I flipped through the news channels, hearing all about the dread and despair, thinking about how unsafe everyone felt (a few weeks before this friends of mine canceled a trip to New York because they had heard about potential New Year's plots on New York City), and about how I got cheated out of the relief I felt entitled to when the Cold War ended. Who was to blame for all this fear? Whom could I confront and say, "Enough already. We get it. The world's a scary place. Leave us all alone." Whom did I have to smack to get some peace around here?

And on the news there he was—the man anointed as the father of all our fears these days. The man who torments and inspires millions around the world from an undisclosed location that even Dick Cheney can't find from *his* undisclosed location. The most wanted man on the planet: Osama bin Laden.

This was the guy who wrecked the carefree, post-Communist party the twenty-first century was supposed to be. The one guy who screwed it all up for the rest of us. If this guy is such a big deal, why haven't we caught him? Why haven't we found him? Is he a nine-foot-tall ninja with mind-control powers? Why haven't we spent every resource and hired every person we can to turn over every rock on earth to find him?

I mean, who is this guy? Why does he like to terrorize us? What does he want? Why do people support him?

Despite all the face time he got in the media, I bet most Americans really don't know much about Osama bin Laden. Be honest. Would you pick him as a category on *Jeopardy!*? He's the Most Wanted Man on Earth, the man who single-handedly terrorized the entire United States, and I bet most of us know more about Britney Spears than we do about bin Laden.

Sure, there isn't an American alive who doesn't know what he looks like. With his narrow, sharp face and long nose, his dark eyes and scraggly beard, emerging from a cave in long robes and head wrap with an AK-47 dangling from one hand, he was the very image of the evildoer I'd heard so much about. The poster boy for fanatics. If he hadn't made himself the global enemy of the West, we might have created him.

But what did I really know about him? What did I know about his life before September 11? Where did he come from? Where did he get his ideas? Why did he decide to start Al Qaeda? Why did he make us his enemy? Was he married? Did he have kids? Did they run and hug him when he came home to the cave after a hard day of global jihadism? ("What did you do at work today, Daddy?" "Oh, I terrorized the West." "Cool!") And what was he doing living in a cave, anyway? Wasn't he, like, a multimillionaire? What drove him to give up the cushy life in favor of waging jihad?

For that matter, what the hell is a jihad? What's a fatwa? What do other Muslims think of Osama? Do they all hate us, or is it just a lunatic fringe?

I wanted to know. And I really wanted to know how we got to this point where the United States, one of the most revered and respected countries around, is now one of the most hated on earth. I needed some answers, and I figured other people might, too.

So there it was. At that moment, in January of 2006, I decided that I would do what no one else could. I would take my complete lack of knowledge, experience, or expertise and put it to good use by looking for the most wanted and most dangerous man on earth. And to sniff him out I thought I had to try to *figure* him out. Like Sherlock Holmes getting inside Moriarty's head. Or that chick in *Profiler*.

Maybe I could fix this mess. Maybe not. Maybe he'd agree to a mano-a-mano cage match to settle this thing forever. Maybe not. At the very least, I'd try to tackle the one question no one else could answer: Where in the world is Osama bin Laden?

Four months later. April 2006. Morning. I opened my eyes to see a beautiful blonde staring at me. It was my girlfriend, Alex. She smiled at me as she came into early-morning focus. I believe I smiled back.

"I think I'm pregnant," she said.

I closed my eyes and said to myself, "You're going to open your eyes and find that this is all a dream."

I opened my eyes and there she was, still smiling.

"How do you know?" I asked her. I was pretty awake now. From the groggy borders of deep REM sleep to a heart-pounding post-marathon dry-mouth sweat in 0.24 seconds.

She pulled one of those little plastic urine sticks out from under the covers and showed me the plus sign in the little window.

"But that's only one test," I said. "You can't be sure with just one test."

She reached under the covers again and pulled out five more little EPT sticks, fanning them out in front of my face. My eyes jumped from plus sign to plus sign to plus sign to plus sign to plus sign, then back to her eyes, glistening and anxious.

I couldn't speak. It felt as if I'd swallowed one of those EPTs. I closed my eyes again, and had another quick conversation with myself: "Pull yourself together, man. What did you think was gonna happen? You're getting married in a month anyway. This is what married people do. Well, this and get very out of shape."

I opened my eyes.

"What do you think?" she asked.

"I think we're going to have a baby," I said. I smiled, rolled over, and hugged and kissed her.

But inside, ten thousand questions and ideas and fears had all started welling up inside me. Me. A dad. What kind of father was I going to be? I just got really good at taking care of myself! I mean, I'd made it through all the pre-planning test stages of responsibility that determine parental aptitude. Stage 1: The plants in my apartment were all still alive. Great sign. I could water and care for greenery. Stage 2: The cat. He was still alive and kicking! He didn't look malnourished or neglected or unhappy. He still slept in the bed with me, so he *must* like me! Stage 3: The dog. Dammit! I missed the dog stage. This is *the* most important stage, especially in New York, because dogs are a *real* responsibility. You gotta walk them and play with them and pay attention to them and pick up their doody off the sidewalk. Great preparation for a kid, and I'd missed it. Crap!

"It's okay," I told myself. "You got two outta three. Still very good signs that you can actually handle some responsibility." Only now this little old-person-space-alien-looking thing is going to be coming into my life, and it's going to be completely dependent on me. Me! Scary.

Fudge. I'd already started the ball rolling on my quest for Osama. The ball hadn't rolled far yet, but I was doing extra push-ups, wearing more sensible shoes, and prepping to leave the country in a few months. What should I do now? Stay home with Alex and discover my nesting instincts, or stay on the path to finding His Scariness?

Double fudge! Being a dad meant that I couldn't just think about what was best for me, or my girlfriend. I had to consider the big picture. And what, exactly, was the big picture? I thought . . . I squinted . . . I started to see something. . . .

Now, suddenly, it came into focus. What kind of a world are Alex and I bringing this kid into? He or she will be our responsibility for at least the next eighteen years. It'll be our duty to nurture her, educate her, protect her. Children are like little sponges, soaking up everything you do and say, everything in their environment—all the good and all the bad, from toxic chemicals to toxic emotions. What sort of world will our little SpongeBob see and hear?

A pretty screwy one, to judge by the news. We'd just marked the third anniversary of the invasion of Iraq. We'd gotten rid of Saddam Hussein, but we'd been caught completely by surprise in the aftermath of his removal—and had compounded the chaos with extraordinary blunders of our own.

The cost of our occupying the country had risen to nearly $10 billion a month. Ten billion dollars! A month! How would I explain that to my kid? You could house all the homeless people in America with what it was costing us to be in Iraq in April alone. And what was all that money buying us? Every morning I looked in the papers and saw more slaughter, more chaos.

How was our *other* war, the one in Afghanistan, going?

Don't ask. Though we'd just passed the fourteenth anniversary of the Soviet Union's final retreat from Afghanistan in 1992, the place was still a mess. In March, President Bush had made a "surprise" visit to Kabul, where he promised that we would "help Afghanistan grow its democracy and defend those who . . . can't stand the thought of terrorism. . . . Our desire is to see this country flourish." But all that had flourished in Afghanistan was the Taliban insurgency, Al Qaeda recruiting and training operations, and the poppy harvest.

Iraq and Afghanistan were being called "the frontlines in the Global War on Terror" (also known as the GWOT, pronounced Gee-wot, as in "Gee, wot a predicament we've gotten ourselves into!"). But there were a lot of sidelines in the news. Countries like England, Saudi Arabia, and Pakistan paid for being our allies in the GWOT by becoming targets for terrorists. Pretty much the entire Middle East had seen even more terrorist violence than we had. Israel and the decades-long issue of the Palestinian refugees were still sources of rage for Muslims around the world, and a handy recruitment tool for groups like Al Qaeda. France, where people seem to hate our culture as much as Osama does, had become a major recruiting zone for young extremists.

Was all this trouble really caused by one guy? Or, at least, by the ideas he'd come to symbolize? Somehow, the fact that I had a little bundle of joy (and fear) on the way made it seem even more important that I get out there and try to find some answers. I had to do this—for me, for my family, for the child I was about to have. I had to face the terror. I had to know what kind of world I was about to bring a child into. What kind of father I could be. What hope we had for the future. You know, all that light and fluffy stuff.

And so, with the tentative blessing of my wife-to-be, I set off on the adventure of a lifetime—a trip that would take me around the world in search of someone people say is the Devil himself. As I stared into Alex's eyes after we'd agreed that I wouldn't give up this quest, I remembered something my grandmother used to say to me: Be careful what you wish for, because you might just get it.

CHAPTER 2

I'LL TAKE OSAMA FOR $200, ALEX

Like most Americans, I knew very little about Islam and Muslims. I grew up knowing only one or two Muslims as a child, and I was never even exposed to their beliefs until I went to college. I never learned about their religion in school and knew nothing of its roots or its heritage. Thank you, public education system. My first real exposure was at the University of Southern California, when I met a guy down the hall from me who was a Muslim. It was he who first enlightened me, if you will.

We're supposed to be in a "clash of civilizations" with Islam, right? I know what American civilization is: football, baseball, hot dogs, beer, guns, four-wheelers, Brangelina—and democracy. But what is Islamic civilization, and why are we so down on each other? All I knew growing up was that Muslims believe in Allah, face Mecca when they pray, and don't dig on the swine. (Which would be a bummer for me, since I find it to be sacrilicious.)

After doing a television show about Islam in America for the FX network, I knew a bit more, but not enough. If I was going to go looking for spooky ole Osama, the first step in my journey should be to talk to more Muslims. Learn a little more about some of the basic tenets of Islam. Find out what other Muslims thought of Osama and his ideas. Do they like him, or does he terrorize them, too? How does his version of Islam fit with theirs?

STAGE 1: GET EDUMACATED

I asked Reza Aslan, the Iranian-American religious scholar, journalist, and author of *No god but God* to teach me about Islamic culture. We arranged to meet for lunch in an Egyptian restaurant in Greenwich Village. The walls were covered in red, almost psychedelic prints. We sat on the softly carpeted floor and leaned back on thick pillows. A low table in front of us was covered with small dishes of traditional Egyptian hors d'ouevres, or *mezze*: baba ganoush, hummus, falafel, pita, olives, cheese. In the center of the table, a large glass *shisha* (or hookah, the Arabian predecessor of the dorm-room bong) bubbled whenever one of us took a drag of the apple-flavored tobacco. We were entertained by a belly dancer, a beautiful girl with lustrous black hair and liquid hips, who turned out to be Israeli.

Ah, New York.

I leaned back and asked Reza, "Is this a good representation of Islam?"

He smiled wryly. "This is a good representation of an Egyptian restaurant in New York," he answered.

Oh, well.

When many of us Americans hear the word *Muslim* we think *Arab*. Or we hear *Muslim* and think *terrorist*, since all good Muslims are taught by the Koran to kill infidels, right?

Both images, Reza explained, are wildly inaccurate stereotypes. Although it began in what's now Saudi Arabia, Islam isn't just an Arab religion. There are probably about one and a half billion Muslims in the world now, making it the second-largest religion after Christianity, which has about two billion followers. Together, they represent more than half of the people in the world.

Many Arabs are Muslims, but it is estimated that only about 20 percent of Muslims are Arabs. In fact, a little more than half of all Muslims actually live in South and Central Asia. The country with the most Muslims: Indonesia, where there are more than 280 million. Who knew?

"What's the biggest misconception Americans have of Muslims?" I asked Reza.

"That somehow Islam is this monolithic thing," he said. "Islam is unquestionably the most eclectic, most diverse religion in the history of the world. You can fly from Casablanca to Cairo to Riyadh to Beirut and see vastly different versions of Islam. And yet, at the same time, I think because of some of these very loud voices—particularly voices of extremism and traditionalism that we hear all the time—there is an impression that Islam is this monolithic idea."

When I asked Reza why Islam is so diverse, he said that, first of all, it's because it started in Mecca, which in the sixth century was "a religious melting pot, a city full of Jews, Christians in all their varieties, pagans, Zoroastrians, even pre-Islamic Arab monotheists. It was a place of great and profound religious experimentation."

Kind of like Haight-Ashbury in the sixties, I thought, with its beaded curtains, handmade rugs, and hookahs.

Muhammad took all that religion around him and, through divine inspiration, delivered "not a new message but a new *kind* of message," Reza said. "In fact, over and over again in his preachings, over and over again in the Koran, there is a reminder that what you are hearing is not new. This is the same message that was given to Adam, and to Abraham, and to Moses, and to Jesus, and to all the prophets. The only difference is that this was the first time this message had been given to an Arab people."

But where does Allah come in? I asked him.

"*Allah* is just the Arabic word for *God*," Reza explained, smiling.

See? I was learning things already.

Islam stayed diverse, Reza went on, because it spread out of the Arabian Peninsula with incredible speed, sweeping through North Africa, the Persian Empire, and into Europe in less than a century. People in all those places adapted the new religion to local conditions and practices. To this day there's no central authority, no pope of Islam. Islam is more like Protestantism, with many different variations and regional or personal interpretations. The two major sects within Islam are the Sunni and the Shia, a split that goes all the way back to the years right after the prophet Muhammad died, when his followers became divided over who should succeed him. About 80 to 85 percent of Muslims worldwide are Sunni. Another variant is Sufism, the most mystical strain of Islam.

"So if there's no central authority, no Muslim Vatican, to whom do you turn when you've got a spiritual question?" I asked him.

Traditionally, Reza said, Muslims have looked to local religious leaders for guidance. These include religious scholars, the ulema, who interpret the Sharia, the body of Islamic religious and legal writings. In most Islamic countries, civil courts and Sharia exist in parallel, and the strictness with which Sharia law is observed differs from one to the other. For example, Sharia has been more strictly observed in Iran, Saudi Arabia, and Afghanistan under the Taliban than in other Muslim societies.

"There are things that all Muslims have in common," Reza explained. "What are sometimes referred to as the Five Pillars of Islam. The first is prayer. The Sunnis pray five times a day, the Shiites, or Shia, pray three times a day. All Muslims pray exactly the same way: they all face Mecca. It's a way of connecting not just with every Muslim in the world but with Muslims throughout time, all the way back to the prophet Muhammad."

The second pillar is fasting during the twenty-eight days of Ramadan. The third is the obligation to give alms. The fourth is making a pilgrimage to Mecca at least once in your life.

"The fifth pillar is the only one that is not about action or ritual," Reza said. "It's about belief. It's the Shahada, the profession of faith: 'There is no god but Allah, and Muhammad is the messenger of Allah.' "

"Got it. Let's get back to those voices of extremism within Islam," I said. "Osama has been one of the loudest. All those tapes he made, issuing fatwas, declaring jihad. Which version of Islam does all that represent?"

To understand Osama bin Laden, Reza said, you first have to understand his birthplace, Saudi Arabia. The land where Islam began, and home to the holy cities of Mecca and Medina.

The United States and Saudi Arabia have been friends since the monarchy was established in the 1930s. Americans helped the Saudis exploit their enormous oil riches and modernize their country, and, in return, the Saudis have helped keep Americans in gas-guzzling SUVs, Hummers, and private jets. The two countries have watched out for each other's interests in the Middle East and in global markets. The royal family, known as the House of Saud, and the Bush family have been friends for decades. Saudi Arabia is one of the most Westernized—even the most Americanized—of all Arab societies.

But, at the same time, there's this huge conflict within their society, because Saudi Arabia is home to—and a major exporter around the world of—an Islamic fundamentalist movement called Wahhabism, a source of inspiration for Osama and a lot of other radical jihadists who don't like America or Western influence at all. (Not to be confused with Wasabi-ism, a religious devotion to sushi.) Wahhabism dates back to the 1700s, when a man named Muhammad ibn Abd al-Wahhab began to preach a purist, fundamentalist interpretation of the Koran. In its most radical form, it includes an intolerance toward other religions, especially Judaism—Wahhabist clerics routinely refer to Jewish people as "brothers of apes and pigs." Nice. But extreme Wahhabists even consider other forms of Islam not to be true Islam.

Al-Wahhab came under the protection of a local emir, Muhammad ibn Saud. Between 1902 and 1932, the House of Saud united all of what we know as Saudi Arabia into a kingdom, bringing all the tribes under its political rule and all sects of Islam—Sunni, Shia, Sufism—under Wahhabism. Wahhabism became, in effect, the state religion, taught in all schools, public and private, and at the universities. Since the 1970s, the Saudis have spent billions of dollars of their oil wealth actively promoting the creation of thousands of mosques and madrassas (religious schools) around the world, from Southeast Asia to the United States, to spread Wahhabist teachings.

"No one would have heard of the Saudis or the Wahhabis if it weren't for the fact that the country struck oil," Reza said. "And now this tiny, backward tribe and this antirational, heretical, puritanical sect is essentially in charge of the global economy."

It's as if Jed Clampett, after finding that bubbling crude, had moved into the White House and picked Jerry Falwell as his VP. Scary stuff.

But the relationship between the House of Saud and the Wahhabist clerics has not always been a smooth one, Reza went on. In modernizing their country and exploiting its enormous oil reserves, the Saudi royal family has often come into conflict with the clerics, who stress the need to keep Islam "pure" from modern and Western influences.

Born in 1957, Osama grew up in a household that was right in the middle of these tensions between reactionary Islam and the Westernizing of the Saudi elite. His father, a poor and functionally illiterate immigrant from Yemen, became a self-made billionaire with close ties to the House of Saud. He founded the largest construction firm in Saudi Arabia, working on many projects for the royal family—airports, highways, railroads—to create a modern infrastructure for the country. He was proudest, however, of the restoration work he was commissioned to do on the Grand Mosque in Mecca, the holiest place in Islam, as well as the mosques in Medina and Jerusalem. He was the patriarch of a family dynasty, the Saudi Binladin Group (SBG), when he died in a helicopter crash in 1967. Osama was ten years old.

Despite their father's observance of Wahhabism, most of Osama's roughly fifty-three brothers and sisters (his dad had about twenty-two wives during his life—four at a time, the maximum allowed by Islam—and kept them busy) embraced the Westernizing process and became international jet-setters. His oldest brother, Salem, studied and married in England and vacationed in places like Disneyland. Salem became friendly with both President Reagan—whom he allegedly helped funnel funds to the Nicaraguan Contras—and the Bushes.

Osama, meanwhile, stuck close to the family home in Jeddah, a port on the Red Sea that's a major entry point for pilgrims to Mecca. Instead of studying abroad, he went to an elite local high school, where he may have been first exposed to radical thought in Islamic study groups. Then he attended King Abdul Aziz University in Jeddah, where the faculty was full of ultraconservatives. One of them was a Palestinian, Abdul Azzam, who would become one of Osama's mentors. He filled his students' heads with the idea that Islam was under attack from Western influences and needed to be defended and purified at all costs. "Jihad and the rifle alone," he told them. "No negotiations, no conferences, and no dialogues."

And that, friends and neighbors, is where Osama began to think the thoughts that eventually made him America's Most Wanted. I made a mental note that if I was going to track the man down, maybe one of the places I should look for him was Saudi Arabia. Even if he wasn't there, checking it out might help me get inside his head, and that might help me figure out where he might be.

. . .

Wahhabism isn't the only fundamentalist movement in Islam, Reza explained, and Islamic fundamentalism needs to be understood in the context of a worldwide spread of fundamentalist movements over the past century or so. "What fundamentalism in all religions, whether Jewish, Christian, Hindu, Buddhist, or Muslim, has in common is that it's not an independent ideology," Reza said. "Fundamentalism is a *reactionary* ideology. It needs something to rebel against."

The term *fundamentalism* was actually coined in America, by Protestant evangelicals in the 1920s. They felt that secularism and science threatened their Christian values, and they "reverted to an older, purer form of Christianity, to the 'fundamentals' of their faith."

In the Muslim world—as in the United States, only more so—fundamentalism has not just religious implications but social and political ones as well. People like the Wahhabis and the Taliban in Afghanistan believe that "Islam is not just a religion but a comprehensive code of conduct," Reza said. "It rules not just your relationship with God but your relationship with your neighbors, your relationship with your state."

This outlook doesn't seem so different from the views of many Christian fundamentalists in this country, who advocate the importance of "Christian values" in society and think that the American government should be run according to their beliefs.

To Reza, bin Laden takes Islam's lack of a central authority to radical extremes. He represents a "rabid individualization that is taking place in the Muslim world . . . where people no longer go to their clerics, their mosques, in order to get the answers that they are looking for."

Osama and others like him are the Martin Luthers of Islam, Reza maintained, "because Martin Luther's point was that the church could not define what Christianity meant anymore, only the individual could." And what bin Laden is saying "is that the clerics, the mullahs, the imams, the people who have essentially had a monopoly over the meaning and message of Islam for fourteen centuries, no longer matter. He tells his followers, 'Don't listen to your clerics. Don't listen to your mullahs. They have nothing for you, nothing to offer you. Listen to me.' But you can't say something like that without opening up a Pandora's box in which anyone—with any kind of agenda, whatever their social prejudices may be, however bigoted they may be, however they see themselves and their role in society—now has divine authority to define not just the Scripture but the religion itself."

Luther's Protestant Reformation, Reza noted, led to a century of warfare and social upheaval in Europe. He believes that we're now seeing the same sort of turmoil in bin Laden's Islamic Reformation. And terrorism is a part of that upheaval.

"There is a criminal, dangerous element of extremists and militants throughout the Muslim world, non-state entities like Al Qaeda, who have a global agenda," Reza said. "They are not fighting against America. They are fighting a war against the Devil, they are fighting an angelic war—a cosmic battle between good and evil." Hey, what works for Mötley Crüe . . .

Every time we turn on the TV, we hear that the extremists have declared a "global jihad" against us. *Jihad* is a new word for most Americans—and most of us have no idea what it means. The first time I heard it, or actually paid attention to it, was in the movie *True Lies*, when the terrorists of Crimson Jihad were going to blow up Miami. I asked Reza what it means.

The Koran defines it in two ways, he said. The "greater jihad" is a personal, inner struggle to better yourself, to resist temptation and evil. This leads to a "lesser jihad," which, Reza said, is "the physical struggle to remove injustice from the world and allow a Muslim to worship in freedom." In the Koran it is "spelled out in black and white" that this type of jihad "can only be a defensive strike. You cannot offensively engage in jihad." Furthermore, he said, only a mullah or an imam is supposed to be able to declare a jihad. Not just any angry Muslim.

Terrorist groups like Al Qaeda have taken the concept of jihad out of context and made it their sole focus and mission. "They have created a new kind of religion, jihadism, that ignores every other aspect of Islam—all of Islamic history, the history of diverse Islamic thought, the diversity of Islamic theology—and boiled it down to one element: jihad jihad jihad," Reza explained.

He also believes that in framing the Global War on Terror in the same terms the extremists do—"this cosmic battle between the forces of Christianity and the forces of Islam"—we play right into their agenda.

"We've completely legitimized the vision of the world that this small group of lunatics have—by our own propaganda, by our own rhetoric, by the way we've conducted ourselves in the War on Terror."

"I've decided to go looking for Osama," I told Reza. "Where do you think he is?"

When he got over laughing his head off, he answered, "I think everyone knows where he is. He's on the border of Afghanistan and Pakistan. The Afghans say he's on the Pakistani side, the Pakistanis say he is on the Afghan side."

I made a mental note to put Afghanistan and Pakistan on my itinerary.

"If everyone knows where he is, why haven't we caught him?" I asked.

"I don't think we are looking for Osama bin Laden," Reza said with a shrug. "I don't think he's much of a priority. I think somehow we are under the impression that he has been marginalized, that because his physical movements have been hampered he doesn't mean as much. This is profoundly mistaken. Bin Laden is no longer even a figurehead anymore. He is something far greater than that. He has become a demigod. And, as such, his living, his existence, and our inability to capture and kill him have turned him into a mythic figure. It is very important that we put an end to that image, and do so quickly."

"Yeah, they keep trying that with Freddy Krueger, too, and look how far that's gotten them," I said.

To hear what other Muslims in America could tell me about Osama, I went to the obvious place to further my education and knowledge: a falafel restaurant. Actually, I went to a mosque on the Upper East Side of Manhattan (although I do love falafels). The Islamic Cultural Center, built in the 1990s, was the first mosque to be erected in Manhattan (other mosques had taken over existing buildings), and boy is it a beauty. From the outside, it's a modern translation of Islam's time-honored dome-and-minaret architecture. Inside, it's a cube of pure white, airy and filled with sunlight in the daytime, very restful and meditative.

Before my visit, I did some research and found out that despite its short history the mosque had already been at the center of controversy. Within a couple of weeks of 9/11, the mosque's first imam, an Egyptian, Sheikh Muhammad Al-Gamei'a, was quoted in Arabic media saying some strange and pretty undiplomatic things about America. He declared, "The situation has gotten so bad that Arabs are murdered in the streets," and "If the Americans knew that the Jews carried out the September 11 attacks, they would do to them what Hitler did." He went to Egypt and, saying that he'd received death threats in America, did not come back. It's hard to win friends as a minority that condones genocide.

The mosque's image has improved greatly under the leadership of Imam Omar Salem Abu Namous. A slight, gentle man of seventy-two with gray hair and a beard, Namous took Al-Gamei'a's place on November 1, 2001.

The imam told me, "It's very crucial for Muslims and non-Muslims to have mutual understanding, mutual respect, mutual appreciation, and to treat one another not only as friends but as brothers. There is no other way."

We quickly sang "Kumbaya" together, then I asked him about bin Laden and his effect on Islam. The imam replied that Osama was isolated and out of touch with "the broad masses of Islam nowadays." But he also wished "that the leadership of the United States of America would try to win him over, try to talk nicely to the Muslim nation."

I doubted that the United States would be sending Osama a Pick Me Up Bouquet anytime soon—unless it was ticking. But I wondered how much it would help if the United States tried to show the Muslim nation some love. Maybe send out a goodwill ambassador?

I went into the mosque for the *jumah*, the Friday-afternoon prayer service that is the equivalent of Sunday service at a Christian church or the Sabbath on Friday at sundown at a Jewish synagogue. I joined the men at the entrance as they removed their shoes and lined up in rows on the carpeted floor, facing east toward Mecca. I noticed that a few men wore white robes and caps, but most were dressed casually—in jeans, T-shirts, some in shorts, some dressed for the office. Imam Namous looked down on them from a raised chair on the eastern wall and preached in both Arabic and English. Women were in a separate area, unseen.

After the service, I stood on the mosque's lawn and spoke with some men as they left. Ahmed Qayyum was a stocky young guy with a full black beard and an easy, friendly manner. He said that he emigrated from Lahore, Pakistan, five years earlier.

"I was in West Virginia before I came here," he added.

"West Virginia! Represent!" I gave him a high five and a manly handshake hug.

I asked Ahmed if he thought bin Laden was a terrorist.

"That I don't know, because I have never personally met him," he said. "He didn't even admit that he did the 9/11, you know. God knows who did it. And since I'm not God, and I didn't see who did it, I'm not going to pass any judgment."

And I wasn't going to pass judgment on my Pakistani-West Virginian brother, but I wondered whether Ahmed thought OJ was innocent, too. I was sure I'd seen on the news or read somewhere that Osama had copped to 9/11. That night I went online, and in no time I found a transcript from Al Jazeera of a videotaped message that bin Laden made in 2004:

"People of America this talk of mine is for you and concerns the ideal way to prevent another Manhattan, and deals with the war and its causes and results. . . . I say to you, Allah knows that it had never occurred to us to strike the towers. But after it became unbearable and we witnessed the oppression and tyranny of the American/Israeli coalition against our people in Palestine and Lebanon, it came to my mind. The events that affected my soul in a direct way started in 1982, when America permitted the Israelis to invade Lebanon and the American Sixth Fleet helped them in that. This bombardment began and many were killed and injured and others were terrorized and displaced. . . . And as I looked at those demolished towers in Lebanon, it entered my mind that we should punish the oppressor in kind and that we should destroy towers in America in order that they taste some of what we tasted and so that they be deterred from killing our women and children."

Ahmed, my man, don't tell me you don't know from Al Jazeera.

Actually, I was grateful to Ahmed for getting me to do that bit of research. If Osama was saying that American support for Israel was a big reason for the attacks on 9/11, I figured I should add Israel to my list of places to go look for him. Maybe he was hiding there, disguised as an Orthodox rabbi, plotting a move against public enemy number one.

Rejan Khan, a clean-cut, almost preppy young man in a black Las Vegas T-shirt, was a college student from Pakistan who had been in the United States for five years. When I asked him why he came to this country, he said earnestly, "As everybody says, it is a land of opportunity. You really get paid back for the efforts you put in, and it really is a good country."

Like Ahmed, Rejan told me "some people" were not convinced that bin Laden was connected to the events of September 11. "Some people really, truly believe he has not done it, and some people believe that it is done by the government over here," he said. He cited the film *Loose Change*, which suggests that 9/11 was a conspiracy perpetrated by the government and Wall Street. "So some people really don't believe that he has done it. So if they think that he has not done it, they are of course mad, because why if he has not done it he is targeted? Or the Afghan land or the Iraqi land is targeted?"

At this point Hamza Murtaza, another Pakistani, who came to the United States in 1999, jumped into the conversation. Clearly, the conspiracy-theory talk had fired him up.

"Pearl Harbor was done by CIA," he insisted. I thought this was completely amazing, considering that the CIA didn't come into existence until six years later. "They knew the Japanese were going to attack Pearl Harbor, but if they would have stopped that, then they would not have had their opportunity to use their atomic bomb. . . . So the same things can happen now."

Rejan tried to speak, but Hamza was on a roll, and I felt as if I had stepped into the middle of a conspiracy-theory conference where everyone had drunk the Kool-Aid but me. Hamza turned to that popular chestnut from the world of lunatic conspiracy theory, Jewish global domination, with the United States and Great Britain as the Jews' partners in this evil plot. At least his version didn't include space aliens or anal probes.

As crazy as it was, Hamza's harangue didn't totally surprise me. As a New Yorker, I was already familiar with the conspiracy theory, very popular among Muslims I had already encountered—even educated ones like him—that "the Jews" were responsible for 9/11. Partly, it's based on the totally false urban legend that four thousand Jewish people didn't report for work at the World Trade Center on 9/11 because they had been forewarned.

That night, I also looked up the list of people who died on 9/11. I was sorry I hadn't had it with me when I was at the mosque, because I could have asked Hamza about, "Adler, Aron, Berger, Bernstein, Cohen, Eichler, Eisenberg, Feinberg, Friedlander, Goldstein, Greenstein, Horwitz, Jablonski, Kestenbaum, Kirchbaum, Kleinberg, Levi, Levine, Mayer, Rosenberg, Rosenblum, Rosenthal, Sachs, Safronoff, Schwartz, Shulman, Shwartzstein, Silverstein, Solomon, Steinman, Temple, Weil, Weinberg, Weingard, Weinstein, Weiss, and Zukelman"—all of whom were on the list. Were they just some nice Irish kids doing an honest day's work for an honest day's pay? Can some conspiracy theorist tell me that?

The only guy I spoke to that afternoon who was an Arab, Mohammed Bahi from Algeria, looked the least like anyone's stereotype of a Muslim. With his close-cropped hair and neat, full beard, he could have been Amish.

When I asked his opinion of the War on Terror, Mohammed began by explaining the concept of the ummah, the worldwide community of Islam. "We believe the whole Islamic world is one land—from China and India and Malaysia, all of this is one Muslim land," he said. "So if any foreign enemy comes inside and starts oppressing the people, if any enemy goes inside that Muslim land, it's every Muslim's duty to protect and defend that Muslim land, either verbally, financially, or physically if you are in that country."

What many people define as terrorism he calls resistance. "America made the first aggressive move by its military presence in the Middle East," he said. "I haven't seen Iraqi tanks in New York City, I haven't seen Iraqi jets flying over New York City. No, Saddam just had a bunch of arrows, little tiny missiles, you know, they aren't going to reach America—they aren't going to reach nothing. So okay, Saddam is the enemy. Take Saddam and his family out. But to stay there three years, four years later, to impose on them a way of life which opposes their way of life—this is not how to rule a country."

"The president has said that certain Muslims hate Americans because they hate our freedoms," I said. "Hate our culture. Hate democracy. Do you?"

Most Muslims don't hate the American people or culture, Mohammed insisted. But they *do* hate the American government and its foreign policy. "Why would people in Iraq hate America?" he said. "Is it because you have nice cars, nice buildings? No, it's not. It's because maybe they see American soldiers come into their land, American tanks and planes, and the next day they wake up and they hear a loud explosion and they see their neighbors all dead, and then they see a little American bomb on the floor. Maybe that triggers their hate for America? It's the same if we saw a missile hit the Empire State Building and we look through the rubble and we see a missile from Finland. We are going to be, like, 'Ah, to hell with Finland!' You would see Americans go crazy. 'Finland, let's attack them, let's bomb them!' So this is how Muslims see Americans overseas."

The Finns—I always knew they were trouble. I wondered if I should add Finland to my itinerary. Then again, in that same taped message from 2004, I did see where Osama objected to ". . . Bush's claim that we hate freedom. If so, then let him explain to us why we don't strike, for example, Sweden?"

Hmm, I thought. I bet nobody has looked for him in Sweden. Maybe I should go there?

Nah, I decided, scrapping all of Scandinavia. It's too cold.

CHAPTER 3

THE FEW, THE PROUD, THE JIHADIS

Now I knew a little more about Muslims and Islam than I did before, but to further my edumacation I wanted to talk to some more experts on Osama and the War on Terror.

So I went to Washington, D.C., to meet first with Steve Coll, who wrote *Ghost Wars: The Secret History of the CIA, Afghanistan, and bin Laden, from the Soviet Invasion to September 10, 2001.* That book won him a Pulitzer, and it's probably the definitive book on the Man. If he couldn't point me in the right direction, no one could.

We met in an elementary-school classroom. I jammed myself into a kid's desk, suddenly realizing that I would be doing this again in a few years at parent-teacher conferences. Blond and bespectacled in a blue blazer and chinos, Mr. Coll looked very professorial as he wrote on the chalkboard and unrolled maps of the Middle East and South Asia. I knew I was gonna get schooled.

To understand how Osama went from being a trust-fund baby to a terrorist-in-a-cave, Steve and most other experts say you have to go back to a specific year: 1979. Three events that year rocked the twenty-two-year-old Osama's world and sent him down the path to becoming America's Most Wanted. In February, a student revolution toppled the regime of the U.S.-backed shah of Iran. They took Americans hostage, totally made President Carter look like a wimp on the world stage, and Ayatollah Khomeini established a fundamentalist Islamic republic. It was a big problem that Khomeini and his followers were Shiites, whom Osama had been taught to despise as much as Western infidels. Still, Khomeini had shown that an Islamist revolution was possible, and it was great for Osama, and a lot of other young Muslims, to see some Western ass get kicked.

In November, in Saudi Arabia, a small group of young fundamentalists seized control of the Grand Mosque in Mecca, calling for the overthrow of the royal House of Saud and the eradication of Western influences in the country. Osama wasn't involved, but he cheered from the sidelines. It took a bloody two-week siege by government forces to take back the holy shrine. One of Osama's older brothers, Mahrus, was arrested and charged with aiding the radicals, though he was released for lack of evidence and went back to his job at SBG.

Then, on December 26, 1979, the Soviet Union invaded Afghanistan. The conservative Saudi clerics, who made no distinction between the modern West and the modern East, saw the invasion as an all-out cultural attack on Islam. They urged young Saudi men to go and fight with the Afghan resistance. Osama heeded the call, with his family's blessings.

In the mountainous rebel strongholds along the Afghanistan-Pakistan border, Osama bin Laden was a multimillionaire among poor and peasant fighters—a trustafarian rebel. He took great pains to show that he could endure the same hardships in the field as they did. He joined forces with Abdul Azzam, his radical professor from King Abdul Aziz University, who'd gone to Afghanistan to put his theories into practice and help the anti-Soviet resistance.

Osama proved to be an indispensable source of funding and support for Azzam's rebels, who were known as Arab Afghans. SBG construction equipment was used to dig the system of tunnels and caves that would later became known around the world as bin Laden's mountain hideout. In addition to the family business, Osama and his colleagues received support from the royal House of Saud, and from an informal group of wealthy and elite Saudis called the Golden Chain. The German magazine *Der Spiegel* reported that a secret list of these funders obtained by the CIA in 2002 was "a veritable who's who of the [Saudi] monarchy, including . . . two former cabinet ministers, six bankers and twelve prominent businessmen. The list also mentions 'the bin Laden brothers.' "

Egypt, Pakistan, and the CIA also supported the Afghan and the Arab Afghan rebels. We gave them money, intelligence, weapons, and training to fight the Soviets. In other words, we were on Osama's side back then. We helped create him. Oops.

In Afghanistan during the 1980s, Osama came under the influence of another mentor, Ayman al-Zawahiri. Zawahiri had helped form the radical group Islamic Jihad in Egypt in 1980. (More about them later.) Its goal was to overthrow President Anwar Sadat by any means necessary, which the rebels hoped would spark an Islamist uprising among the people. In 1981, the group assassinated Sadat, but the revolution failed to happen. Many of those involved in the plot were executed, and others, including Zawahiri, were jailed and tortured. Upon his release, he too went to Afghanistan to help the resistance.

In 1989, in the waning months of the war against the Soviets, Azzam and two of his sons were killed by unknown assassins. Some said Soviet agents did it, others that Zawahiri ordered it. At any rate, with Azzam gone, Zawahiri became bin Laden's chief mentor. Together, they began to look past the immediate goal of getting the Soviets out of Afghanistan, which had nearly been realized anyway. They dreamed of expanding the fight to a global jihad, a holy war against *all* the enemies of what they considered to be true Islam—which included not only the infidel superpower the United States, the rest of the West, and the Western-backed Israel, but also any Muslim society that had been weakened and defiled by Western influences. And those, not surprisingly, included Osama's Saudi Arabia and Zawahiri's Egypt.

Learning all this, I made a mental note that maybe I needed to add Egypt to my list of places to look for Osama. It sounded as though he had friends there who might help him hide out.

Osama and Zawahiri formed Al Qaeda (Arabic for "The Base") as the nerve center of their movement. And they determined to fight their holy war by any means necessary, including terrorism.

"Okay," I said to Steve. "Let's get down to basics. Tell me what terrorism is and why a guy like Osama chooses to use it."

Steve defined terrorism as a tactic "used by the weak against the strong to create effects that the weak couldn't otherwise achieve." In the modern age, terrorists "create spectaculars made for television," to reach the widest possible audience. The PLO "sort of invented modern, made-for-TV terrorism," and Osama took that concept and ran with it all the way to 9/11.

Earlier terrorist groups, like the IRA, tried to minimize the number of civilians who might be killed or injured by their actions. The IRA often called in a warning a few minutes ahead of a bombing, so that the authorities could at least try to clear the area of "non-combatants."

"You couldn't afford to alienate too many of your followers or people that were on the fence about your ideas," Steve said. "They were interested, as one of their specialists put it, in a lot of people watching, but not a lot of people dead—maximum political effect, minimum political damage."

Hmm. I wondered if I should put meeting someone from the IRA or the PLO on my list. Maybe, as fellow terrorists, they'd have some insights.

Osama and today's Muslim terrorists have obviously changed the rules. Or, as a movie trailer would say, "*Global Jihad*™: This time there are no rules." Steve believes that's because, unlike the IRA or the PLO, they're not political resistance organizations; they're religious fanatics out to change the world—and change it fast.

"To them, the victims of terrorist violence were legitimate victims," Steve said. "These were nonbelievers, these were people who in some sense or other deserved to die. So in this strain of terrorism its architects were interested in a lot of people watching, but also in a lot of people dead."

I raised my hand. "But don't a lot of Muslims denounce bin Laden's willingness to kill his fellow Muslims? Even on September 11, dozens of Muslims died, and since then I've seen on the news how Al Qaeda and its allies have stepped up attacks in Muslim countries in the Middle East."

Steve explained that bin Laden has used the concept of *takfir* to justify these killings. *Takfir* is a bit like excommunication for Catholics, or shunning for the Amish; it is to declare a Muslim an apostate, a *kafir*— a nonbeliever.

"It's basically a debate about who is a legitimate Muslim and who isn't," Steve said. "Osama bin Laden and some of his colleagues have decided that they are in a position to answer that question. They believe that some Muslim leaders of countries in the Middle East, such as Egypt and Saudi Arabia, have strayed so far from Islam that they deserve to die."

This also helps to justify the incredible Sunni versus Shiite massacres that have been carried out in Iraq in the past few years. To Sunnis, including Osama, Shiites are heretics.

"The IRA and the PLO were eventually persuaded to abandon violence and work for peaceful political change," I said, hoping to show Steve that I wasn't completely ignorant. "Do you think Al Qaeda can be persuaded to do the same thing?"

"The problem with Al Qaeda is that there are clearly elements of the movement that seem beyond politics, that have devoted themselves to a vision of transformation, a vision of religious ecstasy, that is beyond negotiation," he said. "Trying to separate those who will never negotiate and form a kind a death cult from those who are politically aggrieved and may be prepared to accept ordinary politics as a vehicle for their grievances—that's the key. It's really difficult, because within a movement like Al Qaeda there is no parliamentary party, there is no nation-state. It's a global movement that imagines itself to be representative of a community of believers dispersed all over the world."

"If Al Qaeda can't be persuaded to enter a peaceful political process, can we beat them militarily?" I asked.

"You can't win the War on Terror with an army alone," Steve said. "I think the most obvious lesson of the American experience since September 11 is that we have expected pure military force to be the answer to too many questions."

The military strategist in me thought that we might improve the situation by turning every third armored division into a touring basketball team like the Harlem Globetrotters, with teams deployed across the Middle East spreading democracy, goodwill, and Gatorade showers. Hey, you gotta think outside the box sometimes.

It's true that you probably can't negotiate with a messianic fanatic like Osama, Steve said, but what about the millions of peaceful Arabs and Muslims who are attracted to his ideas?

"Why are they persuaded by his argument that the United States is their enemy? We have barely begun to have a conversation among ourselves in the United States about where some of the legitimacy of the grievance may lie. The first step is to stop accusing anyone who raises this question of, essentially, a form of appeasement or treason, which is too often the case in our political culture."

I was disappointed to learn that Steve was a traitor, but I suspected the turncoat might have a point. Would it be possible to ask questions about terrorism without being labeled a "terrorist sympathizer"? I sure hoped so. I'd hate for Guantánamo to be the only stop on my book tour.

I told Steve that I wanted to go look for Osama.

"Keep your head down," he said, laughing. Like Reza, he told me that Osama was most likely in the mountains somewhere along the Afghanistan-Pakistan border.

I was beginning to wonder when someone would answer Rio or the French Riviera.

Since I was in D.C., I tried to get someone at the CIA to tell me where I could find Osama, but no one would talk to me. You know how spies are. They only like to gather information, not give any out.

But I did talk to a couple of *ex*-CIA guys.

In the public eye, Mike Scheuer used to be known only as Anonymous, author of the 2002 book *Through Our Enemies' Eyes: Osama bin Laden, Radical Islam and the Future of America* and the 2004 *Imperial Hubris: Why the West Is Losing the War on Terror.* Mike created the CIA's bin Laden unit, which he named Alec Station after his son, in 1996. He wrote his books anonymously because he was a twenty-two-year CIA veteran and, you know, spies don't generally write insiders' books about our intelligence operations. Especially books like these, which were quite critical.

Since Mike has been the equivalent of the War on Terror's Deep Throat, I decided to meet him in the garage of the Watergate Hotel. He stood in the shadows as the ghostly vision of a Plymouth Duster glided by.

Mike told me there was no good reason why the United States got caught with its pants down on September 11. "It's not that hard," he said. "Follow the words, listen to his words, listen to what he says. Bin Laden has told us what he's going to do and why he's going to do it, very clearly, since 1996. But no one in the White House listened."

"Why not?"

"You have to forget the myths that are said about the White House.

It's really a bunch of not really bright people who got carried away and lost control of the situation and are now riding the whirlwind."

"Don't sugarcoat it for me, Mike," I said. "Tell me what you really think. What is the War on Terror?"

"It's kind of an un-thought-through situation where we try to apply military force without addressing the basic problems, which are our foreign policies. The military force and the intelligence services can hold the ring for a while, but America will lose this war if we continue to pursue the same foreign policies we have pursued over the last thirty years."

"Who's in charge of fighting this War on Terror?"

"I think that's one of the problems, that we don't have anyone quite in charge," Mike said. "The president leads in rhetoric, the military pretty much does as it wants to do, and since the 9/11 Commission they have fractured the intelligence community to such a state that it's largely impotent."

Since the CIA and the FBI are now supposed to cooperate in fighting the War on Terror, I asked Mike about the notoriously poor relations between the two agencies.

"It has always been a very rocky relationship," he said. "We have two different missions. [The CIA's] mission is overseas, and we break laws. The FBI's mission is internal, and they protect laws."

Since 9/11, the FBI has struggled to be less of a Dick Tracy crime-stopper's agency and more of a domestic counterterrorism service. But it still has a long way to go, in everything from hiring more Muslim agents (there were no more than a dozen out of some twelve thousand agents as of October 2006) to teaching agents how to read and speak Arabic (only thirty-three out of the twelve thousand had even a rudimentary understanding of the language).

I was sort of afraid to ask Mike my next question. "So who's winning the War on Terror?"

"Without question, Osama bin Laden and his forces are winning," he said. "The attacks on the United States have been, by and large, received well in the Islamic world—not because they hate Americans but because there is near-universal detestation of our foreign policies. He has also been a very strong leader in an Islamic world that is virtually without leaders. Islamic governments are populated by dictators, tyrants, families that own countries, like Saudi Arabia. And, among all of those, no one will defy the Americans except Osama bin Laden. So his position in this is extraordinarily important. He is a hero in the Islamic world."

"Why hasn't he been found yet?"

"Well, he hasn't been found because we didn't kill him when we had the opportunity to do it—in 1998, 1999, and 2001. He now lives in an area where the mountains are the highest on earth. He lives with tribes that value protecting their guest with their lives. It's very unlikely that any Muslim is going to turn him over to the United States for money."

I hadn't even thought of that! Right now the reward for information leading to the capture of OBL is a stupid amount of money. If I found Osama, Dick Cheney and the Prize Patrol would roll up to my cave with balloons and an oversized check for 25 million smackeroos! Woo-hoo! I could already see the happy-angry-painful-smirk-grin on Dick's face.

"The final cause of why we didn't get him is quite simply Iraq," Mike continued. "Iraq has drained away so many of our resources, both technical and human, from Afghanistan that bin Laden, in the last several years at least, has been under virtually no pressure at all."

"How dangerous is he right now?" I asked.

"He is an extraordinarily dangerous man. Our leaders continue to say that he is isolated, that Al Qaeda is broken, that he can no longer be anything more than a symbol." None of this is true, Mike told me. Osama himself might be in a remote cave somewhere, but he's still inspiring Muslims around the world to join his global jihad.

"Since November of 2005, we've seen cells taken down—two cells in Australia, two cells in London, a cell in Toronto, a cell in Miami, a cell that was planning to attack New York City from outside America." If they weren't directly connected to Al Qaeda, they had all been "inspired to act, to organize, to plan, by the actions of Osama bin Laden and Al Qaeda."

No single person has inspired others to commit so much mayhem since the satanic back-masking on *Blizzard of Ozz*.

"Are there Al Qaeda cells in the United States?" I asked.

"I think we would be foolish to assume that there weren't," Mike said. "The FBI leadership says there is no evidence within the United States, but I think it's very easy for them to fool us."

Great. I wondered if I should look for the Man right here in the States. He'd pick someplace warm and sunny, I'm sure. I could see him downing piña coladas with the Parrotheads in Key West.

Then I spoke to Jerrold M. Post, MD, a psychiatrist. He now teaches political psychology at George Washington University, but he spent more than two decades at the CIA, interviewing captured terrorists and developing profiles of terrorist psychology. And get this—he edited the English-language edition of *The Al-Qaeda Training Manual* (the original Arabic title was *Military Studies in the Jihad Against the Tyrants*). It was found by British agents in 2000 when they raided a suspected Al Qaeda cell in Manchester, England.

Dr. Post gave me a copy to help me get inside the head of the man I was hunting. He said that he thinks Zawahiri himself had a hand in the writing. It starts with quotes from the Koran, then a jihadist pep-rally speech. ("The confrontation that Islam calls for with these god-less and apostate regimes [is] the dialogue of bullets, the ideals of assassination, bombing, and destruction, and the diplomacy of the can-non and machine-gun.") After that it's your basic terrorist trainee's field manual, full of what Dr. Post called "tradecraft"—how to blend into a crowd, how to set up a safe house, how to write in a secret code (cool!), how to assassinate a target crossing a street, and other warm and cuddly things like that.

I asked Dr. Post to explain how Osama and those like him operate. "Terrorism works," he said, "because otherwise normal people are seen committing acts that so horrify, that are so out of the boundaries of human experience, that they are totally transfixing."

"Normal people? Suicide bombers are *normal?*"

Yep, Dr. Post insisted. Terrorists tend to be normal people who get caught up in a movement for different reasons. For example, he said, most of the Palestinian suicide bombers who have massacred hundreds of innocent civilians in Israel over the years are just desperately poor kids, "seventeen to twenty-two years old, uneducated, unmarried, un-employed—really unformed youth." They're recruited from Palestin-ian refugee camps, which he called "terrorist assembly lines."

The suiciders who carried out 9/11, on the other hand, were all adults in their late twenties and early thirties. "A number of them had higher education," Dr. Post said. "Mohammed Atta and two of his colleagues, in fact, were in graduate school at the technical university in Hamburg. They came from comfortable middle-class families in Saudi Arabia and Egypt, and they had been on their own in the West for upwards of seven years, in this buzzing, blooming confusion of a democracy we live in. And yet, while they were simulating blending in, they were carrying within them like a laser beam their mission that they were going to give their lives while taking thousands of others. They were almost like a cult, followers of the destructive, charismatic leadership of Osama bin Laden. They had subordinated their individuality to that group."

That's what makes terrorists so hard to defend ourselves against, Dr. Post said, and what makes what they do so terrifying. They're not raving lunatics, they're sane people—people just like us—who've been persuaded to do insane things.

Dr. Post made me wonder about bin Laden. I mean, under different circumstances we might never have heard of him. The son of a billionaire, with a job for life in the family business. Like his siblings, he could have become just another high-rolling Saudi sheikh, living it up around the world, with four wives, four private jets, four yachts, four whatever. Instead, he came under the influence of radical fundamentalism, first from his teachers at home, then in Afghanistan. He heard the call of the Dark Side, and he went over. . . . And now he is the poster boy for terrorists around the world.

What Dr. Post said made me think something else: Maybe I needed to look for Osama in England, where that training manual was found. Maybe he was there and dropped it. Or he might be in a Palestinian refugee camp, hiding among supporters.

Man, this was beginning to look like a hell of a trip.

So how do Al Qaeda and similar groups get their ideas out to recruits? Increasingly, they're using the Internet. And Evan Kohlmann showed me how easy that is.

He consults on international terrorism for agencies of the U.S. and other governments—for law enforcement, private groups, and the media. His websites globalterroralert.com and counterterrorismblog.org offer daily updates on jihadist activities worldwide. I met him in his apartment, where he sat surrounded by computers.

"These days, the Internet *is* terrorism," he said. "You cannot have terrorism without the Internet. The Internet plays an integral role in terrorist recruiting, financing, spreading propaganda, you name it."

I asked Evan, "Are our intelligence agencies up to the task of tracking all their communications, coordination, and real-world activities?"

He gave me a bleak look. "Agencies like the CIA or the FBI, generally speaking, aren't picking people on the basis of their experience or skills when they assign them to these units. Someone could be assigned to the bin Laden unit at the FBI, and yesterday they were doing bank robbery in Nebraska. . . . It's a bureaucracy that really wasn't designed to fight against a nimble, fast-moving, transnational enemy. Our system was geared to fight the Soviet Union or the Mafia. We've never had to confront an issue like this."

"Yeah," I argued, "but the CIA et al. have all the technology, all the latest gadgets, like on *24*, right? They're monitoring terrorist websites and reading their e-mails and surveilling the heck out them . . . aren't they?"

Evan scoffed. "I dare you, I triple-dog-dare you to find someone in the U.S. government who has that skill set, that capability. Maybe at the NSA [the National Security Agency], *maybe*. At any other agency? Come on. They can't afford this equipment."

"But you just need a guy in a room with a computer and a mouse," I said.

"You're looking at him," Evan said. "That's what I do. I do work that the U.S. government should be doing on its own."

I pointed out that he was alone. Working out of his apartment. Just one smart young guy with a few computers. He could be, you know, running a porn site, building an army of killer robots, or running a massive über-geek game site. But instead he's trying to make sense of everything.

"It doesn't take a jacket and a tie to understand terrorism," Evan countered. "But that's the problem. The focus so far in the War on Terror has been on pomp and circumstance—on speeches and bombing campaigns. It hasn't been about understanding these people and what motivates them and what will stop them."

"Dude, that's what I'm trying to do, too," I said. "So how do you spend your day? How do you track global jihadist activity on a daily basis?"

"It used to be very difficult to find terrorist material on the Internet," he told me. "But these days, I hate to say, it's become almost childishly easy." He turned to one of his computers and tapped the keyboard. A website with flowing Arabic script filled the screen.

"These days, you have chat forums like this one, alhisba.org." He explained that Al Hisba is a major media outlet for Al Qaeda. "What you are looking at here are the latest releases, up-to-date today, of terrorist material—propaganda videos, communiqués, magazines, you name it. This symbol right here is the symbol for the As-Sahab media wing. That's Al Qaeda's media wing in Afghanistan and Pakistan. Videos of bin Laden or Ayman al-Zawahiri or bombings in Afghanistan—that's As-Sahab right there. This right here is Li Baek media, also from Afghanistan. That's the Taliban's media wing."

"So they have their own full media wings?"

"They have their own media *production companies*, never mind media wing. Al Qaeda has multiple media wings. Al Qaeda in Afghanistan has one, Al Qaeda in Iraq has another, Al Qaeda in Saudi Arabia has another, Al Qaeda in Algeria has another."

"Like CNN," I said.

"It's exactly like CNN."

Evan pulled up one of the videos on the Al Hisba site. Suddenly I was looking at terrorists training somewhere out in a rocky, dusty desert.

"This video is called *They Are Coming*," he said. "It depicts Al Qaeda and the Taliban training in Afghanistan. This individual right here is Abu Yahya al-Libi. He's a Libyan Al Qaeda operative who escaped from U.S. custody at Bagram Air Base several years ago. He has since become a major spokesman for these folks. Notice you don't see too many tanks, tomahawk missiles, Patriot launchers."

He was right. All I could see was some guys doing exercises while others shot at painted rocks with rifles. It looked pretty primitive.

"These guys are using bargain-basement tactics, automatic weapons, explosives, AK-47s. Very simple guerrilla tactics. That's Al Qaeda's philosophy—keep it simple, stupid. Don't overthink things, don't make things too complicated. The idea is to flood us with operatives who have all received mid-level training, who are all capable of carrying out mayhem. So when one gets captured there's another one behind that guy."

Evan noted that the video was probably three or four months old. Which meant that five years after the invasion of Afghanistan—one of the major goals of which was to knock out Al Qaeda and Taliban training camps there—here was at least one camp, where a guy we'd once captured was strolling around, basking in the sunshine.

Evan explained that the pre-invasion camps had been larger and more permanent: "This is the new style of terrorist training camp—mobile, simple, small. These camps are essentially jungle gyms in the desert. So you bomb a jungle gym in the desert, so what? They can rebuild this in ten minutes, and they don't have to go to the same place. The beauty of this is that these types of camps can be built not just in Afghanistan and Pakistan. A camp of this size could even be put up here in the United States—and that's what people have tried doing, setting up training camps inside the United States, and sometimes successfully."

"Wait. Terrorist training camps in the U.S.?"

Yep. I looked it up later. In 1989, FBI agents surveilled a group of men who regularly drove from a mosque in downtown Brooklyn to a Long Island firing range, where they took weapons and survival training from an African-American Muslim. They later moved the training to a firing range in Connecticut. Three of them went on to be involved in the 1993 World Trade Center bombing. A fourth, El Sayyid Nosair, assassinated the firebrand Rabbi Meir Kahane in 1990, planned bombings of Atlantic City casinos and bridges and tunnels around New York City, and was also involved in the World Trade Center bombing, for which he was convicted and sentenced to life plus fifteen years.

There was also a farm in Pennsylvania, owned by an American convert to Islam, where both Boy Scouts and Arab terrorists trained in the early 1990s. Several of those men were arrested for plotting to blow up various New York City sites. Four of them were apprehended while mixing explosives in a house in Queens.

Astounding. Alex would be pleased to hear this. I didn't have to travel halfway around the world to find Osama and his followers after all. I could just take a commuter train out to Long Island and still be back in time for dinner.

But that wasn't the plan. I wanted to get out in the world, to see what kind of impact bin Laden and his ideas had in some of these places everyone had been telling me about. To see what kind of world my little SpongeBob was going to be born into. To hear what they *really* thought of the country I love and its foreign policy. That way, when I found the Man's cave we'd have some things to talk about—if he was home when I rang the bell.

That meant I would be going to some dangerous places. Places where a lot of people might not be happy to see a blond, blue-eyed American. Or else they'd be *really* happy to see me, because I'd be such a good target. So if I was going to come back to SpongeBob in one piece, I needed to learn a few things about how to handle myself in those places.

I packed my bags and reported to a "hostile environment training" course just outside Atlanta. The course was run by the AKE Group, a private security company that (according to its website) "has spent over a decade showing multi-national clients how to assess and mitigate risks and stay safe and effective." Sweet. The course I signed up for was called Surviving Hostile Regions, which was perfect, because that's exactly what I wanted to do.

AKE was founded by some British SAS guys (the Special Air Service regiment of the British army, which is like the Special Forces in the United States) who had found much more gainful employment in the private sector. These were the guys I wanted to impart some knowledge to me. I'd seen *Rambo*, like, a thousand times, and had much respect for anybody who could live solely by eating bark and drinking his own urine. That, however, wasn't part of our curriculum.

I was in the class with journalists from CNN, NPR, *Time* magazine, the Voice of America, and the Canadian Broadcast Company, and in addition to the odd desire to go to a place where we could potentially become cannon fodder, we all shared a desire to stay alive. The days when journalists and documentary crews could wave a white hankie and be given a pass through a battle zone are long gone. Truck bombs and roadside bombs don't distinguish among soldiers, civilians, and film-makers. More to the point, journalists and film crews are now targets, potential Daniel Pearls to be kidnapped, tortured, or killed.

The folks running the program made that clear on our first day, showing us terrifying footage of civilians, cameramen, journalists, even children, being shot, blown up, bleeding profusely, dying. It was shock-ing and sickening: the sort of raw war footage they don't show on the news. I was really glad Alex wasn't there to see it.

I learned some interesting things during the next few days. For ex-ample, a major killer of journalists in combat zones is heart attacks. You're a civilian, older, perhaps, and not in the greatest shape, and you're suddenly under tremendous stress, frightened and exhilarated at the same time—boom goes the ticker. We learned CPR—and also that, in most cases, if medics don't show up soon with the defibrillator pad-dles, CPR is useless.

Oh, the things we learned! About compound fractures, bleeding head wounds, and "penetrating chest trauma," colloquially known as a "sucking chest wound." About how to stuff a shotgun wound with gauze, how to apply a nasty anticoagulant called QuikClot, how to use a tourniquet, and how to tell if the person you've just shot up with peni-cillin is having an allergic reaction and going into anaphylactic shock. We learned about small arms and assault rifles, and the ability of body armor to stop projectiles of different velocities. We learned about all the different kinds of bullets, and all the different ways they can pene-trate you, and all the different things they can do to your body. I was es-pecially taken with "frangible rounds"—soft bullets designed to enter but not exit your body, just rattle around inside causing all sorts of may-hem. We learned about rockets and mortars and plastic explosives, and how to take cover when the shooting starts: Hit the ground, don't duck behind that tree. And if you see a crater from an artillery round, jump into it, because the chances are a million to one against another round landing in the same spot.

It was a scary, scary few days. In the evening I'd call Alex, and even though I hinted at only one-tenth of what I was learning, she was completely freaked out. I wasn't even out of the country yet, I was just outside Atlanta, and she was scared. How was she going to cope when I was in Pakistan? I decided that all I could do while I was there was call her every day and tell her that I was safe and how much I loved and missed her. As my grandma told me when I was a kid, "It's hard to be honest without lying."

Yeah, I'm a terrible husband. But, at the same time, I knew that I was doing the right thing. I was anxious, but excited. It could be completely dangerous and stupid, but it could be really great, too.

At least that's what I told myself when I lay awake at night with visions of sucking chest wounds dancing in my head.

CHAPTER 4

ANARCHY IN THE U.K.

I spent September 11, 2006, in a setting that was about as different from my New York City home as you can imagine: the county of Leicestershire, in the heart of England. When you picture the English countryside as quaint little hamlets nestled among gently rolling green hills and pockets of ancient forest, you're seeing Leicestershire. The Hobbits would feel right at home.

Before getting my hunt for Osama under way, I went to the Leicestershire County Cricket Club. Not because I know anything about cricket or particularly like to watch it—it looked like a really s-l-o-w, Alice-in-Wonderland version of baseball to me—but because a very special cricket match was taking place that day: the imams of the local Muslim community were playing the local Christian clergy. The idea, one imam told me, was "to create better community cohesion." They'd previously played a football (soccer) match, and the imams had kicked some fatherly ass, 5-0.

The referees, or whatever they're called in cricket, were a Hindu and a Jewish rabbi. The Hindu joked that he was "not favoring either faith—I'm sitting on the fence." The Christians were hoping for payback after a humiliating football defeat, but from the looks of the two teams—lots of really healthy-looking young men with shiny black beards on the Muslim team, and mostly gray-haired, pink-skinned older Englishmen on the other—I didn't think they had much of a chance.

It was a warm and sunny day, which, given that this was drizzly England, was clearly an indication of "divine intervention," one imam said. He beamed as his team once again beat the pants off the Christians, who took their loss in a proper spirit of interfaith fun and didn't declare a new Crusade at the end of the match.

STAGE 2: HIT THE OSAMA TRAIL

I decided to start my trip in England, rather than jump straight to the Afghanistan-Pakistan border, for a few reasons. One was purely personal: I didn't feel ready to dive straight into the deep end of the terrorist pool. I wanted to start out in a country where I spoke the language and understood the customs. And I still needed some time to practice my bomb-ducking moves.

But that was just me and my comfort level. There are plenty of other reasons that England is a good place to look for Osama. For one thing, did you know that he had an office in London in the 1990s? Steve Coll told me about it. In fact, Osama even wanted to move to England. Blimey! It couldn't have been for the sausages—Osama don't dig on the swine. So what was it?

According to Steve, when the Soviet-Afghan War ended in 1989, Osama returned to Jeddah and took a desk job in the family business. Somehow I don't think he was planning to stay there until his retirement kicked in, but at any rate another big event came along to steer him toward the Dark Side. On August 2, 1990, Saddam Hussein invaded Kuwait, which is wedged between eastern Iraq and northern Saudi Arabia. Bin Laden wrote to the Saudi king, King Fahd, offering to put his seasoned Arab Afghan fighters—whom he called "my mujahideen"—at the disposal of the House of Saud to repel the Iraqis if they decided to invade Saudi Arabia as well. Instead, King Fahd let his old friend George Herbert Walker Bush use Saudi Arabia as a staging area for U.S. ground troops launching Operation Desert Storm.

Osama was both personally insulted that his offer was rebuffed and outraged that the king allowed "Crusader" troops, "the most filthy sort of humans," onto sacred Islamic soil. He was convinced that Desert Storm was just a pretext for a U.S. military takeover of Saudi Arabia. He started to speak out about it publicly. The king was not amused, and had Osama basically put under house arrest in Jeddah.

That was the last straw. Convinced that the House of Saud had completely sold out to the Americans—for Osama, *we* were the Dark Side—he left Saudi Arabia in 1991. He went to Sudan, where he was warmly greeted by the archconservative Muslim government. It was there, over the next few years, that he got serious about Al Qaeda, gathering and training fighters, making plans with Zawahiri, and building a network with other radical Islamists around the world who felt as he did—that the time had come for global jihad. They got the ball rolling with the first bombing of the World Trade Center in 1993, killing six people and injuring more than a thousand. It was just one part of a larger plan of attacks inside the United States that would have included flying a plane into CIA headquarters.

Meanwhile, Osama continued to issue public statements denouncing King Fahd for allowing Saudi Arabia to become "an American colony" and a Crusader garrison. Some of those statements came from an organization he'd started called the Advice and Reform Committee, and were issued from its office in London, which opened in 1994. The Saudis didn't seem to be listening, however, so Osama sent messages they couldn't ignore: a series of deadly truck and car bombings in the Saudi capital of Riyadh.

In 1994 the Saudi government revoked Osama's citizenship and took steps to freeze his considerable assets. His family publicly disowned him. The United States and Saudi Arabia pressured Sudan to expel him and his followers. Osama started looking for somewhere to go. And in 1995, through one of his contacts in London, he applied for asylum in England! The British government turned him down—big surprise—and in 1996 he went back to Afghanistan. But can you imagine how different the world might be now if the Brits had let him in? (Wait, I think there's a movie idea there, or at least a sitcom.)

Reza Aslan gave me other reasons that I should check out the situation in England. The United Kingdom is home to an estimated two million Muslims, out of a total population of about sixty million. Reza argues that, as one of the world's great imperial powers for several centuries, England played a major role in creating the violent, fractured world of today. Wherever they went in the world, the European colonial powers were experts at divide-and-conquer rule, intensifying existing tribal, ethnic, class, or religious differences among their subjects to "curb nationalist sentiment," keeping people separated and unlikely to organize rebellions. The Belgians played the Hutu off against the Tutsi in Rwanda. The French played up class frictions in Algeria. The British set the Hindus against the Muslims against the Sikhs in India, the Catholics against the Protestants in Ireland, and the Jews against the Arabs in Palestine. Cheers, mates!

As the empires crumbled in the twentieth century, local rivalries that had been built up over centuries erupted across the postcolonial globe—in the bloody partition of Hindu India and Muslim Pakistan, in the tribal genocide in Rwanda and Sudan and other new African states, in the Troubles in Northern Ireland, in Israel and Palestine. In fact, the 1960s and early 1970s were like an ethnic-clash-a-palooza, with conflicts spanning the globe. Many nations are still reeling from the conflicts that grew out of that era.

England's colonial chickens came home to roost. The United Kingdom experienced terrorist violence long before the United States did. The IRA was killing British civilians a good three decades before September 11. After 9/11, as Prime Minister Tony Blair made England President Bush's most loyal ally in the GWOT, the British people once again found themselves targets of terrorist attacks, including the July 7, 2005, suicide attacks in London—remembered in the United Kingdom as 7/7. Three subway trains and a bus were bombed, killing fifty-six people (including the four suicide bombers).

What was particularly troubling about 7/7 was the fact that the bombers weren't foreigners, like the 9/11 bombers. They were young Muslim men born and bred in England. Homegrown terrorists. Two of them had taped statements declaring their allegiance to bin Laden. After the bombings, Zawahiri said, "To the British, I am telling you that Blair brought you destruction in the middle of London and more will come, God willing."

So Osama may not have actually moved to England, but his ideas and his influence certainly have. The authorities in England and throughout Europe are very concerned about this development, the spread of extremist beliefs among young people born and bred there. The European edition of *Time* has dubbed them "The Enemy Within" and "Generation Jihad."

As the United Kingdom became as deeply mired in the GWOT as the United States, resentment and protest spread, and calls for Blair to step down increased. In a November 2006 poll, when UK voters were asked which world leaders posed "a great or moderate danger to peace," 87 percent named Osama bin Laden, 75 percent said George Bush, and 69 percent said Kim Jong-Il. (Results may have been skewed by Ahmadinejad's unpronounceable name.) In the same survey, seven out of ten voters said they thought the invasion of Iraq was unjustified.

All of this is why I decided that England was a good place to begin my travels. Britons may have had more experience dealing with terrorist threats, but I wasn't sure they had the situation any more under control. If I (and other Americans) felt scared of the big O-sam, did Britons shrug him off the way they do orthodontia? Or are our more worldly cousins just as worried as we are?

I looked all over London for Osama. Hey, you never know. Maybe he'd sneaked in without an official invitation. I looked for him in Westminster Abbey. I scanned the crowd watching the changing of the guard. I checked out the Tower of London. It seemed like the sort of grim, dark place he might enjoy. I walked around Hyde Park to see if he might be standing on a soapbox, lecturing a crowd about the evils of Western civilization. I heard several wacky Englishmen lecturing about various wacky topics, but no Osama. I looked for him in pubs. Lots and lots of pubs.

I never found him. But since I was in London I looked up a guy I'd been told might give me some helpful clues to what makes the Man tick. Maybe they would help me find him in my next port of call.

Sitting in a conference room in the office building for Members of Parliament, waiting for Shahid Malik, I looked up at a TV monitor in the corner and saw this on the screen:

WEDNESDAY 13TH SEPTEMBER
THREAT LEVEL
SEVERE

It seemed a weirdly appropriate prelude to my meeting with Shahid. In 2005, at the age of thirty-eight, he was elected Labour Party Member of Parliament (MP) for Dewsbury, in West Yorkshire, a region of northern England. Traditionally, you might say West Yorkshire has been England's West Virginia, a poor, hardscrabble coal-mining and factory area. But in recent decades it has also become home to a sizable community of both immigrant and British-born Muslims, like Shahid, who was born and brought up in Burnley, a town not far from Liverpool in Lancashire. In the 2005 election, Shahid's main opponent was also Muslim.

We talked about why "homegrown terrorism" might be more of a problem in the United Kingdom than in the United States. Shahid agreed with what I'd heard from other people—that Muslims in the United Kingdom and Europe have had a much harder time assimilating into the mainstream culture and thriving economically than have Muslims in the United States.

"If you compare the Muslims of the United States with the Muslims in the UK, they are different beasts," he said. "In the U.S., you have Muslims amongst the most affluent, the most educated, the highest percentage of home ownership. In the UK, they're the least educated, the least affluent." The poverty rate among Pakistani and Bangladeshi Muslim children in England is around 60 percent, more than twice the national average.

"You've probably got the best Muslims in the world in America," Shahid went on. "In America, it's easy to be American. In this country, it takes some time. In America, you go there as an immigrant and you can just about say, 'I'm American.' We're a bit different."

The mix of poor whites and poor Muslims in Yorkshire has had some volatile results. Yorkshire has England's highest per-capita concentration of activists in the British National Party, a white supremacist organization (oh, but they don't call themselves white supremacists or racists anymore; they're "ethno-nationalists") that has stepped up its attacks against local Muslims in recent years. Meanwhile, three of the four 7/7 suicide bombers were young Muslims from Shahid's district.

The 7/7 bombings happened just a couple months after Shahid was elected. "It was an incredible shock," he recalled. "If somebody had said to me before the seventh of July, 'You're gonna have suicide bombers in this country,' I would have found it hard to believe. If you had said they were all *homegrown* suicide bombers, I would have said, 'No, never, I don't believe that at all.' It was a wake-up call for me and for everybody else."

"As a Muslim, how do you feel about these people?" I asked him.

"These people didn't reflect or represent Islam," he said. "They only represented evil, and evil has no religion whatsoever." Thinking that all Muslims commit or support terrorism, he said, is like thinking that Timothy McVeigh represented all white, Christian Americans. "But he didn't. He represented evil."

Terrorists and extremists are just the lunatic fringe of Islam, he said. "These people believe that they could kill themselves and kill other innocent people and somehow go to heaven. Now, that's nonsense. They're not martyrs going to heaven. *My* Islam tells me these people are sinners going to hell."

"How should the rest of the Muslim world deal with them?" I asked.

"Condemning these people isn't enough. We've actually got to *confront* them. That means when we hear things that we know aren't quite right, we've got to deal with it. We've got to create zero tolerance. We've got to be very clear that no matter what's going on in the world, violence, terrorism, extremism cannot be justified and cannot be legitimate."

Shahid believes that the key to stopping the spread of extremist ideas in the Muslim community in the United Kingdom is to increase Muslims' social and political integration into the larger society. When Shahid and I spoke in September of 2006, he was one of four Muslim MPs. He compared that with the U.S. Congress, which had *no* Muslim members despite the estimated four to six million Muslims in the United States. Proportionally, he noted, there should be two Muslim senators and eight Muslim representatives. (A couple of months later, we got our first Muslim congressman in history: Keith Ellison, the Democratic congressman for Minneapolis's Fifth District. He was also the first African American congressman from Minnesota.)

Shahid believes that Muslims in America, at least before 9/11, were content to do well, look after their own community, and keep a low profile politically. "There was no real need, as they saw it, to have influence over politics," he told me. "In the UK it was very different, because we were the least achieving, you know, really the underclass. . . .

We don't have the political power, therefore we need more Muslim MPs. We'll get more. In 1997, we had one. In 2001, we had two. In 2005, we had four. In 2009 we'll have eight, in 2013 we'll have sixteen, and at this rate"—he laughed—"in fifty years the whole Parliament will be Muslim!"

Shahid, like most people I would meet on my journey, also quickly offered up his criticism of the United States. He believes there is a gap between what America's leaders say and what they do in the world. "President Bush, for example, when he speaks about freedom and democracy as the way forward—George, I'm 100 percent with you."

Great, I thought. Shahid loves America.

"But you can't be selective in this," he went on. "You can't say that we will make sure we will have a democracy in Iraq, then be dismissive when democratic elections in other places yield results we don't like—for example, when Hamas won control of the government in the Palestinian Authority."

Fantastic, I thought. Shahid hates America.

"I was there with Jimmy Carter," Shahid said, as he began telling me about the Palestinian Authority elections. "Nearly an 80 percent turnout, and you wouldn't believe the scene—it was like a carnival. Unbelievable. More women on the streets than men. Colors flying, kids everywhere, brilliant election result in terms of the process. The result *itself* wasn't one that anybody [in the West] wanted. It's not one that I wanted. But that is the will of the people, as Jimmy Carter said. And then for us to deny them funding—which means that for the best part of nine months they haven't had any pay for civil service—that's a mockery. I remember the pride on the faces of the Palestinians, because they were leading the Middle East in terms of democracy. They really loved that day—but that's the only day they loved. Every single day after that, they really dreaded."

But the real question that everyone asks, especially after an election like that, is can terrorist organizations like Hamas actually become viable, trustworthy political parties? Can extremists really be drawn into the political process? I asked Shahid.

"I served as a commissioner in Northern Ireland following the Good Friday peace agreement," he said. "Who would have said that Sinn

Féin, which effectively was the political wing of the IRA, could form a pact with the government in Northern Ireland?"

I don't know. Maybe Up with People saw it coming, but I'd have to say that's it.

Two of the 7/7 suicide bombers came from the city of Leeds, a short drive from the town of Dewsbury. They grew up in a dreary working-class neighborhood called Beeston Hill, a place that, I was told, was well known for its high unemployment, drug use, drinking, and low expectations. It's a neighborhood where whites and Asians live near, but not with, one another, and street clashes between Asian youths and white tattooed skinheads lead to beatings and stabbings. As educated but directionless young men, the two would-be bombers were as alienated from their British homeland as they were from their parents' Pakistan. Looking for roots and a purpose in their lives, they came to Islam almost like converts—but it wasn't the peaceful, mainstream Islam their parents practiced at most of the city's mosques, which they found boring and too conciliatory. It was the radical, politicized Islam of global jihad, which they learned on the Internet, in Islamic bookshops, and, most surprising, in the juiced-up, testosterone-fueled environment the locals jokingly called "the Al Qaeda gym." No, I am *not* making that up. It was a real gym where radical guys pumped iron, spotted one another, and, in between power sets, plotted global jihad. And here all I ever talked about in the Body Garage back in West Virginia was how good my biceps looked in the Weider Arm Blaster.

Not far from Beeston Hill, the Makkah Masjid, the first mosque built in Leeds and completed in 2003, stands like a fragment of the old empire brought back to the heart of England. It was built, not coincidentally, on the site of an old Christian church that had fallen into ruin. The red-and-tan striped minaret soars over a quintessentially English neighborhood of redbrick Victorian row houses lining narrow streets, their chimneys pointed at the drizzling gray clouds. If Mary Poppins had landed on one of those chimneys, I wouldn't have been a bit surprised. The interior of the mosque is an extraordinarily beautiful and peaceful space, with a high dome pierced by circular windows that would let in streams of sunlight if the sun shone more often in north-ern England. Almost as if to make up for the gloomy clouds outside, the dome, the walls, and the carpets on the floor are all sky blue, and the dome is inscribed with intricate Arabic script.

Imam Asim, a soft-spoken young man who looked like an angel in his brilliant white outfit, told me that since 7/7 he has taken great pains to distinguish the mosque and its constituents from the acts of the two young bombers, which he condemns as contrary to all the principals of Islam. It didn't help that when the BBC ran stories about Leeds in the days after 7/7 it kept showing footage of the Makkah Masjid, which the bombers did not attend. At the mosque, the religious community has been working to show their British neighbors that the negative images of Muslims they see constantly "on telly" are inaccurate stereotypes.

"We're opening the mosque for people to come in," Asim said. "People have seen the mosque from the outside. They've never actually been inside."

"Are people afraid to come in?" I asked him.

"Yeah, I think people are afraid to come in," Asim said. "Even though there are over fifteen hundred mosques in England, and only one mosque so far has been portrayed as being associated with terror-ists." The local bombers attended another mosque in Leeds, he told me. "But the image is so powerful that people are afraid to come in any mosque. We need to dispel those kinds of images and break the barri-ers and reach out to people."

Like Imam Namous in New York, Imam Asim stressed the need for people of all faiths and cultures to reach out to one another, commu-nicate with one another, and work together to save the planet from chaos.

"At the moment, the political climate is such that it's us and them," he said. "And we are on a *Titanic*, a huge *Titanic*. And the ups and downs, the waves of emotions—it's just, you know, some people are rocking it more than others. We need to make sure that it doesn't sink."

As long as I was in the United Kingdom, I decided that I might as well cross over to Northern Ireland for the next phase of my edumacation:

STAGE 3: MEET A "TERRORIST"

Walking with Martin McGuinness among the crosses, headstones, and stone angels in the Derry City Cemetery in Northern Ireland (aka Ulster), I remembered a story I'd read in a biography of him—about how he once eluded a would-be assassin's bullets at a funeral by ducking behind a gravestone. Today, all was quiet and peaceful, the grave markers and the green grass shining beneath a soft and sunny blue sky. No assassins in sight. But that's not to say that McGuinness doesn't still have enemies.

McGuinness explained that one row of white stone crosses we passed marked the graves of "members of the IRA who were killed in active service." The dates of their deaths spanned the 1970s into the mid-1990s—the period known in Northern Ireland as the Troubles, a euphemism that hardly does justice to a quarter century of bloodshed and sorrow.

"Many of our closest friends are buried here," he said. "If the situation in Derry and Ireland had been normal and there wasn't injustice and conflict, these people would have been living about this community now. Married, with their families, living in perfect peace and harmony."

True enough. But I couldn't help wondering how many other graves held people who hadn't been McGuinness's friends but his enemies and victims. I was, after all, walking with the man who was once called "Britain's Number One Terrorist."

He didn't look or speak the way you'd think a terrorist would. A gray-haired, handsome man in his mid-fifties, he looked and spoke more like what he is: a Member of Parliament, representing constituents in Northern Ireland. Yet his party is Sinn Féin (pronounced "shin fane"), the political wing of the Provisional Irish Republican Army. And as a leader of the PIRA from the early 1970s onward, he was definitely associated with years of terrorist activity, and directly or indirectly involved in a lot of killing and maiming. Since several people had spoken to me about the IRA's shift from violence to politics, I wanted to hear McGuinness's thoughts on whether the same thing could happen with groups like Hamas and Al Qaeda.

Many experts say that terrorism is rooted in poverty, alienation, and anger. That was certainly true of the circumstances in which McGuinness grew up. There's a line from the movie *The Commitments*, about how "the Irish are the blacks of Europe," that was particularly applicable to Catholics in Protestant Northern Ireland. They lived in separate ghettos, unemployment was rife, and their voting rights were legally restricted. In 1968, large groups of Ulster Catholics began a series of freedom marches modeled on the civil-rights marches in America. The Ulster police cracked down brutally. By 1969, with riots pitting Catholics against both official security forces and Protestant militia groups, the British army was called in to further suppress Catholic agitation. The IRA (whose origins go back to 1916) and the more radical PIRA reemerged to oppose them.

McGuinness was a Catholic teenager in Derry while this was going on. His radicalization began when the British sent in troops. Like a lot of Catholics in the North, he saw them as an invading army of occupation. In January 1972, on the day memorialized as Bloody Sunday, McGuinness watched as British troops fired on marching Catholics in Derry, killing fourteen of them in the space of fifteen minutes. The PIRA lashed back after Bloody Sunday, attacking British soldiers and Ulster forces throughout the North. At first, they fought with small arms, nail bombs, booby traps, and homemade mines. It was like their own mini-Fallujah. Before long they were smuggling in automatic weapons manufactured in the United States.

By 1973, the PIRA had grown into a full-on terrorist organization. It took the conflict to the British homeland, launching a series of bombings in pubs, subway stations, and other public places, including Harrods department store in London, in which a number of innocent men, women, and children were killed or maimed. It also targeted Britain's political leaders for assassination. In 1979, it blew up the yacht of Lord Mountbatten, Prince Philip's uncle, killing him and two of his children. In 1984, a bomb detonated in a hotel in Brighton, where Prime Minister Margaret Thatcher was meeting with top members of her Conservative Party, killing five people. Thatcher was unharmed.

The madness of attack and retaliation dragged on, year after year after year, and McGuinness was right in the thick of it. In the early 1970s, he quickly rose to a position of leadership in the PIRA. He allegedly planned and directed bombings, gunfights, and assassinations during the Troubles.

Serious peace ·efforts began in 1994, and in 1996 President Clinton sent former senator (and Arab American!) George Mitchell to mediate. The negotiations culminated in the Good Friday Agreement of 1998. Signed by all parties, it provided a basic road map for reorganizing the political situation and addressing civil-rights grievances. By 2006, the PIRA had announced that it had totally "decommissioned" its military force and surrendered its weapons; it now operated solely through its political party, Sinn Féin. There remained some questions about whether this was entirely true, but the consensus was that the organization really had disarmed. (In fact, after the signing of the Good Friday Agreement, the IRA was removed from the U.S. State Department's terrorist watch list.)

In an age when we think *Islamic* whenever we hear *terrorist*, it's amazing to see how much the Provisional IRA—a bunch of white folks in Northern Ireland—prefigured what we see going on today. Just as many Muslims see the U.S. presence in Iraq and Afghanistan, both locals and foreign sympathizers saw the British army in Northern Ireland as an oppressive occupying force; and, like the Sunni versus Shiite violence in Iraq today, the Troubles, at least in part, reflected an age-old religious split between Catholics and Protestants.

The PIRA had perfected the use of car bombs and roadside bombs decades before these became daily facts of life in Iraq. The group also invented its own incredibly cold-blooded version of the suicide bomber, called the "proxy bomb." A man and his family were taken hostage, then the man was strapped behind the wheel of a car filled with explosives and told to drive it to the target. He was informed that if he failed to reach the target his family would be massacred. When the poor man drove up to the designated spot, the explosives were detonated by remote. All that was left of one proxy bomber after he successfully completed his mission was the back of his hand. At least it appeared to be his hand.

As a partner with Sinn Féin's longtime party leader Gerry Adams, McGuinness worked the political angle as well as the military one, and was instrumental in the PIRA's transition from guerrilla and terrorist organization to legitimate political party. He was elected MP for the constituency known as Mid-Ulster in 1997, and reelected in 2001 and 2005. But when we met in September 2006 he had never actually gone to Westminster to sit in Parliament. Like Woody Allen and the Oscars, none of Sinn Féin's elected party members had ever gone, because—as staunch Republicans—they refused to recognize England's rule in Ireland.

"People say you're loved by old women, children, and animals," I commented. "What about everybody else?"

McGuinness laughed. "Well, I think everybody wants to be loved by everybody, but that's not the sort of world that we live in," he said. "It's probably a minority of people who think the work that Gerry Adams and I have been involved in over the last ten years has brought huge gains for society and for themselves."

"People have called the IRA a terrorist organization. Is it?" I asked.

"No. The IRA are freedom fighters. I was one of them for some time at the beginning of the Troubles. I'm proud that I was. Our willingness to stand up against the British army and the British government inspired an awful lot of people in our community, educated an awful lot of people—it's one of the most politically astute communities in all of Europe."

I asked McGuinness if he thought a period of violent resistance is necessary in such situations before the warring parties can move toward a peaceful political resolution.

"When you're involved in a conflict, the predominant thought of those enmeshed in that conflict is survival from day to day," he said. "When you are involved in a conflict over a long period of time, you say to yourself, 'Well, this is my life, this is the way it's going to be, should I live to be sixty, seventy, eighty years of age.' " (In America, we get to look forward to hip surgery in our eighties, although running from bombs might be better exercise than shuffling your walker down the hall to watch *Golden Girls* reruns.) As that thought sinks in, he said, you begin to think about the need to "break this cycle of conflict." Which is what he and Adams began trying to do, by offering cease-fires and asking the British and the Protestants to sit down and negotiate.

"One of the things that we hear from President Bush all the time is that he won't negotiate with terrorists," I said.

"Margaret Thatcher used to say that all the time. I think people who are not prepared to talk or to resolve conflict through peaceful and democratic means are absolutely doomed to failure."

Along with becoming Members of Parliament—Adams represents West Belfast—one of the most remarkable developments in the careers of the two Sinn Féin leaders is that in recent years they have been asked to advise on peaceful conflict resolutions in other parts of the world that are experiencing their own Troubles. When McGuinness and I spoke, Adams had just returned from a trip to the Palestinian Authority, where he'd been invited by the president, Mahmoud Abbas.

During the year, McGuinness had made his own consulting trip to Spain, where he met with the Basque separatist organization ETA, and had twice been to Sri Lanka at the invitation of President Kumaratunga to talk to the separatist Tamil Tigers, who've been called the most organized guerrilla army in the world.

"When you meet with these groups, what do you tell them?" I asked.

"We don't go there because we think we can solve the problems of Sri Lanka or the problems of the Middle East," McGuinness said. "Our message is very consistent: 'People can fight here for another fifty years. How many people are gonna die in those fifty years? Why not recognize that there cannot be a military victory? That the only way forward is to have a dialogue and negotiations?' We don't go there to put down a template. All we say is 'This is what we did in Ireland. If that helps you in any way, then we are overjoyed.'"

And what about Osama and Al Qaeda? Did McGuinness think they could be brought to the bargaining table?

"First," he said, "I have to say that I think the Middle East [meaning the Israeli-Palestinian conflict] needs to be resolved, and the Western powers need to be seen as fairly involved in that, recognizing the great injustices that have been done to the Palestinians over the course of many decades. Slowly but surely, the West is then seen to be a positive influence in resolving conflict, whether it be in Africa or the Middle East. Then more and more people in the East can be encouraged to challenge the bin Ladens of this world, and stand against them. Maybe it's not possible to negotiate with Osama bin Laden, but you have to identify the big conflicts in the world and see how a resolution can be found."

He added, "I have no time whatsoever for Osama bin Laden. I think he is a threat to world peace. But I think the U.S. administration has to consider whether or not their response to him represents as great a threat to world peace as Osama bin Laden does."

I'd made it overseas and even met my first alleged terrorist. If I learned anything in England and Ireland, it was that terrorism isn't the exclusive province of the purely evil. At least some of the time, terrorism was what happened when politics got ugly. It sure seemed that the past hundred years had seen a whole lot of ugly all around the world. And while ugly has a tendency to stay ugly, the progress in Northern Ireland showed that there might be an outside chance for us to fix some of the worst of it.

What I learned in the United Kingdom also reminded me of what Steve Coll and Evan Kohlmann had told me. Osama may be holed up in the mountains somewhere in Afghanistan or Pakistan, but if he is, he certainly isn't having any trouble spreading his ideas and his influence far and wide, even to dear old Blighty. And, as Dr. Post said, those ideas could persuade normal, sane people to do insane, horrible things. Especially if they already had grievances and felt that they were being mistreated by the rest of society.

I was told that the situation was even more volatile elsewhere in Europe, especially in France. It's another country that Osama and his followers have reached out to in a big way. I doubted that I'd find him hiding there, wearing a beret and eating croissants on the Left Bank. But I was determined to leave no stone unturned, so that's where I went next.

CHAPTER 5

THE FRENCH CONNECTION

- - - - - - - -

Why are your governments allying themselves against the Muslims with the criminal gang in the White House? . . . Why are your governments, especially those of Britain, France, Italy, Canada, Germany, and Australia, allying themselves with America in its attacks on us in Afghanistan? . . . This is unfair. It is time that we get even. You will be killed just as you kill, and will be bombed just as you bomb.

Audiotaped message from Osama bin Laden, November 12, 2002

Every cliché you've ever heard about Paris at night is true. Even for a smart-ass, goofball American male like me, it really is enchanted, magical, and romantic.

At least, the Paris that the tourists see is. And Alex and I were behaving like total tourists, real Americans in Paris. My lovely six months' pregnant bride flew there to meet me before the real crazy of my journey kicked in, and while it was still comfortable for her to fly. One night we went all out and had a candlelight dinner, with champagne (all for me, since she was preggers) and foie gras (none of that for my vegan girl, either) on a bateau making its leisurely way up and down the Seine, gliding almost silently under one beautifully arched, lamplit bridge after another. The floodlit majesty of Notre Dame . . . the Eiffel Tower rearing up high above us, its spidery steel tracery lit up with ginger-ale-colored carnival lights . . . a little farther along the opposite shore, a small replica of the Statue of Liberty holding up her torch, built by homesick American émigrés in Paris in 1916.

Hmm. Eiffel Tower on one side, Statue of Liberty on the other . . .

"Honey," I said, "it's just like Las Vegas!"

It was great having Alex with me for a few days. When I wasn't working, we did everything people in love are supposed to do in Paris: le purr, le meow, le rau-rau. Except now we were a ménage à trois. Which I guess is okay in Paris, too.

Little Spongey wasn't so little anymore. I loved running my hand over Alex's big, round belly. When I put my ear to it, I could both hear and feel Spongey shifting around in there, stretching, kicking, doing a little kung fu, counting the days until he/she could bust outta that joint and start living in the real world.

After some of the things I'd heard, I had half a mind to put my lips to Alex's belly and whisper, "Hey, you know what? Don't be in such a rush. You may want to stay put for a while. Like five or ten years. We still got a lot of problems out here. We're working on them, and I'm optimistic, but it could take a while. Why don't you just kick it in there? Work on your kung fu. I'll ask your mom to eat some Crayolas. There's no meat in Crayolas. You can doodle on the walls."

STAGE 4: GET TO KNOW GENERATION JIHAD

Shahid had told me that there were millions of young Muslims in Europe who were in the same situation as the ones in England. What I knew about them you could fit into a small escargot shell, so when I wasn't grossing Alex out by eating foie gras in front of her and little Spongey, I was in the hotel room doing some homework. For instance, did you know that an estimated fifteen million Muslims now live in Western Europe? Islam is now Europe's largest minority religion; in the Protestant north, there are more Muslims than Catholics, and in the Catholic south, more Muslims than Protestants. The future of Europe and that of Islamic Arabia have become so intertwined that a term was coined for it: Eurabia.

France, which has a population of sixty million, is home to an estimated five million Muslims, almost as many as there are in the United States (an estimated six million). They're mostly from two former colonies, Algeria and Morocco. The estimated million and a half Muslims in Spain are also largely of Moroccan descent. Germany's estimated three million Muslims are largely Turkish, along with some from the Balkans. The parents and grandparents of these Muslims came to Germany in the 1960s and 1970s as *Gastarbeiter*—"guest workers," a polite euphemism for what we'd call migrant workers in this country.

When the original Muslim immigrants came to Europe, it was to take low-paying jobs, or as refugees dependent on the state. Their European-born children, though well educated, have had trouble finding any work at all. They say they are discriminated against in Europe's already squeaky-tight job market. In the Swedish city of Malmö, Muslim immigrants make up 25 percent of the population—and up to 90 percent of them are unemployed. These young Muslims have no choice but to go "on the dole," living on handouts from social-welfare networks that have been stretched to the breaking point. And some, like the Pakistani suicide bombers in England, turn to radicalism in protest. In fact, in one article that I read Europe was described as "a hunting ground for Al Qaeda recruits." Homegrown jihadists were responsible for the 2004 assassination of the Dutch filmmaker Theo van Gogh, the painter's great-grandnephew (for making a film about Muslim women in abusive relationships) and the bombings of the Madrid rail system that same year, which killed almost two hundred people.

I figured that if anyone knew whether Osama might be hiding out in Gay Paree it would be one of France's leading counterterrorists, Judge Magistrate Jean-Louis Bruguière. Judge Bruguière was a very serious older man dressed in a dark-blue suit with a red power tie. He looked somewhat like Pat Buchanan and sounded a lot like Inspector Clouseau. I just knew Cato would burst in at any second.

We talked about the fact that France has been dealing with terrorism longer than the United States has. A *lot* longer. In fact, the French even invented the word—*terrorisme*—back in the 1790s, during the Reign of Terror, when the radicals who had won the French Revolution rolled out the guillotines and chopped off tens of thousands of their countrymen's heads. That type of terrorism, where a government terrorizes its own citizens, is different from what we're faced with now, but the French weren't the last to practice it. Hitler, Stalin, Pol Pot, Saddam, and plenty of other tyrants have put their own stamp on *terrorisme*. As French exports go, it's as successful as red wine and as repulsive as mimes in striped shirts.

But, even in modern times, France has had much more experience than we've had, going back to the 1960s, when the people of Algeria didn't want to be a French colony anymore and used terrorism to get the French out. Algerian terrorists continue to be a problem for France to this day. And, much as some Americans like to think that the French have been wussies about the War on Terror, on their own soil, at least, the French have been tough as nails. Their intelligence and security agencies are top-notch, and their laws are really firm. They've made a lot of arrests and stopped a lot of deadly plots.

Judge Bruguière has been in the thick of things since the mid-1980s. In 1994, he recalled, the radical Algerian Armed Islamic Group, known in France as the GIA, "hijacked a commercial plane in Algiers, and was intending to crash this plane over Paris. So that's the first attempt of an attack with a plane," à la 9/11. The GIA was also responsible for several deadly bombings in the Paris Métro in the 1990s.

As a judge magistrate, Bruguière operates very differently from the way judges in U.S. courts do. He doesn't just hear cases in court; he initiates and runs his own investigations, authorizing surveillance and other activities, overseeing the arrests and interrogation of suspects, and building a case against them. One of his most recent victories began, ironically, on September 10, 2001, when he started an investigation that culminated in the 2005 conviction of six Islamic militants conspiring to carry out a suicide bombing attack on the U.S. Embassy in Paris. They were part of a European terror network linked to key Al Qaeda leaders. The convicted ringleader was born in Algiers but brought up in Paris. Other members of the group, all males in their twenties and thirties, ranged from working-class North African immigrants to French-born, middle-class, homegrown jihadists. Some had come to Paris by way of radical mosques in England; others had trained in Al Qaeda camps in Afghanistan. One was a Tunisian ex–soccer player. When the ring was busted, one member fled France—for Leicestershire! Where I saw the cricket match! British agents nabbed him there.

Judge Bruguière agreed with Dr. Post that terrorists "look like normal people." There's no set "criminal profile" to work from, he said, which makes them hard to spot and track.

"Are they hiding in your society right now?" I asked him. I was picturing Osama in his beret.

"Yes, of course. But we have a very long experience with them. We have many published in a database, many names," and "update our information day by day."

I remembered Mike Scheuer and Evan Kohlmann complaining about how badly the FBI lacks this sort of data in the United States. Not a cheery memory.

In doing my homework, I'd read statements from Osama and Zawahiri like the one at the start of this chapter, threatening France as one of America's allies. (Funny how Osama sees the French as our ally, while most Americans see them as cheese-loving pansies. But I digress.) I also read that in the past few years Al Qaeda and Algerian terrorists have become good buddies. So I asked Judge Bruguière if Al Qaeda has stepped up its operations in France, or Europe in general, since September 11. Maybe Algerians were hiding Osama in Provence.

He said that the situation is very complex. There has been a proliferation of many different organizations operating in Europe, and based in many different places—Morocco, Algeria, Tunisia, Turkey. Furthermore, he told me, sometimes they join forces with each other or with Al Qaeda.

"It looks like a web, evolving very rapidly, very quickly, on the horizontal scale, not on a vertical one," he said. "You don't have a central structure which gives orders and plans all the actions. [These] networks composed of North African elements [and] others in fact compose what I call the outside circle, with Al Qaeda being the core. That's the difficulty—to know the exact relationship between the core itself and other circles that are surrounding and revolving around the core."

Hearing that, I asked him, "If Osama bin Laden was killed tomorrow, how much of a difference would it make?"

"Tomorrow, if Osama bin Laden is captured or killed, unfortunately, that event will not have any specific impact on the revolution."

I still figured that if Osama was hiding in France it would be among those young French Muslims the terrorists were supposedly recruiting.

To find out, I had to get out of enchanted, magical, tourist Paris. Way out, to a gray, dreary part of Paris that few visitors to the country see.

The French term *les banlieues* is usually translated as "the suburbs." But forget whatever images of split-level homes with green lawns and driveways the word conjures up. Think, instead, of miles of grim public housing towers, like the Bronx in the 1970s. The banlieues that ring Paris and other major French cities are satellite ghettos where France segregates its poorest minority populations to keep them out of the picturesque, tourist-swamped central cities. Like America's ghettos, they're cauldrons of poverty, crime, despair, and resentment. Unemployment runs around 20 percent, twice the national average, and among people in their twenties it's closer to 30 percent. The average household income is only 25 percent of the national average. There are many single-parent households. Lots of young people in the housing projects have lived on welfare all their lives.

These bleak projects are where the majority of French-born, second-generation children of African and Arab immigrants—known by the slang term *les Beurs*—grow up. And grow angry. Since the early 1990s, the Beurs' pent-up anger and resentment have periodically boiled over in street riots that have left large swaths of the banlieues in smoking ruins.

Meaux is a banlieue well east of the tourist and business sections of Paris, beyond the farthest reach of the Métro system. It really did remind me of the Bronx. Dull public-housing towers rear up twelve, sixteen stories, identical as giant ice-cube trays stood on end, looming over large parking lots strewn with more overturned shopping carts than cars. Cracked concrete paths wandered aimlessly across patches of scraggly grass edged with a few low bushes.

Habib met me and my camera crew at the entrance to one of the towers, where he had lived all his life. He jokingly said that he was fifteen, but I thought he was probably in his early twenties. A big, very likable dark-skinned guy in a Che Guevara T-shirt, Habib showed me around the bleak environs, pausing periodically to smoke a joint. He liked his dope—both for personal use and because dealing it to others in the projects was his main source of income.

We spoke through a translator, François.

"What was it like growing up here?" I asked him.

"There's always been a great sense of solidarity here," Habib said. "If I need a tomato for a salad, I go knock on the neighbor's door and get it. Solidarity."

"Is it all types of people, a lot of races, that live here?"

"Yes. All, all, everything. Algerians, Tunisians, Moroccans, Congolese, Guadalupe, Zaire, some Portuguese, too. And that is the strength, for all of us to be together. We learn from each other, a language here and a language there. He learns Arabic, I learn Malian. That's one of the cultural, enriching features of living together. One of the positives."

"What do you think is the hard part of growing up in an environment like this?"

"The hardest part is seeing other people in the shit, the misery, rather than being in the shit yourself."

I asked Habib about claims that the banlieues are where all the trouble in France comes from.

"It's the government's fault, in the sense that it's a self-fulfilling prophecy," he said. "The government says the young steal bags, they burn cars, they do bad things, and then the young, after reading about themselves in the paper, about how bad they are, they decide they might as well be as bad as they are depicted. That's the first problem."

Sure, I thought, that happens—look at Jodie Foster in *Taxi Driver*.

"It's true that people steal," Habib went on. "But basically it's to make do. There's not a lot else you can do here to make money."

"So how hard is it for you to find a job?" I asked.

"It's very difficult. It's really hard for a dark young Arab to get work. Even your address—when you say that you live here, you're considered scum. . . . My parents are from Algeria. We fought for the French in World War II. Then, to reconstruct, we came here and reconstructed. So we've done everything that we were asked to do. And now they want to send us back home."

"What's the way out for you?"

"There are two ways out. One way is to do a big heist, get a lot of cash, and you fuck off. Or, the second way is religion. Because when you embrace religion, then money does not become such a problem.

You find wisdom inside yourself. But until you find that, money is the first thing. I could have said go and study, of course. But school means money. If you want to go study, it will cost your family money."

As for terrorists, he said, "I don't even have words for them. I feel like insulting them. Cutting heads in the name of Islam—you're not a Muslim. All you do is dirty the name of Islam. Islam has never told anyone to cut heads. If I killed in the name of the Bible, it would be the same; I would be desecrating it. They aren't Muslims."

Okay, so Habib was one young French Muslim who wasn't going to be joining Osama's crusade anytime soon. I was glad to hear it.

Inside, the building looked like a prison the guards had abandoned to the inmates to run for themselves. One of the two elevators in the lobby was out of service, and had been for five years, Habib said. The lights in the lobby had been torn out. One of them was hanging by a lone wire, begging for someone to finish ripping it out and put it out of its misery. The floor was wet with urine, and the smell followed us as we headed up the stairwell. On the floors above, long hallways with dirty cinder-block walls and dull linoleum floors ran straight into pools of darkness where the fluorescent strips in the low ceiling had burned out. Apartment doors were gray metal, like the doors to prison cells. Habib said this was to prevent squatters from breaking into empty apartments.

"What do you want for yourself?" I asked him.

"I want a house and a car. That's it, a house in the suburbs with a backyard. I don't want that my kids grow up in a place like this, with neighbors upstairs, downstairs, next door, back there. Because when you live up here your education is out here, on the streets. And I don't want that for my kids."

"When you see people who have kids here, what do you think?"

"What strikes me is that here it's even more difficult to be a parent than anywhere else," Habib said. "The courage that these parents have. When you're a mother and you try to make your son be perfect in this environment, you know?

"Here you have nice people doing not very nice things. Because you're here, you want to buy your coffee, you want to buy your cigarettes, you want to try to pick up a chick or whatever—you need some money. You need to get the bills in, and the way to get the bills in is to do illegal stuff."

"What kind of stuff?"

"Everything. Drugs, stealing, scams. Everybody has a specialty."

"How do you get up in the morning and feel good?" I asked.

"Hope. The hope that I'm going to get out of it, the hope of leaving."

"Are there people who get out?"

"The ones who do, you never see them again," he said.

"And are they few and far between?"

"Three out of fifty."

We stepped out to a graffiti-tagged open stairway and Habib smoked a joint while we chatted about music. He said he liked all kinds— hip-hop, R & B, soul, funk, even classic French dance-hall music, the sort of stuff Edith Piaf used to sing on *The Ed Sullivan Show*. He did a few hip-hop dance moves, humming that Rick James "Superfreak" riff that MC Hammer sampled, and giggled. I didn't want to blow his mind with my phat kick worm, so I held back.

"How do you deal with your frustrations, or your aggression?" I asked him.

Habib chuckled and looked a little shy. "I smoke a lot," he said in French. And then he added in English, "Smoke smoke smoke," as he mimed toking a joint. "And I think the government is happy to have a lot of hash around here, because then people stay on the corner. They stay quiet, they don't start a lot of trouble."

We went down the stairs and crossed a wide parking lot leading to the next building, where a bunch of young guys were hanging out. They shouted greetings to Habib as we approached. It was all in French, though I did hear one kid call out, "Fifty Cent!" All African and Arab kids in their teens and twenties, they did look an awful lot like a bunch of American ghetto boys—hoodies, baggy jeans, Yankees caps, Puma baseball jackets. A couple of them even flashed hand signs, which Habib said stood for 7-7, their district. One of them did some freestyle rapping in French for the camera.

As we headed back across the parking lot, I asked Habib what he thought would become of those guys.

"Some of them will land in jail," he said, disarmingly matter-of-fact. "Or die. A cell or a coffin, basically."

I then asked him something I'd been wondering about. "How much of the ghetto is in the head?"

Habib thought for a long moment and smiled slowly. "No one's ever asked me that question before," he said. "Sure, maybe it's partly in the head. But for me, I see it—it's visual." He gestured all around. "So it's not in my head, it's there for me to see. It's real. You're standing in it. When every morning the same guy tells me the same story, I sometimes wonder, Am I in a psychiatric asylum? There's concrete everywhere, the same thing everywhere. Sometimes I wonder if I'm in a crazy hospital."

"And you still have hope?"

"Always hope, yes." He smiled. "It's hope that allows me to smile. And we're all in the same boat, so I know that we're having the same shit, and we can take it."

We walked around to the back of his building. Half a dozen young guys were standing around back there, too, just hanging out, since there was nothing to do. But their mood was more serious and wary than the other guys'. It was time for business.

I watched as Habib led a guy through the rear doors and a short way down an empty hallway. The guy handed Habib some bills, and Habib gave him a small block of hash, brown and soft, like an unwrapped candy bar. They shook hands, and the guy left. Habib told me that a chunk of hash that size was worth 170 euros, or about $220.

Another young man, heavy-set, black, very serious, wearing an African-looking tunic and ballooning trousers of sky blue, walked farther down the dark corridor with Habib. In a corner where the hall made a left turn, he pulled a handgun out of his waistband. He and Habib inspected it, exchanged a few low words, and the guy put it back in his pants and left.

I thought about what Habib had said. He was such a bright, personable young guy, but I also knew that he sold drugs and was involved with guys who carried guns. I hoped he would get his house in the real suburbs someday, but as I drove away I thought the odds of "a cell or a coffin" seemed much greater. In this environment, you couldn't help feeling that his hand had already been dealt. He made me realize how much I take for granted the advantages Spongey will have.

Ali was a very different guy from Habib, more thoughtful and more worldly. When he was nineteen, he wanted to get some answers about the meaning of life, so he went to a Catholic church, a synagogue, and then a mosque. He liked the mosque best and went to Saudi Arabia for two years to study. He also visited the United States once, driving from New York City to Miami. He liked it well enough, but thought it was too full of temptations and distractions.

Married, with no children, Ali lived in the banlieues and was working at the airport temporarily when we met. We sat at a picnic table in a little parklike area and talked.

"Is it hard being a Muslim today in France?" I asked him.

"Of course, we have the freedom of being whatever religion we want," Ali said. "But the contradiction between democracy and Islam makes it complicated. In democracy you give the power to the people, and in Islam you give the power to God."

"Do you vote in the elections?"

"No. I don't want to participate. It's just something so that the masses don't think about anything. You elect a guy, but in fact he is supported by a group of people."

"If there was a Muslim running for office, would you feel that he represents you and your point of view?"

"I wouldn't vote for him, but it would be great for the dialogue. Dialogue is very important. But again, from my religious point of view, I don't believe in democracy and I want to stay away from that."

"So you don't believe in democracy, but you live in a democracy?"

"I didn't ask for it," he said. "I didn't ask for it."

The sun came out and shone in our eyes. I suggested moving to the shade, and made a joke about the eyes being the window to the soul. "And television is the window of the Devil," Ali shot back, with an unhappy glance at the camera.

"I am using my powers for good," I argued.

"Yeah, that's good," he said. "It depends on how you use it, like a knife. You can cure or you can kill."

I thought that was a good segue into what he thought of Islam. "Is Islam a religion of peace?" I asked him.

"Islam is a religion of both peace and war. It's perfectly balanced. As long as there are people who want war, there will be war. As long as there will be a fight between good and evil, there will be war."

I wondered if I was talking to one of those "radical Muslims" I'd heard so much about in the States, and I asked Ali as much.

"What is a radical Muslim?" he said. "I don't know if I am, but if you tell me what it is, then maybe I am. But I don't like the words. I don't like labels. It's just words. What do you mean by 'radical'? I have no idea. . . . I don't think I'm radical. Maybe in the mind I can be radical sometimes, sure. But not in my actions."

I figured I wouldn't be finding Osama tucked away in Ali's apartment. Still, I wanted to know where he stood on the guy.

"On which level?" he asked. "The way he acts, or the way he thinks? The way he thinks, I would agree. The way he acts, no. . . . Bin Laden wants respect for Muslims. That's what he's fighting for."

"Is he making things better or worse for Muslims, in your opinion?"

"From a material point of view, he's making it worse. From a spiritual point of view, he's making it better. He's like a big brother. Bin Laden is there, part of the world. He restores the pride of the ancient Muslims. It makes people think about Islam. Without him, we wouldn't be here to speak together. So, in a way of thinking, he has his benefits. Even if his way of doing things is not correct, at least we are together."

I couldn't argue with him there. If all that insanity hadn't happened, I wouldn't be here today, connecting with someone halfway around the world, talking to him about things most of us never discuss. If this is the "good" that can come from tragedy, then so be it.

Walking down a street in Paris, I happened upon an Arabic butcher shop—a *boucherie-charcuterie*—and went in. Alex would have been disgusted, but for a carnivore like me it was heaven. Giant slabs of beautiful raw red beef, sausages (*merguez*) piled like rope, tubs of livers, mountains of chicken legs. *Mmmmm!* One of the butchers explained to me that all the meat was halal, the Islamic equivalent of the Jewish laws of kosher. Like kosher butchering, the animals have to be killed, bled, and cut in specific ways—and facing Mecca. Muslim cows. Who knew?

A photo of the Kaaba in Mecca hung next to a framed Koranic verse. There was also an ad poster for something called Mecca Cola.

"Mecca Cola is economic war against Coca-Cola," one of the butchers said, grinning.

"Is it popular?" I asked.

"Very popular. If you go to an Arabic country, you'll see it a lot."

A little way down the street, a Muslim woman wearing a *hijab* (head scarf) squatted on the sidewalk with her palm out, begging. This struck me, because it was the first time I had ever seen someone who was obviously Muslim begging on the street. Poverty is an equal-opportunity non-employer, and I'd see a lot more of it later in my travels.

In Saint-Germain, tourists and locals flock to quaint little cafés and bistros to enjoy the end of a beautiful Parisian summer day. It was at La Grille Saint-Germain that I met Olivier Roy, a scholarly, bespectacled middle-aged man, who is another of France's best-known and most respected terrorism experts. Olivier approaches the issue from a different angle than Judge Bruguière. He taught school in the banlieues for eight years from the 1970s into the 1980s, and still lives out there. Now he's a professor and the author of several books on Islam and terrorism. Like Shahid in England, he believes that better assimilation into French society is a way to keep young Muslims from going over to the Dark Side.

We sipped red wine, enjoyed the sunset, and he spoke beautiful English as we talked about all the things most people think but never say.

"What's happening with Islam in Europe?" I asked him.

"The issue is not about Islam," he corrected me. "The issue is about *Muslims.* It's about concrete people. What matters is how people adapt. And I am quite optimistic. I think, in fact, that most of the second-generation Muslims did find a way to adapt to the West. . . . But it doesn't mean that they are well integrated, or that they have a job. Many of them are jobless, many of them are school dropouts, many of them consider that they are victims of racism."

"Are they?"

"Yes," he said, but "it's more to do with social factors than to do with purely ethnic factors." Stuck on welfare and ghettoized out in the ban-lieues, "they have little hope, little expectation."

I noted that they sounded like black American kids in the ghetto—and that they dressed the same way, too.

"They are fascinated by the American black subculture in terms of dress, in terms of music, so they take their models from the American street culture—fast food, hip-hop, things like that," Olivier said.

"But some French Muslims do manage to succeed and assimilate, right?"

"Of course. We have success stories. A lot of success stories. At the moment, we have more schoolteachers, physicians, surgeons, lawyers, engineers coming from these neighborhoods. But they *leave* these neighborhoods and they go to other towns. And, in a sense, they have become French, because they are individualistic and anarchistic. They don't care about organizing themselves. They don't care."

"Did you just describe every French person?" I asked.

He smiled. "Yeah. Anarchist. So they are not organized. They are not trying to lobby or to make pressure on politicians. They just want to be ordinary people. . . . They want to be in the mainstream; they don't want to create an Islamic political party, an immigrant political party."

I asked him about the law passed in 2004 forbidding the wearing of the *hijab* in the classroom. It was amended at the last minute to also for-bid the wearing of any large or ostentatious religious symbol—a cruci-fix, a Star of David, a yarmulke, a Sikh turban—but still, I told him, to an outsider it looked like a petty, racist slap at France's millions of Mus-lim citizens.

"It's very French," he explained. "It is not just secularism. It is an op-position to religion in the public sphere." He noted that the French re-public was born a century ago, in a struggle against the Catholic Church. The "separation of church and state" that we hear so much about in the United States is taken *very* seriously in France. You can practice any religion you want in private, but keep it out of the civic, public sphere.

"I've got one last question," I said. "I'm about to become a father, and I'm curious—from your point of view, what kind of world am I about to bring a child into?"

"I have two children," he said, with a very Gallic shrug. "I am not worried. That's their problem."

"But I'm younger than you," I protested.

"Yeah." He shrugged again. "Every generation has their own apocalyptic story. It's the end of the world. And the world is still there." He raised his glass. *"Insha'Allah."*

Which means "God willing" in Arabic.

CHAPTER 6

DIAL-A-FATWA

STAGE 5: ENTER THE LAND OF DENIAL

Alex flew back to New York, and I flew on to Cairo. She was more than halfway through her second trimester. If I was going to find Osama, and get home in time for Spongey's grand entrance, I needed to giddyap.

Osama has all sorts of connections to Egypt. Some of his most influential mentors were Egyptian. Many of his radical ideas originated there. It was home to plenty of extremists who would probably love to put him up.

So yeah, I could easily picture him hiding out there. Who knew? Maybe I'd spot him riding a rent-a-camel at the Pyramids. And, if not, I figured I'd get more clues about how he thinks that might help me track him down.

The terminal at Cairo International Airport was new and shiny, and contained a massive Air Mall. The one right next to it showed years of wear and tear. It was an interesting contrast: one spanking new, the other Third World shabby-sheikh. Nice of them to show you the contradictions of the Middle East the minute you arrive.

I walked through the airport gawking like any other American tourist setting foot in this part of the world for the first time. Some of the people bustling and swirling around me wore Western clothes, but a lot of them were in traditional Arabic and Muslim clothing—women veiled and covered from head to toe, some men in the *shalwar kameez*, some in long white robes (called *jallabiyas*, a local man told me when I complimented him on his) that swept the floor as they walked. Some wore Arafat-style scarves (the *shemagh*) on their heads, some didn't, and everyone was speaking Arabic. For the first time in my life, I felt like—and was—the minority.

An amazing feeling of trepidation overcame me at that moment. I was excited, but to suddenly be surrounded by people who spoke no English was beyond intimidating. My comfort zone was being pushed and expanded. And this was only the first night.

My camera crew and I gathered all of our luggage with no problem, but there was a long line to get it out of the airport. The security crew was giving travelers a seriously hard time before allowing them to leave. Thank God our fixers had met up with us. A fixer is a local person who works with foreign film and news crews, and a good fixer is indispensable: a combination translator, tour guide, diplomat, sometime chauffeur, and all-around go-to person who will keep your ass out of trouble.

The security crew were riffling through everybody's bags, making skeptical faces at passports and visas, having loud arguments in Arabic, waving their hands, and shaking their heads. One security guard was an older woman in a long black dress (an *abaya*) with a black head scarf (a *hijab*). She reminded me of the classic Italian grandmother who's the last person you want to mess with. You could see that she was very maternal, but also very stern and not about to take any guff from anyone. They were giving one poor guy a really thorough going-over, dumping stuff out of his bags, tsk-tsking over his passport. As he whined and argued and cajoled, she just stood there with her fist on her hip and her head cocked, giving him a look that made it clear she wasn't buying a word he was saying. I was waiting for her to pick him up by the scruff of his neck and throw him out the door like a naughty kid. It took us more than an hour, with our fixers running interference, to get through the gauntlet.

I kept gawking as our taxi crawled into Cairo in bumper-to-bumper traffic. It was the last night before the beginning of Ramadan—if Ramadan is Islam's Lent, this was its Fat Tuesday—and the streets of the city were mobbed with millions of people enjoying one last night of eating, drinking, and strolling. I couldn't get over the massive, relentless traffic jam. It was amazing that we were moving at all. And the honking . . . In New York, out-of-town visitors always comment that New Yorkers "drive with their horns." But it's nothing compared with the cacophony in Cairo. The other thing I couldn't help noticing was that police officers were everywhere. I mean everywhere, on every corner—cops in stiff white uniforms and berets, huge black machine guns slung from their shoulders. And they were all business, seriously scanning everything and everyone around them.

We finally got to our hotel at about midnight. It was a Hilton, right on the Nile. It looked like any big, new Hilton you'd see in the West—except that there was a gate at the entrance, with two armed security guards and a bomb-sniffing dog checking every vehicle. In my room, I stood at the window and stared out at the Nile. The Nile! Just seeing that drove home to me that I had stepped into the cradle of a civilization that was thousands of years older than my own. And Egypt was definitely an Islamic country. From my window I counted the minarets of three, five, seven mosques, just in my line of sight.

The next day, news of Osama's death, as reported by a French network, flashed around the world. I called Evan Kohlmann, who instantly said that he never trusted anything from the French media or French intelligence. Steve Coll left me a message saying he didn't think there was anything to the story, either. There was no mention of it on Al Qaeda's websites, neither to confirm nor to deny it, which convinced Steve that it was bogus.

At first it was a shock to think that my journey might be taking a very dramatic turn, and that my search for this one man might end before it had really begun. Then it occurred to me that bin Laden's death might take some of the wind out of Al Qaeda's sails, but it might also turn him into a more powerful, almost mythical figure. His death certainly wouldn't end the world of violence he had helped create. Which made me realize that I wasn't searching just for Osama but also for what he represented.

Today was also the first day of Ramadan, so I decided to try fasting. Ramadan is the ninth month of the Muslim year, the month in which it's believed the Koran was given to the prophet Muhammad, and it's seen as the holiest time of the year in Islam. You're supposed to fast from dawn until sunset—and they do mean fast. Not a bite of food, and not even a sip of water until after the evening call to prayer at sundown. Smokers aren't supposed to smoke, which, like drinking alcohol, is *haram*—forbidden—even when it's not Ramadan, but doing it during Ramadan is even worse. I was told by my fixer that Ramadan made most Muslims *really* cranky. You can't even chew gum. And there's no sex during daylight hours. No afternoon delight!

The evening meal is called *iftar*, which means "breaking the fast"—and which, I was told, shouldn't be confused with the Western "breakfast," which got its name from being eaten after an involuntary fast (aka sleep). And you don't gorge yourself at *iftar*—it's a light meal. Then you're supposed to visit family and friends, and say extra nighttime prayers. Some people read the entire Koran during Ramadan, and speedy readers may crank through it a few times. At the end of Ramadan there's a three-day holiday, *Eid al-Fitr* (or simply *Eid*), the Feast of Breaking the Fast, when everyone can start eating, smoking, and having sex at noon again. Woo-hoo!

I soon realized that if Osama was hiding out in Cairo, finding him would be a lot harder than finding a needle in a haystack. The city is vast, sprawling for miles in all directions, and it's home to something like fifteen million people—20 percent of Egypt's total population of seventy-five million. It is far and away the biggest city in Africa. And it's not actually called Cairo, at least not by the locals. They call it Misr, the same name they have for Egypt. *Egypt* comes from the Greek name for the place, Aigyptos. So Egyptians don't call their country Egypt; they call it Misr, which I guess means they're not Egyptians at all but . . . Misers? It's all kind of confusing when you think about it, so don't.

I took a bus, thinking that would be a quick way to see a little of the city. Maybe I'd spot Osama strolling down the street. He's very tall—he'd stand out.

The bus driver, Ashef, was a chubby, jolly man with a round and wide jack-o'-lantern head, complete with just a few crooked teeth in his mouth, and he was playing Arabic pop on the tape deck. At one point, he did a kind of belly dance—and this guy had some belly—with his hands in the air, not touching the wheel. The traffic was so slow that it didn't matter. Then he changed the tape to somebody chanting the Koran and settled down. I guess he remembered it was Ramadan, or maybe the people scowling at him as we sat in traffic made him rethink his jubilation. He forgot that he was supposed to be cranky like everybody else.

The sidewalks were teeming with pedestrians, and those cops in their gleaming white uniforms with their black automatic weapons were everywhere, keeping a stern lookout. I watched a little boy in a

T-shirt and baggy shorts carrying a huge tray of bread loaves on his head, delivering them somewhere. The tray was longer than he was tall, and he was all business, paying no mind as he rushed past a crippled old beggar squatting against a wall with his wooden crutches leaning beside him.

I searched for Osama in vain. Terrorist-hunting on an empty stomach is no joke. By early afternoon my stomach was growling, and my throat and mouth were parched. It's hot in Cairo in September, over-one-hundred-degrees-every-day hot, and the air is terrible, a visible fog of diesel exhaust and dust that stings your eyes, clutches at your throat, and makes your lungs feel weak and dirty. I was dying for a bottle of water, or one of those imperialist machine–fighting Mecca Colas the guy had told me about.

I continued to scour the city as the sun, a bright spot somewhere up there above the brown smog, slid slowly toward the horizon. By late afternoon, the prospect of *iftar* was even more exciting than the possibility of stumbling upon the Man. I realized that's one of the great things about fasting—it makes you so happy and grateful to eat. A way of reminding yourself not to take your daily comforts for granted. On the street, I got out my cell and called Alex in Brooklyn. I told her how ecstatic I was to be able to drink a simple glass of water.

"I think you're crazy," she told me.

"You just now figured that out?"

I was invited to join a group of local men for *iftar*, right out on the street, in front of their tiny cigarette-and-soda stand. They set up a few folding tables and plastic chairs, brought out dishes and silverware, then we sat in the lengthening shadows of the setting sun and waited for the evening call to prayer, to let us know that it was okay to eat. I rubbed my empty stomach and smacked my dry lips. One man smiled and explained to me that fasting was good for me. "It makes you stronger," he said.

This makes me stronger? I thought. Sweet. By the end of Ramadan I should be Hercules.

Then the haunting voice of a muezzin, the Muslim equivalent of a Jewish cantor, wafted over us from nearby loudspeakers. Then another, at a short distance, and another and another, until their voices echoed throughout the city, like a strange, Arabic version of air-raid sirens.

Allahu Akbar . . . God is great.

And then we ate and drank. I gulped down my cup of tamarind juice before the guy next to me had taken three sips of his. In my mind, I could hear the hissing sound and feel the cold water hitting the hot spots all the way down to my stomach. This fasting thing was going to take some getting used to.

Next, we ate some dates. I had never been a big fan of dates, but let me tell you, after a day of not eating anything, I think dates are now one of my favorite foods. They were so sweet and delicious. Maybe the reality was that I had never truly appreciated dates. Well, I sure appreciated them now. I made a note to myself to be thankful and appreciate every single thing I was fortunate enough to eat for the remainder of Ramadan.

I looked for Osama all over Cairo. I looked for him at the Pyramids. I looked for him at the Sphinx. Why not? A lot of people think he sphinx.

While I didn't find him, I did use my time there to study up on his ideas some more. Everyone I asked said that many of Osama's most important ideas and beliefs came from Egypt.

"Egypt?" I said. "As in King Tut and Cleopatra?"

No, dummy, they said. Egypt as in the birthplace of the Muslim Brotherhood.

"Okay, I give up," I said. "What is the Muslim Brotherhood?" I was picturing an Egyptian version of the Freemasons or the Moose Lodge. Which, it turns out, wasn't entirely wrong. I have my moments.

Steve Coll explained it to me. He said that the Brotherhood is widely considered the ideological fountainhead of much of the Islamic fundamentalism in the world today. It was founded in 1928 by a young Egyptian schoolteacher, Hassan al-Banna, who, like the Wahhabis in Saudi Arabia, "argued that Islamic societies could never achieve their potential until they threw off secular ideas and secular constitutions and remade these societies in keeping with the Koran." The angrily anti-Western writings of Egyptian Brotherhood member Sayyid Qutb became the philosophical underpinnings for Osama and Al Qaeda's jihad.

The Brotherhood started out as a nonviolent organization, limiting itself to verbal attacks against Egypt's secular government. That was enough to get it banned anyway, at which point some members, impatient with talk, turned to violent action. In 1948, Brotherhood members assassinated Egypt's prime minister as punishment for not doing enough to eradicate the new nation of Israel. In retaliation, Egyptian government agents assassinated al-Banna. Then, in 1954, the government really cracked down on the Brotherhood after members tried to assassinate President Gamal Abdel Nasser. Along with other members, Qutb was imprisoned that year and wasn't released until 1964.

The 1954 crackdown started the Brotherhood's diaspora to more than seventy countries throughout the Middle East, Europe, and the United States. Brotherhood members were welcomed in Saudi Arabia, where their ideas were very similar to the Wahhabis'. Many Muslim Brotherhood members became teachers in Saudi schools and universities, where they spread their reactionary creed. Abdul Azzam, who was preaching jihad at King Abdul Aziz University in Jeddah when Osama was a student and later became his first mentor, was a Muslim Brotherhood member.

Brotherhood members had a similar influence on young Muslims everywhere. Khalid Sheikh Mohammed, who claims to have masterminded the September 11 attacks for Osama, was first radicalized as a teen by Brotherhood refugees in Kuwait. In the Palestinian territories, Brotherhood members formed Hamas. And they were influential in Algeria, Jordan, Iraq, Iran, Sudan—pretty much anywhere that radical Islamist movements grew.

At home in Egypt, the mainstream Brotherhood continued to pursue a peaceful, political path. But others, like the ones who fled, and the ones who were dissatisfied with the slow-moving bureaucratic process, broke ranks and formed one of the most violent terrorist organizations that has ever existed, Islamic Jihad. One of its biggest achievements was the 1981 assassination of Egypt's president, Anwar Sadat, whom they despised because he'd made peace not only with the United States but with Israel. Two Islamic Jihad members who were arrested for involvement in the assassination but later released went on to become superstars of global terrorism, as well as two of the most important figures in Al Qaeda. One was "Blind Sheikh" Omar Abdel-Rahman, who is currently serving a life sentence in a supermax prison in Colorado for masterminding the 1993 World Trade Center bombing. The other is Ayman al-Zawahiri, the founder of Islamic Jihad and Osama's closest adviser.

International terrorism—it's a small world after all.

Today, the Brotherhood in Egypt still renounces violence, at least in its official statements, and fields political candidates for municipal offices and seats in the Egyptian parliament, much like the IRA's segue into Sinn Féin. Because the organization is still banned, Brotherhood candidates run as independents or on other parties' slates, but it's no secret who they are. In 2005, the Brotherhood's stealth candidates won a pretty impressive 88 of the 454 seats in the parliament, making them the leading Islamist opponents to President Hosni Mubarak's secular government. Which makes them a huge thorn in his side.

"Well, okay then," I said to myself. "I guess I need to meet some Muslim Brotherhood guys. Maybe they can tell me where Osama is, or at least give me some helpful insights into how he thinks and where he *might* be."

Leading Muslim brother Dr. Abdel Monem Abou El-Fotouh looked no more like a terrorist to me than Martin McGuinness did. In his fifties, he looked like what he is—a hospital administrator, amiable, silver-haired, wearing a smart dark-blue suit and matching tie. We sat in a well-appointed conference room lined with little flags on a dais, like a mini United Nations, and he alternated between English and Arabic as we discussed his current role as head of the Brotherhood's Guidance Council, as well as the concept of promoting peaceful, democratic change in Egypt.

He seemed a far cry from the young man who, as a student at Cairo University in the 1970s, helped found Al-Gama'a al-Islamiyya—the Islamic Group, which became one of the most notorious of all Islamic terrorist organizations. It was Islamic Group members who massacred fifty-eight foreign tourists at Luxor in 1997, one act in a wave of terrorist attacks during the decade. They also call Sheikh Omar Abdel-Rahman their "spiritual leader."

Dr. El-Fotouh had moved away from the group and its terrorist activities long before those events. He seemed to have grown from an angry, radical youth into a calmer, wiser adult. Still, as we spoke Dr. El-Fotouh made some interesting distinctions between terrorism, which he denounced, and other forms of political violence that he felt were justified—including suicide bombings.

"The main aim of the Muslim Brotherhood," he told me, "is to reform society, but peacefully and on a democratic basis. We are not a radical movement." Change was sorely needed, he said, because the Mubarak government is a corrupt tyranny, "contradictory to democracy, and to the basis of human rights and freedom."

Tyranny? "Are you saying Mubarak is a dictator?" I asked.

"Of course. Completely," Dr. El-Fotouh said. "I was put in prison for five years, from '95 to 2000. Not only me but about sixty-two of the leaders of the Muslim Brotherhood. Without any crime. Why? Because of our opposition to Mubarak. Nothing else."

The more people I talked politics with in Egypt, the more I kept hearing the same thing. In Egypt—one of the Middle East's shining examples of a "Western-style democracy," one of America's "closest friends" in the region—if you dare to speak out against the government you can be thrown in prison—or much worse.

The United States' two biggest friends in the Middle East are Egypt and Israel. Well, they're the friends who get the biggest allowances from their Uncle Sam, anyway. Between them, Egypt and Israel get 93 percent of the U.S. aid that goes to the entire region, more than $5 billion a year. Egypt's share is its reward for developing peaceful relations with Israel in 1979 (that is, after Israel beat it in three wars—in 1948, 1967, and 1973); for being a buffer against nations in the region that our government doesn't like very much, like Syria and Iran; and, more recently, for backing Bush's play in the GWOT. (That's the Global War on Terror, in case you forgot.) So what kind of a friend have we bought in Egypt and its leader, President Hosni Mubarak? Let's just say that with friends like these it's a wonder we work so hard to make enemies.

Egypt is a democracy—sorta . . . kinda . . . well, not really. Parliament members run in elections that have some semblance to being free and open, though there are restrictions on who can run and who can vote. At the presidential level, though, it's a strongman dictatorship.

After the assassination of Anwar Sadat in 1981, former air-force officer Hosni Mubarak, who had been Sadat's vice president, took over under a state of emergency. Twenty-five years later, not only Mubarak but the state of emergency were *still* in place.

President Mubarak ran unopposed in three elections starting in 1981. Then, under pressure from the United States, he finally ran for reelection in 2005, in an ostensibly open race against two opponents. But he banned the main opposition party, the Muslim Brotherhood, from fielding a candidate, and arrested Brotherhood members before and during the elections. The police beat protesters and jailed journalists and civil-rights advocates who spoke out too loudly for democratic reforms.

In the end, Mubarak ended up with almost 90 percent of the votes in an election that many observers believed was rigged. Hmm, ya think? The ongoing state of emergency grants the Mubarak regime broad powers to arrest and detain anyone it claims to suspect of seditious activities. Supposedly, this is to keep a lid on Islamic extremists, like the Muslim Brotherhood, whose members are constantly being harassed and arrested by the government. But Mubarak's government will arrest *anyone* who merely expresses disagreement with government actions—and may hold detainees indefinitely without trial. It also often tortures them. So why are we friends with this guy? He has survived *six* assassination attempts! People obviously don't like him, but during the Cold War the United States decided it needed an ally like Mubarak. At the time, all of America's foreign policies were colored by our belief that the fate of the world hinged on stopping the spread of Communism. If we had to support dictators to stop the Red Menace—even if that meant overthrowing freely elected governments—that's what we did. So we supported the likes of Mubarak, Pinochet, and Saddam Hussein. And we overthrew elected governments—like Iran's in 1953, and Guatemala's in 1954.

Once the Cold War ended, in the early nineties—or, as I like to say, "once we kicked the Bolshevik out of those guys"—it probably would have made sense to reassess our foreign-policy priorities, and think about how we might help the world become a freer and safer place. Well, that didn't happen. We sent money where we'd always sent it, chose status quo over change, and as freedom broke out across the world we reacted behind the curve. Even when *chaos* broke out, we were behind the curve. Still, we did eventually try to do the right thing in places like Bosnia, Kosovo, Ireland, and even in the Israeli-Palestinian conflict under Clinton.

After September 11, we opted for radical change in Afghanistan and then Iraq. It was like a roll of the dice to see what might happen. But even now, when it looked as if we'd made a bad bet, we were still following a Cold War foreign policy in much of the world; it had been rebranded as the Global War on Terror, but we were supporting the same kinds of people in the same kinds of ways, with the same kinds of oppression and conflict rampant across the globe. Our lack of foresight had helped foster a major distrust of America around the world, making it hard to broker political dialogues between our traditional friends and their political opponents.

Which brings us to Egypt. In today's world, we no longer prop up dictators to halt the spread of Communism. We do it to halt the spread of Islamism. Otherwise, it looks like business as usual to me.

I pointed out to Dr. El-Fotouh that the United States gives Egypt about $2 billion a year in aid. "What role does that money play in the politics of Egypt?" I asked him. "What does Egypt give back?"

"America doesn't give aid to Egypt, or even to Israel, for the love of God," he replied. "It gives for the sake of its interests. It's natural. But the danger is in putting these interests above ethics and the great human values that the American Revolution called for, such as freedom and democracy. Who could imagine that the United States, the mother of democracy and freedom, supports regimes like these tyrannical Arabic ones in the region—regimes that kill people, practice corruption, and steal the wealth throughout the region? This doesn't honor America or the American people who support these regimes. . . . This is not the face of America."

It was weird to travel all the way to Cairo to get a civics lecture on the principles of the American Revolution. Little did I know that I would soon get used to it.

Since he mentioned Israel, I noted that Egypt and Jordan are the only two Arab nations that have officially recognized Israel. I asked Dr. El-Fotouh if he personally recognizes Israel.

"It's a very complicated problem," he answered.

Somehow, I wasn't surprised.

"I compare the state of Israel to a bastard child," he went on. "This is my opinion. Would it be allowed to kill a bastard? What is his sin? He doesn't have any. So it's not allowed to kill or eradicate him. Would it be allowed to deny him? What's his sin? He doesn't have one, so you can't deny him. He didn't form himself. He came out of wrongdoing and incest."

I asked him about Hamas, which is classified in the West and in Israel as a terrorist organization but has a political wing that had broad popular support within the Palestinian Authority. Like the guys back at the mosque in New York, Dr. El-Fotouh believed that what groups like Hamas do is not terrorism but armed resistance to injustice. I didn't agree.

"So when Hamas sends a suicide bomber onto a bus in Tel Aviv to massacre women and children, that's not terrorism?" I asked.

"We as the Muslim Brotherhood are against targeting civilians, whatever their religion or nationality," Dr. El-Fotouh said. "But when a young Palestinian blows himself up inside a bus in Tel Aviv, is there a difference between this act and the bombing of [Palestinian] villages by [Israeli] F-16 jets? Is killing people with the F-16s not terrorism and violence? If the Palestinians had the F-16s—if you Americans gave them the F-16s—they would use them to attack their occupiers, and they wouldn't be viewed as terrorists. So give them the F-16s so that they can liberate their land. And they will attack with them the same as the Israelis attack with them, so that they will not be terrorists."

Although there was a twisted logic to this, somehow I didn't think more F-16s were the answer. I was curious to hear what Dr. El-Fotouh thought he could do politically if the Brotherhood was actually able to gain enough power. "If the Brotherhood got to run Egypt," I asked, "would you establish a country ruled by Islamic law? I mean, would people get their hands chopped off for stealing or be stoned for adultery, as we've heard happens?"

"First," he said, "the crime of adultery is punished in Islamic law with eighty lashes, not stoning."

Only eighty lashes! Phew.

Dr. El-Fotouh explained that such extreme punishments are meant as deterrents, and are carried out only in extreme situations. The way the death penalty is justified by folks in America, you might say.

Just for the hell of it, I asked Dr. El-Fotouh, "Where is Osama bin Laden?"

"I don't know," he shot back with a grin. "You should ask Mr. Bush, the only man who knows where he is."

"There's a rumor that he's dead. Will it change anything if he is dead?"

"Nothing. Osama bin Laden is an individual. His existence or nonexistence doesn't change anything. He is the scarecrow that George Bush and the extreme right used to fool the American people."

Well, I thought, if he's the Scarecrow that's perfect, because even with the civics lectures I'm definitely not in Kansas anymore.

Dr. Kamal Habib is another middle-aged Islamist who has renounced the violent associations of his youth—with certain qualifications. As a college student in the 1970s, he became a member of Islamic Jihad and was involved in President Sadat's assassination. A gray-haired man in a tan suit and brown loafers, he showed none of Dr. El-Fotouh's easygoing charm as he sank into a stuffed chair and avoided my eyes. He dangled a loop of prayer beads from his right hand, and distractedly ticked the beads off one by one between his thumb and forefinger the whole time we spoke. It was very choreographed, something I'm sure he had witnessed other Islamists do numerous times in the media—a surefire way to reinforce his piety to viewers. I would see this happen many times on my journey. In Muslim countries, as in the West, public figures know how to use the media to build their persona.

I asked, "Were you involved in the murder of Anwar Sadat?"

"Yes, I participated in it," he said. "I was a member of the organization. Only five people executed the operation, but I participated. I mean, I knew what was going on, I knew what time the operation was going to be executed."

So there it was again, this fine line between "never committing violence" yet "participating" in it.

Following the assassination, hundreds went to prison—including

Dr. Habib. "I was convicted and served ten years, from 1981 to 1991," he told me. "I was twenty-four at the time."

His decade in prison gave him plenty of time to reevaluate the use of violence as a way to bring about change. He still believed that he and his colleagues were acting "within Islam" by seeking to remove a ruler they perceived as working against Islam. But, he said, he came to "the opinion that the use of force to change regimes has dangerous consequences for society, for Islam and unity, and we advise our youth now not to go that way. . . . We call for participation within society and the political process, and in the formation of parties."

I noticed that he wasn't exactly saying he thought political violence was immoral, just ineffective. So I asked him flat out, "Do you condone violence now?"

"No, it's not condoning it," he said. "I am against individual violence. But if there is a historical moment that demands a real change involving a kind of revolution, like civil disobedience or political struggle, then I'm with this."

When I asked him what he thought of Al Qaeda, he described the organization as "a response to the unjust Western policy towards the Islamic world."

He went on, as if by rote, "Of course, in the end I don't want violence. But the unjust foreign policy of the United States requires the involvement of new generations of young Muslims and Arabs with ongoing violence. This crusade reminds us of the Crusades that happened before. Therefore they are just defending their countries, their societies, their identity, their culture, and their civilization."

Yeah, that's exactly what Osama has said, many times. In 1998, Osama, Zawahiri, and others, calling themselves "the Global Islamic Front for Jihad Against Jews and Crusaders," issued one of their homemade fatwas, declaring, "To kill the American and their allies—civilians and military—is an individual duty incumbent upon every Muslim in all countries. . . ." And in October 2001, right after we began bombing Afghanistan, Osama again declared, "I have only a few words for America and its people: I swear by God Almighty who raised the heavens without effort that neither America nor anyone who lives there will enjoy safety until safety becomes a reality for us living in Palestine and before all the infidel armies leave the land of Muhammad."

"So," I asked Dr. Habib, "do you think the killing of innocent Americans on American soil was justified?" Dr. Habib fumbled his words a bit, and ticked off a few more prayer beads, before answering. "You are in a war, and the war has a universal aspect. This war was announced by George Bush. Therefore the other side can do whatever the law of war allows. So [bin Laden] can vow to attack the Americans in the United States, or in Europe, or in London, or in Spain, because this war has a universal aspect. And as the United States doesn't make exceptions for anyone in this war, Al Qaeda also doesn't make exceptions for anyone."

I got back to my hotel room very late that night, and was very depressed by what I'd heard. Both of these men were supposed to be "moderates." Both paid lip service to having renounced terrorism (after doing heavy prison time for supporting it, I couldn't help noticing). But I didn't have to push very hard to get them to admit that they thought it was justified, as long as it was in defense of Islam against the West and Israel.

These guys were moderates? They were the ones who were going to help bridge the gap between the extremists on either side? The ones who were going to reform the corrupt world? Not with the kind of talk I'd heard, which I was sure had been watered down for my benefit. There's a better way to try to change the world than by regurgitating rhetoric like that. I wanted to have a dialogue, but I felt that I was getting only justifications and veiled threats.

Alex called at 3:45 in the morning. "I'm just so worried about you," she said. "I want you to come home. I just started thinking about these people you're meeting. You never know what's going to happen."

I was starting to get worried about being an American in the Middle East. I didn't tell Alex that I'd given those guys my business card. I didn't want her wondering if I might someday get a ticking box delivered to my office. Or would it just be a truck pulling up in front of the hotel that night and taking out the first twelve stories? Or a guy on a motorcycle pulling up alongside our van the next day?

I truly believe that it is a small fraction of people who want to go out and kill for an ideal that may or may not lead to whatever goal they have. But that doesn't negate the fact that there *are* people who would like to see me dead simply because I'm an American.

We'd gotten a lot of sympathy from across the world after September 11, but that didn't last. Everyone I had talked to so far on this trip either wanted to tell me that America was a justifiable target because we were wicked, or that we'd placed the GWOT equivalent of a "Kick Me" sign on our backs by acting recklessly, ignoring or misjudging the long-term effects of our choices. As one person told me, we were doing as good a job of recruiting terrorists as Al Qaeda ever could. The War on Terror was creating more enemies for the United States than it eliminated; it was turning millions of people around the world against Americans, radicalizing them.

And as much as we think those guys are crazy for saying that God told them to fight against us, I was reminded by people I spoke to that our current U.S. president, the most powerful man on the planet, George W. Bush, said that God told *him* to invade Iraq. Well, amen brother, and pass the ammunition.

I certainly don't want my kid to wake up every day thinking, Is today the day somebody walks on this bus and blows it up? Kids are waking up and wondering just that every day in the Middle East, in Asia, in Africa. Americans have been very, *very* lucky that this has happened only a few times in the United States. We don't know how lucky we are. I was reminded of that every time I drove into my hotel there on the Nile, where bomb-sniffing dogs walked around the car and two guys with M-16s peered inside and checked our papers before raising the gate just so that I could drive to the front entrance. Inside the hotel, the ritual continued, with more security, instructions to empty my pockets, show my room key, walk through the metal detector, get patted down. The whole city is like a vast airport check-in.

Unless we change our opinions and actions for the better, I wonder how much longer our luck will hold out. The anger and hatred we've generated in this part of the world is festering and boiling. There are both cruel regimes and radical opposition movements that benefit from making America the scapegoat for their country's problems—that's becoming an easier card to play these days.

I didn't get much sleep that night. I was depressed, paranoid that the hotel might explode, afraid that I was slipping down a rabbit hole so deep that I might never make it out.

The next morning, as we got ready to leave the hotel, we were met in the lobby by officers of Egypt's Tourism and Antiquities Police—the same guys who patted me down and made me empty my pockets every time I returned to the hotel. Ostensibly, their job is (a) to safeguard the security of foreigners traveling in Egypt; and (b) to safeguard Egypt's incredibly rich heritage of antiquities, ensuring that no ancient treasures are smuggled out of the country.

I applaud both activities, especially the first one. But a large part of what their job really entails is keeping an eye on all foreigners in the country, especially film and news crews, in order to control what they see, hear, and record. Controlling information and protecting Egypt's image abroad—most notably in the United States—is every bit as important to the Mubarak government as protecting mummies and tourists.

So the T & A police wanted to accompany us everywhere. I'm usually all for T & A following me everywhere, but not here, and not these guys. They wanted to know where we were going, whom we were speaking with, why, the goal of the project, everything. They wrote down everything we told them in little notebooks. They told us they had to "escort" us around the city, that it was for "our protection." We couldn't leave the hotel without one of them climbing into the van with us. Sometimes he'd be in a white police uniform, with a pistol on his hip. One guy, more undercover, wore a dark suit and carried a submachine gun in a shoulder holster. It was all very police state for a country that's supposed to be a democracy. Sometimes we'd ask the guy to go inside and get something from his supervisor and then we'd drive off, but they got wise to that one fast. Other days, we'd try to change our departure time in the hope that the officers wouldn't be there yet. It never failed, though; someone was always there, writing things down, asking questions, demanding that he come with us.

. . .

When I'm riding the subway in New York, I often see Hasidic Jews reading the Torah on their way to the office, and every once in a while you might catch somebody reading the Bible. But in Cairo people read the Koran aloud, everywhere, all day. Maybe this was just because it was Ramadan and everybody was trying to keep up appearances, like the folks who go to church only on Christmas and Easter, but it was a little strange to see people reading Scripture all day long.

Imagine walking down the street in the United States and seeing everybody reading the Bible and quoting Scripture. Furthermore, suppose the people you met told you that whenever they do something it's based on a quote in the Scripture, and they quote the Scripture to make their point, because they had to memorize the whole Bible as part of their schooling. As if this weren't enough, five times a day church bells come out of loudspeakers all over Kansas, everything stops, and everyone goes to pray. It would take you by surprise, let me tell you, no matter what your beliefs. I'm a very open-minded guy, but this still took some getting used to.

I also have to admit that it was strange that almost every woman I saw in Cairo wore the *hijab*, the head scarf. And it's not draped casually but sealed tight across the forehead, so that not a single hair escapes. This was true even of female TV newscasters.

I also saw lots of women wearing the *niqab*, the face veil. Most Egyptian women abandoned the custom with Egypt's modernization in the twentieth century. But it's been making a comeback, along with fundamentalism, and the government and other Egyptians condemn it as a symbol of political extremism. A university in Cairo banned the practice right around the time I was in Egypt, and several of the big newspapers printed editorials against it.

Since Osama is so fond of issuing his own do-it-yourself fatwas, I went to see Sheikh Ali Gomaa, Egypt's Grand Mufti, one of the most revered spiritual leaders in Islam. People from all over the Muslim world come to him for fatwas, both in person—for personal guidance on things like marital affairs—and electronically, for more general guidelines on things like how to fast during Ramadan. His offices at the Sultan Hassan Mosque have a staff of forty who are equipped to answer questions by telephone (you leave your question, wait forty-eight hours, and call back to get the answer) or via the Internet, in Arabic, French, or German. They issue more than seven thousand fatwas *a month*! Call it Dial-a-Fatwa. I was told that the most original question ever directed to them was about space travel: If a Muslim went to Mars, which way should he turn to face Mecca during prayer?

I sat with the Mufti in his beautiful, wood-paneled office. A small, gray-bearded man, he wore a very nicely tailored *jubbah*, the ankle-length jacket favored by imams, in black pinstripe, and a white cap, a *kufi*, with a red turbanlike cloth wrapped around it—the sign of a religious scholar.

I asked him, "When you hear a phrase like 'Islamic terrorists' or 'Islamic radicals,' how does that make you feel?"

"I feel that I am oppressed," he said in Arabic, "because it's a kind of injustice to describe Islam, which is a religion of peace and mercy, as a religion of terror. . . . Those people basically didn't study Islam. They do what they're doing for social and political reasons. They don't represent Islam, either as a school or as a movement."

When I asked him what he thought of the way Islam is portrayed in Western media, he said, "I think that they don't miss a chance to defame the image of Islam."

"Why?"

"You have to ask the Western media," he shot back. "But they do this, and we're surprised. And we are surprised by them also, not just by their words but also with their silence, because anytime we have a conference against terrorism, or a conference for peace, they don't talk about it in the Western media. They shut up on it. So they don't talk about all the advantages, but they talk about all the misfortunes. And why? I hope to get answers from you, because we are confused."

Believe me, Big Mufti, nobody's more confused than me—especially since whenever I turn on the TV I hear about terrorism, every single day.

I asked him what he thought of America's foreign policy.

"The people on the street are shocked by these strange behaviors," he said. "The United States declares the war against terrorism and causes all this bloodshed in the world. You kill people in order to save people. And it becomes contradictory. It's a laughing matter. And it's not understood. We are in general sadness from the American behavior. Do you have any explanation?"

"I'm trying to find one," I said with a smile. I wanted to see if he had any new ideas about how to get the world out of this mess. He didn't.

"I hope that when America calls for democracy that doesn't mean that our world has to be like America," he said. "For one simple reason only—that the world is not America. And we pray to God that the world doesn't become America. We live in happiness. We have our problems, we try to solve them. Leave us alone. When God created the universe, he didn't make the United States our mother. Or our father. Let America take care of itself and let America go back to itself so that she can take care of her people. We have a civilization that surpasses the existence of America hundreds of times, because our civilization spans ten thousand years. And the genes that are in us are genes of civilization. So America, the strongest country in the world, should care about itself and leave the world to care about its interests."

Saad Eddin Ibrahim is a *real* Egyptian moderate. A sociology professor at the American University in Cairo, he spent years living and studying in the United States and returned to Egypt with the intention of helping to spread a little more U.S.-style democracy around. In 1988, he founded the Ibn Khaldun Center for Development Studies, whose mission is to advocate civil rights and democracy in Egypt and the Arab world in general.

In 2000, when Dr. Ibrahim announced that the center would monitor and report on the fairness of the upcoming national elections, the Mubarak regime imprisoned him and twenty-seven of his colleagues, and shut down the center. Sentenced to seven years in prison, he was acquitted and released after a three-year appeals process. Those sure aren't the winds of freedom blowing across the Egyptian desert.

The center, which has been reopened, occupies a plain, suburban-looking house in the Mokattam Hills, a working-class neighborhood on the eastern outskirts of Cairo. The wide street was unpaved and dusty in the Egyptian heat. Nearby, ugly housing towers crumbled under the blazing sun, reminding me of Meaux in France. In the rubble-strewn lots separating them, stray cats and even a stray white donkey foraged.

Dr. Ibrahim is a small, scholarly-looking gentleman with ruffled gray hair and a neat gray beard. He led me through the house, past shelves lined with books and magazines, and walls covered with photos of himself meeting a host of world dignitaries.

"This building was sacked, everything here was looted, all our documents, all of our books—everything was destroyed," Dr. Ibrahim told me, recalling what it was like when the government shut down the center and arrested him and his staff. "We had to rebuild it from scratch. What is in a building like this? What is in a research center? Except books and ideas? Why would the Mubarak regime destroy it? It's like destroying a library, a museum. But that is what despotism and tyranny are all about. They cannot stand an idea that is different. They cannot stand criticism. They cannot stand alternative visions, even if you are carrying them out peacefully."

Dr. Ibrahim is a full-on advocate of participatory democracy, and has pressured Mubarak to grant equal political rights to the poor, to women, to the Coptic Christian minority, and to the Muslim Brotherhood. I asked him about the fear that if Islamists come into power in a country like Egypt they will repress people's rights, enforce Sharia law, and engage in or support violent extremism.

"Well, that depends on how they come to power," he answered. "If they come to power through elections, I think that fear will be exaggerated. If they come through a coup d'état or a revolution, then that fear would be justified, and I would be one of the people who share that apprehension."

He compared a country like Turkey, a stable Islamic democracy where people live freely, to places like Iran and Afghanistan, where Islamic extremists seized control and imposed repressive regimes on their people.

"When Islamists come to power through an election, they know there will be another election and they know they will be held accountable," he said. "And that's when they begin to moderate their rhetoric and to behave in a more responsible manner."

I asked him, "If change can occur through the political process, why do some of these guys feel the need to join radical groups?"

Dr. Ibrahim said that's what happens when people don't have access to peaceful political power: "People are not born radical. People are born 'normal,' and they lead a normal life, and they want to participate in shaping their future—educationally, politically, and in every other respect. If you block channels of fair and equal participation, people become radicalized. They become outraged and angry."

"A lot of folks seem to think that the Muslim Brotherhood is the answer to Islamic reform in this country," I said. "Do you think they've really changed?"

"Yes, of course they have," Dr. Ibrahim said. "Humans do change. If you give them respect and dignity, they will act respectable and dignified, and they will be responsible."

Dr. Ibrahim had given me a new perspective on my earlier meetings with Dr. Habib and Dr. El-Fotouh. They certainly weren't the ideal partners for making a better Middle East, but at least they were willing to talk, and even talked a decent game on democracy. If Dr. Ibrahim was right—that these men would have to be less radical if they hoped to consistently win votes in order to remain in power—maybe it would be best for the United States to begin a dialogue with them, and even to pressure Mubarak to back off. If the Muslim Brotherhood is the alternative to creating more Mubaraks *and* more bin Ladens, maybe we should consider giving it a shot?

But then again, like I said, the roots of some of the most violent terrorist groups in the world have sprung from the Muslim Brotherhood. We may never be able to stop all the crazies, but we could at least try to limit the things that push them in the wrong direction.

Egypt was a real eye-opener for me. It was my first time in a Muslim country—and one where people are trying to deal with all the conflicts of modernization versus fundamentalism, democracy versus repression, moderation versus extremism. I learned a lot about Egypt and the Arab world, and some things about how Osama became Osama. But I also learned how little I really understood. I was starting to develop some opinions about the situation, but most of my opinions contradicted each other. My edumacation was making my head hurt.

Was I getting any closer to understanding Osama? Maybe. I'd

learned that he wasn't alone in hating the United States. But I was also learning that even in Egypt people were more interested in joining America in the democracy club than in joining Osama in a global war.

I was confused and overwhelmed as I tried to figure out how we might go about navigating all the questions and choices facing Egypt and the rest of the region. I'd heard about another man who was trying to lead his country through this tricky path, with mixed results. It was time to pack my bags.

CHAPTER 7

IN THE LAND OF SPEEDY MOHAMMED

Walking the twisty, narrow paths of Sidi Moumen, the shantytown that sprawls outside Casablanca, I expected to be met with suspicion, anger, even hate. After all, it was from this poor slum that fourteen young Moroccans fanned out across Casablanca and unleashed the worst night of terrorist killings in the city's history—May 16, 2003, Morocco's 9/11 or 7/7. But in Sidi Moumen I found that I was welcomed with warmth, curiosity, and generosity.

I don't know if anyone else ever thought of looking for Osama in Sidi Moumen, but I could definitely picture him hiding out in its maze of shacks and hovels, hanging with its desperately poor young Muslims, who, like the Casablanca bombers, might be wooed over to the Dark Side. Osama the trustafarian jihadist liked rubbing elbows with the poor. In a 2004 poll, almost half of the Moroccans questioned expressed favorable views of Osama, so I thought I should search for him there.

I'd also come to Morocco because several people told me it's got the whole spectrum of issues facing Islam today, in microcosm. It's been held up as an example of a Muslim country that has a thriving, open culture and participatory democracy. It's one of America's best friends in the Muslim world (and the oldest—Morocco was the first country in the world to recognize the United States, in 1777). But, at the same time, it has a growing fundamentalist movement—people who would like to see the country go in pretty much the opposite direction from which it was now moving. And because of those tensions it's been both a target of and a source for terrorist violence.

When you think of Morocco, terrorism is probably not the first thing that comes to mind. I've always thought Morocco was where the Spanish and French go to let their hair down. Morocco has always been one of North Africa's more international, cosmopolitan societies. It's 99 percent Muslim, but that never stopped it from having a good time. All of Moroccan society, or at least its well-to-do and educated elite, has traditionally been open to Western influences, from the trivial (blue jeans, DVDs, scotch) to ideas like women's rights. In cities like Rabat and Casablanca, few women wear the *hijab*, and the ones who do are usually older matrons. Sometimes you'll see a girl in shorts and a T-shirt walking with her mother, who's covered from head to toe: the old alongside the new. But this is a large part of what the radicals say they're fighting—this is "the problem." Too much Western influence. Or, as one man told me, "too much freedom."

And life isn't all fun and games for these people. I was told that close to a third of all Moroccans live in extreme poverty, and unemployment is more than 20 percent. Fully half of Morocco's thirty million people are illiterate, and the illiteracy rate for women in rural areas is as high as 90 percent. The infant-mortality rate among the poor is high, and Morocco's prisons and police have a well-earned reputation for brutality.

Morocco is a constitutional monarchy, with an elected parliament ruled by a hereditary king. In his early forties, King Mohammed VI represents a dynasty almost four centuries old—only Japan's imperial dynasty goes farther back—but he's also a very new kind of monarch for Morocco.

Only thirty-five when he took the throne, King Mohammed is a young, swinging, hipster monarch. He went to school in Europe and earned a Ph.D. in political affairs. He prefers to drive himself around rather than be chauffeured. He smokes Marlboros. He's hung with Elton John and P. Diddy. He's athletic and fond of jet skis, for which he has been nicknamed "His Majetski." And because he's been in a hurry to reform and modernize some aspects of Moroccan society, the people gave him another nickname: "Speedy Mohammed." I'm not kidding. Morocco's kings claim direct descent from the prophet himself, yet Speedy's program of "adaptive modernization" has met with a lot of resistance from his religiously conservative subjects. Like young Muslims everywhere, many of Morocco's youth have heard the call of the "Islamic Reformation," as Reza called it. In recent years, young Moroccans have become much more conservative in their faith than their moderate elders.

In Casablanca one night, I went to hear the Koran being recited at the Grand Mosque, built by King Hassan II in the 1980s. It is immense—the largest mosque in the world outside of the one in Mecca, built on a rocky cliff right on the sea, with a towering minaret that, I was told, is the tallest in the world. The mosque can hold twenty-five thousand people inside and another eighty thousand in its vast courtyard, where Daniel, my cameraman, and I stood with an enormous crowd listening to the Koran. It was the Islamic version of a rock concert. I'd seen Bon Jovi at Giants Stadium a few weeks earlier, and there were almost as many people here, listening to someone read from one of the holiest books in the world. I was blown away. An estimated forty thousand people came that night, and many of them were young people dressed in their Ramadan best; some of the men wore suits and ties, others were in long white robes. They stood there respectfully, all of them listening, their heads bowed, literally hearing the call of Islamic tradition.

I was very moved by the scene. It would stay with me for weeks, watching these peaceful people, many of whom smiled or nodded at me as they walked inside, the power of the word washing over them.

And then there are the ones who hear the call of extremism. The young men who dispersed from Sidi Moumen with explosives strapped to their bodies that night in 2003 struck two restaurants, the five-star Hotel Farah, the Belgian consulate, a Jewish community center (which was empty that night), and near a Jewish cemetery. Forty-five people, including twelve bombers, died, and more than a hundred were wounded. A few were Europeans, but the majority were Moroccans.

It turned out that they'd been recruited and trained by a terrorist organization called Salafiya Jihadiya. It means "Salafist jihad," and Salafism is the equivalent of Wahhabism. It was interesting to learn that the organization was begun in the early 1990s by North Africans who, like Osama, went home radicalized after fighting the Soviets in

Afghanistan. The group fished for recruits in slums like Sidi Moumen, and sent some to Afghanistan for training in Al Qaeda camps. In a weird demonstration that there are only six degrees of separation in terrorist circles, some of the Casablanca bombers were trained by a French guy, Pierre Richard Robert, nicknamed "the blue-eyed emir of Tangier." A tall blond youth from the French countryside, Pierre got interested in Islam while playing soccer at a Turkish cultural center, converted, and then went all the way over to the Dark Side. In 2005, a Moroccan court sentenced him to life in prison.

So terrorism travels in both directions between Morocco and Europe. Some of the perps of the 2004 Madrid train bombings were members of Salafiya Jihadiya. Zacarias Moussaoui, serving a life sentence for his role in the September 11 attacks (he's in the same Colorado prison as the Blind Sheikh, by the way), is a French Muslim of Moroccan descent. The assassin of Theo van Gogh was Dutch Moroccan.

In an audiotaped message of February 2003, Osama told all "true Muslims" that they "must motivate and mobilize the ummah to liberate themselves from their enslavement to these oppressive, tyrannical, apostate ruling regimes who are supported by America, and to establish God's rule on earth. The areas most in need of liberation are Jordan, Morocco, Nigeria, Pakistan, Saudi Arabia, and Yemen." The Casablanca bombings happened three months later.

Coincidence? I doubted it. I had a feeling that Morocco was just one more place where Osama, wherever he was hiding, had reached out and touched someone with a vengeance. Later, I'd learn that my instincts were correct.

There's one other alleged Osama-Morocco connection that's just so frickin' weird and funny I gotta mention it. In 2005, a mysterious Sudanese-born novelist and soap-opera scripter, writing pseudonymously as Kola Boof, claimed, in her book *Diary of a Lost Girl*, that for several months in 1996—a time when everyone else says he had returned to Afghanistan—Osama kept her as a sex slave in Marrakech. She described his S&M tendencies, his great admiration for Whitney Houston, and how he veered between being a devout Muslim and "this devout party boy who wanted to hear Van Halen or some B-52's." Not surprisingly, her story was widely discounted. Still, you gotta love the image of Osama bopping to "Rock Lobster."

STAGE 6: SEE WHERE TERRORISTS COME FROM

With the Casablanca massacre, Sidi Moumen earned a reputation as a hotbed of terrorism, and in the following weeks the king's security forces made repeated arrest sweeps through it and Morocco's other slum areas. By 2005, more than two thousand people had been brought to trial and nine hundred convicted of various extremist activities, including seventeen who got the death sentence. Human Rights Watch reported that many detainees were abused or tortured. Clearly, Speedy Mohammed could be pushed only so far.

I wanted to see Sidi Moumen for myself. As my guide, I had Aboubakr Jamai, who had also felt the king's displeasure. Aboubakr was the outspoken editor and publisher of two weekly Moroccan newspapers, the French *Le Journal Hebdomadaire* and the Arabic *Assahifa al-Ousbouiya*. The king had shut down the papers more than once for being critical of his regime, and Aboubakr was once convicted of defaming the king's foreign minister in an article charging him with corruption. He evaded a jail term but was hit with a huge fine. For persevering, he won the International Press Freedom Award in 2003.

Sidi Moumen's shacks and huts would probably all fall down like a big house of cards if you leaned too hard on one of them. Their walls are haphazard piles of cinder-block, or sheets of rusty corrugated steel, or even slabs of old billboards slapped together. There are no roads, just paths, barely wide enough for two adults to pass each other, that twist and burrow deeper and deeper into the rabbit warren. Wash is hung everywhere, and kept slapping us in the face as we navigated the labyrinth. Women get water from outdoor pumps and hoses and carry it home in jugs on their heads. There are no sewers. Trash and garbage collect in huge piles. This being the twenty-first century, however, jerry-rigged electrical lines loop over the rooftops, and behind one hut I glimpsed maybe a dozen small satellite dishes. No running water, no glass in the windows, but they've got satellite TV. I was reminded of places in West Virginia.

An army of kids descended on us the moment we arrived; there must have been a hundred or more. They surged all around us, laughing, shouting, flashing the peace sign, racing ahead of us down the winding paths. They may have been dirt poor, but they weren't dirty, and there was nothing about them that seemed downtrodden. In fact, they glowed with joy and life. I've never seen happier, more excited kids.

But they were just kids. How will the realities of their situation change them as they grow up?

Aboubakr told me that as many as three hundred thousand people lived in Sidi Moumen. Mostly they were very poor, often illiterate people drawn to the city from the countryside—a process he called the "ruralization" of the cities.

"The dangerous thing," he said, is that "in the countryside you have the tribe, you have families which were established for a long time, so they have this solidarity system that works as a safety [net]. . . . Here you don't have that."

The average income for those who had jobs was well under $100 a month, and many of those jobs were in an underground economy. Which means no rights. You get hurt? Too bad. You get sick? Sorry, can't help you. It's every man for himself in this jungle, and many are just barely surviving.

"Our social ladder is completely broken," Aboubakr explained. He gestured toward one of the smiling boys trailing us as we proceeded farther along the maze of narrow alleyways. "What's the hope of this kid to go to a good school, to become literate and live in downtown Casablanca in a nice neighborhood? The chances are pretty slim, almost nonexistent, because we have failed them as a society. They go to school, but the quality of the school is so low. Basically, it is a machine to produce unemployment."

We walked past a home whose wall was made of rusty sections from an old Perrier billboard. In a place where the only running water comes from hoses, it was a striking embodiment of the immense gulf that separates the rich and the poor in Morocco. "You can find outrageous, luxurious places, and you can find the most miserable places a few miles away," Aboubakr said. I thought I'd seen huge gaps between the richest and the poorest in New York City, but it was much worse here. In Sidi Moumen, even the bare necessities became sacrifices.

After the 2003 bombings, Aboubakr said, the government announced a raft of new programs, like the construction of new public housing, aimed at improving the lot of the people in slums like Sidi

Moumen. But in three years nothing much had happened. "They are still complaining about the fact that they are completely forgotten by the state in general. No electricity, no sewer system, no running water, et cetera."

The 2003 suicide bombers came not only from Sidi Moumen but from "the same street even. . . . They were either unemployed or had menial jobs, and they were completely outcast in their own society. Of course, on top of that you have the religious element, which is important. It allowed them to use this anger in this socially hopeless situation."

Aboubakr told me that in a 2003 poll Moroccans were asked which leaders they thought were most able to solve the world's problems. Osama bin Laden came in second, with 40-odd percent. Jacques Chirac came in first. (In America, Jacques Chirac could have come first only in a poll asking which politician hates freedom but loves funny accents.)

"So you think that people are pro-Islamist, pro-terrorist, then you look at who's first and you are completely surprised it was Jacques Chirac, who is no Muslim, no Arab, no Islamist," Aboubakr said. But what he and Osama have in common is that "they are against the American administration. That's the common link between Jacques Chirac and Osama bin Laden, and that explains it."

Aboubakr said Osama wasn't just a popular figure among the poor. "I had discussions with very wealthy businessmen in this country, very modern," he told me. "You know, their daughters went to university, they are unveiled, et cetera. And they like Osama bin Laden. Which is weird. Which is horrific. . . ."

Aboubakr explained his personal views on bin Laden: "On a moral ground you can't support Osama bin Laden. And, even if you take a utilitarian point of view, what did he achieve? I don't think he achieved much—except, and that's the sad thing, to awaken the Western public opinion to the dire situations maybe of the Palestinians and the rest of the [Arab] world."

So there it was again—Palestine, Palestine, Palestine. And now the rest of the Muslim world was being thrown on top of it, just to sweeten the pot. I wasn't so sure that Osama had brought more attention to Israel and Palestine. They had always been in the news in America, although everyone I met said we hadn't gotten the whole story. And now that story had to compete with Iraq, Iran, and Afghanistan for media attention. But still, there it was again.

Aboubakr told me about another poll (they like polling almost as much as we do) in which something like 80 percent of Moroccans indicated that it was important that their leader be Muslim. But when they were asked whether this person should be a religious scholar or an imam, the overwhelming response was no. They didn't want someone who would be telling them how to interpret the Koran.

"They want someone who's Muslim in the sense that they want him to have an ethical behavior," Aboubakr said. "Because in our societies Islam is linked to that. When someone is a practicing Muslim, it tells you something about his behavior. It allows you to know that he has a minimal level of honesty, et cetera."

"He has some sort of moral compass."

"Exactly. I would suggest that it is the same thing that's going on in your country. I would think that a lot of people who are not exactly Christian extremists think that way. There was a similar poll in the United States, where people said they wouldn't vote for someone who wasn't a Christian for president. . . . It's astonishing, the similarities between the United States and the Middle East, in the perception of religion and state."

In the West, Morocco is held up as an example of a Middle Eastern nation that has managed to preserve its own version of democracy against the rising tide of Islamic extremism. But Aboubakr's experience suggested that there were definite limits to how much democracy King Mohammed VI was willing to tolerate.

So I asked Aboubakr, "*Is* Morocco a democracy?"

"Well," he said with a rueful smile, "the regime likes to think and say it's a democracy, but obviously it's not. A very cursory reading of the constitution would tell you that it's not a democracy. It would tell you that it's an absolute monarchy. We have a political life, we have political parties, a measure of freedom of the press and of expression. But it is not a democracy in the sense that Moroccans have the power to change their ruler, because they certainly can't."

I thanked Aboubakr for his time and continued exploring Sidi

Moumen on my own. A few months later, in January 2007, I'd be sorry to hear that, to spare the paper the crushing fine Speedy Mohammed's court had hit him with, he had been forced to resign from *Le Journal*. One more voice for free speech and democracy silenced.

I pressed on farther into the labyrinth of shoulder-wide paths to the home of Ahmed Sadri, his wife, Zora, and their three kids, where I was invited for *iftar*. It was just three tiny rooms and a tinier kitchen, and it was very spare, but it was spotless. The walls were smooth plaster painted a soft yellow. A TV stood in one corner of the central room. A velvet painting of a stag, which looked just like one from any of the ninety-nine-cent stores on Fourteenth Street in Manhattan, hung over one doorway, and inexpensive Persian-style rugs covered the floors. In the kitchen, Ahmed's wife, a shy, sturdy woman in a red traditional robe and a *hijab*, was frying half a dozen sardines in an iron skillet on a two-burner stove. Soup was steaming in a pot on the other burner. The stove was fed by a propane bottle on the floor. She had already laid out small salads, hard-boiled eggs, dates, and bread. It was all very simple and, after another day of fasting, everything looked and smelled delicious.

Ahmed and I went into a closet-size space off the central room. We sat on the carpeted floor, leaned back against small pillows, and chatted while his wife cooked. His four-year-old son, Saed, came in and greeted me with shy kisses on both cheeks while his dad beamed proudly. His other kids were eleven and seven years old.

"You have a beautiful family," I told him.

"*Alhamdulillah*," he said with a smile. It means "Thanks be to God," and I heard it a lot in Muslim lands. It's what you say when someone asks "How are you?" or if you want to express thanks and graciousness to something someone has said to you. Then, through the translator, Ahmed added, "I want just to be happy in my life and have a very good family. That's it. And sleep without any problem."

Ahmed drove a truck and did day-labor construction work when he could find it. He said the money wasn't good—usually it came to about $50 a month—but he thanked God for it. He said he hoped that his kids would study hard so they could better themselves. After the fifth grade, he'd left school to start working. But things were changing so fast in Morocco—he threw his arms up in a *whoosh*, like a jet taking off—that if his kids didn't study they'd be left behind. He added, however, that in the end it was all up to God. He noted that there were people in Sidi Moumen who had graduated from college and they couldn't find jobs, either.

I asked Ahmed to advise me as a soon-to-be dad. He told me that patience and honesty were a father's most important virtues. And that it was the father's responsibility to teach his children about life, culture, and religion. God would judge me harshly if I failed, he warned.

Ahmed said that the suicide bombers who had come from Sidi Moumen were "not Muslims," because Islam forbids terrorism. He believed that outside agitators had bribed the young locals by promising them cash for their families and rewards for themselves in heaven when they completed their mission. As to who the outside agitators might be, he thought maybe they were—ready?—Zionists. Yes, apparently the Jews and their supporters somehow caused this catastrophe as well. The conspiracy theories were alive and well throughout the Muslim world, fueled daily by the local media and by rumors.

Ahmed was pleased and impressed that I was fasting during Ramadan. It is "the first step of Islam," he said, smiling. His brother joined us about halfway through the meal, and more and more people came in until the tiny house was packed; Ahmed and his wife welcomed them all. We all shared *iftar*—plates and bowls of food and glasses of tea, and a drink that was like a thick banana shake but was made from some kind of yogurt and tasted nothing like a banana.

Ahmed literally had almost nothing but his tiny home, his beautiful family, and his faith. Clearly, that was plenty. I've never met a man who seemed happier or more content with his life. Let me put that another way—I've met plenty of rich and famous people who had a lot more and seemed far less content, *and* who were a whole lot less open and generous. I couldn't believe how warmly I had been welcomed into this little home. Ahmed and his family didn't know me. They didn't know or care about my religion or my politics. It was an honor for them to share what they had with this stranger, and I was blessed to be there. *Alhamdulillah*.

. . .

One of the most vocal and visible critics of King Mohammed's adaptive modernization program is Islamist Nadia Yassine, the daughter of the conservative sheikh Abdesalam Yassine. Sheikh Yassine and Nadia call for an end to the corruption and Western-style decadence of the royals and the wealthy elite, and for more social and economic justice for the millions of desperately poor Moroccans—but carried out within a context of traditional Islamic values of compassion and charity, not through Westernization.

Nadia is a compact forty-something with a serious but not stern demeanor. Both she and her husband are university graduates, and she speaks impeccable French. Wearing a *hijab* and a tailored, very businesslike version of the traditional robes, with matching handbag, she projected the very image of a modern-but-not-Westernized Muslim woman.

We strolled in the late-afternoon shadow of Rabat's Hassan Tower, a tall twelfth-century minaret that stood alone in the center of a vast plaza where the rest of the mosque was never completed. The courtyard is filled with broken shafts of Greek-looking pillars that surround it like huge chess pieces. King Mohammed VI's father and grandfather are buried there.

"So here we are in the shadow of the kings' tombs," I said to her. "How do you feel, walking through this place?"

"I am not very happy to be walking here," she said in French. "I am an opponent of the current regime. And this is a symbol of a monarchy that I'm not particularly fond of."

"I hear that Morocco is 'a democracy with a king.' Is it a democracy?"

"Oh, no no no," she said. Her opinion echoed Aboubakr's. "It is not a democracy at all. Morocco is a disguised autocracy. My father wrote thirty books denouncing a regime that was imposed on us by our princes and not by the Koran or the Islamic tradition. So we have a responsibility to awaken the political consciences and say that the monarchy is not one of Islam's ends."

"So what do you hope to achieve?" I asked her. "What do you see as the perfect government?"

"I think that we have the right to democracy, of course. [But] we do not want to import Western or even Persian [Iranian] democratic models. I think that Islam has universal values that can be very well conjugated with universal democratic values."

"So when my president says the Middle East wants democracy, it's true?"

Nadia sighed. "Listen, these statements made by George Bush have shading to them that doesn't suit me, very frankly. Because it is true, there is democracy, but when it is Bush defending this democracy, when we know what your president is worth, despite all the esteem I hold for the American people, in his mouth this democracy makes me uneasy. I think that there is a democracy to be reckoned with that Bush is proposing. There is a very interesting author, Octavio Paz, who speaks of a 'Nescafé democracy.' "

It's also known as "decaf democracy," meaning instant, easy—just add voters. Me, I like my democracy leaded, filled to the brim, and all jacked up with caffeine. I thought Nadia, with her rapid-fire self-assuredness, would be the perfect person to tackle the issue that continued to pop up in my discussions: the coexistence of democracy and Islam in government.

"I believe that they can do better than coexist," she said. "I think they can merge together. Because Islam has kept spiritual values that democracy really needs. As we see, there is a crisis of democracy, and the wise Westerners recognize this. But Bush will never recognize that."

Nadia mentioned the conspiracy theory that the Republicans provoked or faked 9/11 as an excuse to go to Iraq and get hold of its oil. It was a little depressing to hear this line again, but I was getting used to it. I asked how she'd felt about September 11 when it happened.

"I said to *Le Monde* that if it were truly Osama bin Laden that had done this, then he dealt us a bad hand. . . . He legitimized the American presence in the Middle East. He was the reason for the adoption of all the antiterrorist laws that have pushed us further under the yoke of our own local political leaders. I was astonished on many levels. It's horrible, what happened is horrible."

"Do you believe Osama bin Laden committed 9/11?"

"I don't know," she said. "Frankly, I have no idea. I'm going to look like I'm paranoid—a lot of people look like they're paranoid—but this whole idea of Al Qaeda and bin Laden, I don't know how much of it is true and how much of it is an American creation."

Wow. We've made up some pretty good fake stuff in America: E.T., *Star Wars*, Rock Hudson as a leading man. But I didn't think we made up Osama or his connection to 9/11.

Nadia wasn't afraid to tell you what she felt. I really wanted to hear what she thought we had to do, as a world culture, to end the fighting. "I have lost all trust in official governments, all trust," she told me. "All we have left for a peaceful future and world is one possibility—it is civilian societies. . . . The American civil society is not made up of strictly enraged or mad Bushians."

Mad Bushians! We both laughed.

"We have to reach out to each other," she went on. "And ignore official political lines, and create unofficial bridges between civilian societies in order to bring about change. The only way, or at least one of the ways, of efficiently changing the future is to . . . recover a true democratic life and not a semblance of a democracy, or a democracy of theater, as seems to be happening now in several Western countries."

I told Nadia that most of the people I had talked to had found some way to tie the Israeli-Palestinian conflict to the conditions in their own countries. I asked, "If Palestine had a state tomorrow, and Palestine and Israel coexisted, would everything suddenly end? Or would radical groups still find something to fight about?"

"The wound is so deep that it would be difficult to say that everything would change overnight," she said. "And I think there are economic factors that will always ensure Israel's advantage over a dawning Palestinian state."

As I was leaving town, I thought it was a good thing that at least Nadia and her people were trying to pursue their goals of change and reform through politics, protests, and persuasion, rather than through violence—it worked for Gandhi—unlike some of the Egyptians I'd met, who paid only lip service to that idea.

. . .

Traveling the highway between Rabat and Fez one day, I saw what might be one little metaphor for Morocco's current situation. We stopped at a very modern-looking gas station called Afrique. And where its equivalent in the United States would have a 7-Eleven or a Stop-N-Shop and maybe a game room for weary parents to drop their pent-up kids for a few minutes, this one had a mosque. Out there on the road, in the middle of nowhere, a Coke, a smile, and a mosque. Sitting for a minute in the garden outside, getting a caffeine fix from a cup of Arabic coffee, I watched some men who had stopped as they filled their tanks, washed themselves as instructed in the Koran, and then prayed in the peaceful solitude of Afrique. It was just what I'd expect to see in the land of Speedy Mohammed.

Then it was time to hit the road again. I knew that if I was gonna find the Man I needed to get outta Dodge soon.

CHAPTER 8

LOOKING TOWARD THE PROMISED LAND

The Jordanian regime is an infidel regime. . . . Some people think they are a lifeboat, when in fact all they are is a sinking ship.

Message from Osama bin Laden, December 16, 2004

From Morocco we had to fly back to Paris to catch a flight to Jordan. At Charles de Gaulle, I went to get a cup of coffee and passed a bar that was filled with a bunch of Muslim guys I recognized from our flight, some of whom would also continue on to Jordan with us. A few of them were knocking back drinks at the bar; others were quietly smoking in a dark corner. Both groups must have known that Paris would be the last place they'd be chastised for either vice, even during Ramadan. Hey, when in Rome . . . or Paris, for that matter. I'm pretty sure they weren't going to find a bar open in Amman, where buying, selling, and drinking alcohol would all be *haram* and, from what I'd heard, strictly enforced. So they were living it up while they could. Hey, it could've been worse. At least they weren't devouring big platters of BBQ pork ribs as well.

It was then that I was reminded of a guy we worked with in Egypt, who said that he couldn't wait for Ramadan to be over so he could drink and have sex with prostitutes again. I guess it's the same in all religions; there are the devout, observant, obedient believers who live every day by the letter of the law, and there are folks who just go through the motions. In Islamic countries, though, the added twist is that the second kind of people *must* go through the motions, because the religious observances are intertwined with civil law.

After flying into Jordan, I went straight from the Amman airport to my hotel, the Radisson SAS—a place with a gruesome significance in modern terrorism. On the night of September 9, 2005, suicide bombers simultaneously struck the Radisson and the nearby Grand Hyatt and Days Inn. At the Radisson, a husband-and-wife suicide team walked into a wedding celebration in the ballroom. The pack of explosives the woman wore malfunctioned, so the husband sent her out of the room before leaping onto a table and detonating his. He killed thirty-eight people besides himself, including the groom and the bride's father. His wife survived, and was arrested and sentenced to death. The bomber at the Hyatt was also a walking bomb; at the Days Inn it was a car bomb.

Abu Musab al-Zarqawi, the Jordanian-born leader of Al Qaeda in Iraq, claimed responsibility. In all, sixty people were killed and more than a hundred wounded, most of them Jordanians. Among the dead was Moustapha Akkad, the Syrian-American director of the Oscar-nominated 1976 film *Mohammed, Messenger of God* (aka *The Message*) and producer of the *Halloween* movies. All sorts of terrible ironies in that, I guess. Here's this guy who wanted to do something great for his religion through his art, and he ended up getting killed in a brutal attack.

The hotel had been completely refurbished since the attack, but the security was intense. Concrete barriers and steel road spikes gave the entrance the look of a military fortress. Soldiers with M-16s at the steel gate added to the sense of fear and paranoia that I now lived with daily. Over here, as a bellboy expressed to me at the hotel, you can't help feeling as if you're living in a time bomb.

Al Qaeda attacked Jordan because it's everything guys like Zarqawi and bin Laden *don't* want in the Middle East: a voice of peace, tolerance, and moderation, especially a local one that's speaking in Arabic. (Zarqawi also had some personal grudges, which I'll explain later.)

And that's why I was there. I figured that if Osama was really foxy he might be hiding out in the one country where you'd least expect to find him. So I went to have a gander.

STAGE 7: LOOK FOR OSAMA AMONG THE ARAB PEACENIKS

Back in D.C., I had interviewed *Los Angeles Times* reporter Josh Meyer, who's been covering the War on Terror since 1999. It was Josh who first told me that I might want to see Jordan on my trip, and he explained why.

Jordan wasn't always at peace with its neighbor Israel. During the 1947–48 war that followed the creation of Israel, Jordan fought along with other Arab countries, and grabbed a large piece of what's called the West Bank, which included the holy city of East Jerusalem. It also became a refuge for something like four hundred thousand Palestinian Arabs fleeing Israel. When Israeli troops later occupied all of the West Bank in the 1967 Six-Day War, still more refugees fled across the Jordan River.

In 1994, though, the Kingdom of Jordan became the only other Arab nation besides Egypt to recognize Israel's right to exist. The current king, Abdullah II, has openly called for peace and for resistance to extremist violence. Prince Hassan, Abdullah II's uncle, founded the Royal Institute for Inter-faith Studies, and there's an interfaith ministry in the government that promotes harmony among Muslims, Jews, and Jordan's Christians, who make up about 8 percent of the total population. King Abdullah has also endorsed a program called We Are All Jordan, which aims to further curb violence in the region.

There's even a new Jordanian-produced cartoon show for kids, *Ben and Izzy*, that teaches religious and cultural tolerance. Ben is American, Izzy Jordanian. The boys meet when Ben's father takes him to an archaeological dig, and proceed to have all sorts of adventures together. They have yet to join forces with their new Jewish buddy, Moishe, but maybe they're saving that for season three.

Domestically, the Jordanian government has tried to distinguish between the Islamist movements it can deal with and the ones that are too extremist and dangerous. The Islamic Action Front, the Muslim Brotherhood's political wing in Jordan, is the largest party in Jordan's parliament. Although the group strongly opposes the king's conciliatory stance on Israel, it operates like a peaceful, loyal opposition party in any parliamentary government. It might be a model for what could happen in Egypt if Mubarak would let it.

Depending on who's counting, Palestinian refugees now make up an incredible 40 to 50 percent (anywhere from two to three million) of Jordan's total population. So no Arab nation has a higher stake in seeing that the Israeli-Palestinian conflict is resolved than Jordan. If what Dr. Post told me was right, Jordan's refugee camps would give me a chance to see one of those "terrorist assembly lines" up close and personal.

I'd also been given one more reason to visit Jordan: to look up a Palestinian-Jordanian journalist who may have better access to Al Qaeda's leadership than anyone else in the media. If anybody could tell me where in the world Osama was, it was that guy.

But first I wanted to hear those voices of peace. Southwest of Amman, in the dry brown hills that rise up from the eastern shores of the Dead Sea, is Mount Nebo (in Arabic, Jebel Nebo). Ancient tradition says that this mountain is where Moses looked out across the Jordan River valley toward the Promised Land that he would never enter. It's been a Christian pilgrimage site since at least the fourth century, and the beautiful stone church that marks what's said to be Moses' tomb looks about that old.

It was the perfect spot for me to meet Father Nabil Haddad, a Jordanian priest of the Middle Eastern branch of Orthodox Christianity known as the Melkite Church. He's a founder and the executive director of the Jordanian Interfaith Coexistence Research Center in Amman, an NGO begun in 2003 to promote understanding and tolerance. In his mid-fifties, with a round face accentuated by a trim gray beard and sparkling blue eyes, Father Haddad radiated a peaceful, positive energy that I found instantly calming.

Father Haddad showed me how Mount Nebo got its reputation. If Moses did stand there and look across to the Promised Land, he certainly had a breathtaking view. We stood facing west, looking out across the valley, rumpled and brown. To the north, our right, it was cut by the glinting ribbon of the Jordan River, where John baptized Jesus—and the border of modern Jordan and Israel. Straight ahead, the northern tip of the Dead Sea glistened. Bethlehem and Hebron were over to the left somewhere, just beyond the haze that rose from the hills on the Dead Sea's western shore. Much farther along in that direction lay the Sinai Desert, across which Moses led his people to get to where I was standing. Jerusalem was on the horizon just about due west of us, Jericho stood at the northern tip of the Dead Sea a little to our right, and farther in that direction lay the troubled West Bank.

It was moving beyond words to stand here in this place, looking out over the land that as a child I'd heard and read about in Bible school. This was the place "of historical legend" I'd learned about from Reverend Frank Bourner at the United Methodist Temple in my hometown, where I was baptized at sixteen. This was sacred ground. And, whether you are a believer or not, I think it would be difficult not to revel in the power and significance this place has had in the present-day world.

Commenting on all that incredible history spread out before us, Father Haddad said, "In this very holy land we have the responsibility not to compete over who belongs to Abraham, who belongs to heaven, who belongs to Moses, or to the prophets, or the core of the religions. The idea is that we have to compete in helping each other to live peacefully." He pointed to the horizon a little to our left, in the direction of Hebron. "At Hebron, we have the tomb of the great patriarch, Abraham. Abraham came from Iraq, he came to Jordan, and he ended up being buried in Hebron. That is of great significance. Are we really doing what we're supposed to be doing as children of Abraham, as brothers? As grandchildren of Abraham? Are we bearing witness to the whole world that from this land came all these nations, and we should stop fighting?"

I worried about that, especially with a kid on the way, and I also worried about Father Haddad, in his long black robes and priest's round cap, standing out under the blazing sun. So we went and sat on the stone steps of the church, in the shade.

I asked him if it's hard to be a Christian minority in a Muslim region.

"Being a minority is what my Lord said about the salt," he replied gently.

He was referring to Jesus telling his disciples they were "the salt of the earth." Salt was a highly prized commodity in biblical times, not just because it added flavor to meals but because a little salt sprinkled on food prevented it from going bad.

"We have to be the good salt. I never felt [any] kind of prejudice being a Christian. Sometimes I believe I am considered by the Muslims as the elite. I say this because in the holy Koran we are the ones who are closest to the hearts of the Muslims. So this gives me a kind of prerogative. . . . The authority of love is the authority that prevails. It is the best, the victorious, and the winning authority."

"But if religion is love, why is there so much religiously based violence in the world?" I asked him.

"I don't think it is religious-based. I think religion is being used as a mask to hide the cruelty, the ugliness of violence. I don't think that anything that comes from God is anything but beauty."

I wanted Father Haddad to give me his thoughts on how September 11 had affected the Middle East.

"The number one victim was Islam," he said. "And Islam is paying the high price. I think our Muslim brothers have the responsibility to clarify that they are against violence. . . . The moderates are the majority, but their voices are not loud enough to override the screaming of the violent, the extremists, and the terrorists. Those are the ones who are using religion as a mask. And I think there is extremism on both sides of this equation, but 9/11 should be an alarm to all of us. Did we do enough in all the last five years? I honestly, frankly, sincerely think we did not do enough."

As an Arab Christian, Father Haddad believes he is in a unique position to heal rifts between religions and cultures. "I think Arab Christians are the good agents to make this change," he told me. "If we have these misperceptions, stereotypes, the wrong image that everybody has about the other, we have the responsibility to clarify that. The Arab Christians can understand the West easily. And we can understand the Muslims easily, too. So, rather than sitting back here and saying we are the minority in the Arab world, I think we have the responsibility to work on building bridges."

On September 12, 2006, the Muslim world exploded in rage over comments made by Pope Benedict XVI in a lecture at the University of Regensburg in Germany. It was a scholarly lecture about the crucial influence Greek philosophy had on early Christianity, especially the Greek idea that faith and reason are not incompatible. Early in the lecture, the Pope talked about a conversation recorded in the 1390s between "the erudite Byzantine emperor Manuel II Paleologus and an educated Persian on the subject of Christianity and Islam, and the truth of both." The Pope quoted this line from the Greek emperor: "Show me just what Mohammed brought that was new, and there you will find things only evil and inhuman, such as his command to spread by the sword the faith he preached."

The way it was reported in the world press, it sounded as if the Pope himself were saying that Islam was evil and inhuman and had been spread by the sword. That's how many people in the Muslim world heard it, anyway. Hundreds of thousands protested in the streets. Mobs firebombed Christian and Catholic churches. An Italian nun in Somalia was murdered. The Mujahideen Shura Council in Iraq declared that Allah would help Muslims "conquer Rome" and "slit their throats." How's that for a peaceful response? Even Speedy Mohammed recalled his envoy to the Vatican, denouncing the Pope's "offending statements."

"It was all a gigantic misunderstanding," Father Haddad said. The media misreported what the Pope said, and then violent extremists used it as an excuse to whip their followers into a rage. Some people "were trying to take advantage of this misunderstanding. And they started, as usual, to throw the seeds of hatred. . . . But in times like these you need wisdom. You need understanding. You need people who are willing to sail against this current."

Ultimately, Father Haddad told me, he was optimistic that "love and respect will prevail," adding, "It is stronger. The people of hatred, the people of ugliness, the people of blood—they are the ones who are going to be defeated. They are the enemies of the good."

One evening I was invited to *iftar* by His Royal Highness Prince El Hassan bin Talal. He's King Abdullah's uncle, the late Hussein's brother. Prince Hassan is an avid and astute scholar of religions, one of the very few Muslims to hold an honorary degree in Catholic theology (from the University of Tübingen in Germany), and the founder of the Royal Institute of Inter-faith Studies, promoting peaceful coexistence and understanding. A small, dapper gent in a custom-tailored blue suit, he's the epitome of the sophisticated, cosmopolitan Arab elite, an easygoing man who really does seem to believe that we can all live together in peace and harmony, regardless of religious or political differences.

To give me a glimpse of his belief in action, he arranged a small demonstration for me in Salt, one of the oldest and most picturesque towns in Jordan. With its centuries-old and beautifully maintained homes climbing up gentle hillsides above a lush green valley, it reminded me of the Amalfi Coast in Italy. In a long, narrow banquet room, I dined with Prince Hassan and maybe thirty other men. They were truly a cosmopolitan, interfaith bunch—imams and Orthodox priests, sheikhs in full traditional gear, businessmen in handsome suits, even a guy from Austria.

It felt like a Chamber of Commerce dinner, Arab style. The meal was a traditional dish, *mansaf,* which consists of lamb and pine nuts on a big bed of rice, with the lamb's head in the middle of the platter. The men all stand around and eat with their fingers. It's pretty caveman—or more to the point, I guess, very Bedouin. At one point a sheikh grabbed the lamb's head by the jaw and cracked it open, the way you'd pull apart a lobster. Then he reached in and yanked out the meaty root of the tongue and popped it into his mouth. I couldn't decide if I was disgusted or really impressed. There was also a dried yogurt, *jameed,* which is preserved and shipped around the world to relatives. You just add water to warm it up and it becomes a sharp, spicy cream sauce that's poured over the lamb.

After the meal we all sat around drinking coffee and tea, smoking hubbly-bubbly (hookah pipes), and talking about the world at large. Tonight we were saving the world. Tomorrow may be another story. But I did hear some pretty amazing things from Prince Hassan.

He studied Hebrew at Oxford University, and is the only Muslim member of the university's Center for Hebrew Studies. "My friends at Oxford were Jews, Christians, Arabs of Israel who were caught between the Israelis on one side and the Arabs on the other," he told me. "The Israelis were suspicious of them, as were the Arabs." Also, "my wife was born in Calcutta, so my in-laws are from India, Pakistan, and Bangladesh. So pluralism is not an academic concept for me, it's a part of my life." He's working on a book on Christianity in the Arab world, "because unfortunately there is a wrong impression that Muslim and Arab are synonymous, forgetting the fact that Christianity was born in the East."

He has known Pope Benedict XVI, another avid theologian, since back when he was Cardinal Ratzinger. "We've been working together on producing the three holy books in their original languages, and then, hopefully, producing an analytical concordance of values. So the average layman can immediately say this is the position of a Muslim, a

Christian, a Buddhist, or whomsoever. This is what we have in common, which may be the ethical basis for a law of peace. Because we have a law of war, and, unfortunately, we work with concessions for the law of war, and how we treat prisoners and how we treat refugees and misplaced migrants, and so forth. But we don't have a law of peace."

The prince said he thought the biggest obstacle in the world today is "the fear of peace." So many people have profited by what he called the "no-war, no-peace situation, from the forty or so 'low-intensity wars' that have taken place since World War II ended." He believes that what President Eisenhower famously called the military-industrial complex—everything from arms merchants to aerospace, and all the politicians who support them—thrives on this constant state of conflict.

"I am a member of the Nuclear Threat Initiative, with Sam Nunn and Richard Lugar," he went on. "NTI has spent $8 billion dismantling weapons of mass destruction in the former Soviet Union, and finding new employment for people who used to work in that industry. That's what we should be doing in different parts of the world."

Not everyone agrees. "I was told once by a senior member in the American Congress, 'Folks like you are bad for business,' " the prince said, smiling. "I said, 'It depends on how you define business.' "

In terms of finding solutions to the threat of terrorism, the prince believes that we need to distinguish between groups like Al Qaeda—"people that are just anarchists and bloodthirsty killers who are decapitating children, doing all kinds of atrocities nationally and internationally"—and organizations like Hamas and Hezbollah, which he sees as populist movements similar to the IRA. "Isn't it about time we started turning some of these organizations by engaging them as potential political actors?" he asked.

Ultimately, the prince said, "living together harmoniously doesn't happen through immaculate conception. You simply have to work on intercommunal relations. . . . There has to be a new initiative in the world. A moral imperative. A call for the law of peace. It's about recognizing human dignity and bridging the human-dignity divide."

Build that bridge, my brother!

Now, there is one thing about the meal that I feel compelled to mention, especially in light of "bridging the human-dignity divide": there were no women present. They were in another room somewhere, with the kids. I was told by someone at the event that it's just the culture. This is how it is, and how it will always be. But then a member of our production crew told me something I found a bit disturbing. He said that the women get to eat only after the men have eaten. When the men have had their fill of the dishes we were digging our hands into, the platters are taken to the women and kids, who eat the leftovers. I couldn't believe this was true. That might be the case in the rural countryside. But here? The men sitting in big, comfy chairs drinking tea, talking about how to change the world, while the women were in another room getting, you know, sloppy seconds? I think this gathering was a bit too swank for that. At least, I *hope* it was too swank for that.

That night, the prince sent a gift over to my hotel for the baby. It was a little necklace with a charm on it, the Khamsa (or Eye of Fatima), which wards off any danger or evil. Considering that I was on a hunt for the Most Wanted Man in the World, I could have used one, too.

I woke up the next day like a shot, looking around my hotel room, trying to remember where I was. This happens to me a lot when I travel, especially when I'm in a different city every few days. I feel disconnected. I feel uneasy. All the rooms start to look the same, with the stiff comforters on the bed and the fire-retardant curtains, and you can't remember where the bathroom is when you wake up in the middle of the night. I have almost peed in the closet a few times. The only thing that stopped me was the voice in the back of my head asking, "When did they carpet the bathroom?"

I'd had the first in a series of bizarre dreams that would soon make regular appearances on my journey. Some were nightmares, and others were just real enough to wake me up in a fit of confused despair, wondering if what just happened was real or if this room with the stiff sheets and industrial carpet was the nightmare. In this dream I was in the 1600s or 1700s, being led to the gallows through a screaming crowd of spectators who threw rotten food at me and spat on me through equally rotten teeth. The town square, where the execution would take place, was packed, and the crowd grew louder as I wormed my way through, my hands bound in front of me as the executioner jerked me through the noisy throng. On the wooden platform in the center of the square was a well-used guillotine, its blade shining some twenty feet above me. The executioner wasn't wearing a mask or a black robe but regular clothes, and he seemed to be a bit cleaner than everyone else in the square.

When we reached the top of the wooden platform, the crowd fell silent and the executioner yelled something that I paid little attention to. In my mind, all I could think was This is it. This is the day I die. I looked around the crowd, but I didn't see Alex, and my heart began beating so hard that I thought it would jump out of my chest.

The executioner grabbed me by the arm, pulled me behind the guillotine, and shoved me to my knees. He pushed my head through the opening and secured the wooden slats around my neck. The crowd stared back at me in silence. This was it. Seconds away now. Below me was a wicker basket, old stains spotting its bottom. Out of the corner of my eye, I saw the blade fall. It made a smooth, *shush*ing sound. I felt no pain when it struck my neck. My eyes went out of focus . . . then . . .

Brown. I saw brown. And I felt a hand grab me by the top of my head. The executioner pulled me from the basket and showed my head to the crowd. There were cheers and applause. I couldn't speak. I couldn't do anything. The executioner showed me my own body, crumpled on the other side of the guillotine, and then he turned my head so that I could look him in the face, my scalp still gripped firmly in his hand. He screamed and laughed in my face, and as he laughed the entire world around me slowly faded away. . . .

I don't think I'll tell Alex about that dream.

I'd read that Osama had called the Palestinian cause "the mother of all causes." So I figured one place to look for him was in a Palestinian refugee camp. After hearing so much about the Palestinians, the Palestinians, and the Palestinians, I was finally going to meet some.

Driving along the Jordan River valley toward the Palestinian refugee camp at Baqa'a, I envisioned it as a bunch of tents and temporary shelters pitched in the dirt, with bedraggled people waiting in long lines for a bowl of soup or a spot at the latrine ditch. You know, a refugee camp.

In fact, it used to look like that, fifty-odd years ago. But what I saw as we drove in looked much more like a small town, poor but permanent. Simple, whitewashed buildings lined dirt streets. I saw little shops, and small houses with windows and doors trimmed in sky blue.

The elementary school where we pulled up looked pretty much like any public school in the United States. The kids were just heading out for recess as we entered. They stared or smiled shyly as they filed by in their blue, Catholic school–style uniforms. Many of the girls wore white or black *hijab*s.

According to the United Nations, about two million people of Palestinian heritage live in Jordan. Other estimates are higher. Only a handful of those alive today actually fled across the Jordan River from the West Bank during the creation of Israel in 1946–48, or again as a result of the Six-Day War in 1967. These kids, as well as many of their parents and grandparents, were born and had lived all their lives in Jordan, with full Jordanian citizenship.

But it is undeniably a second-class citizenship. Most of them are still ghettoized either in the ten refugee camps set up by the United Nations in the late 1940s and still UN-funded (Baqa'a is the largest, with about seventy thousand residents) or in urban neighborhoods that are de facto camps. Israel refuses to let them return to the West Bank until an agreement between the territories is reached. But many wonder what they will be returning to anyway. For Palestinians who fled Israel in the 1940s, their land and their homes are long gone, having been absorbed by the government and citizens in the newly formed country. And for those who fled the West Bank there are just as many concerns. Some have heard that their homes have been bulldozed to make way for Jewish settlements; others say their homes were overtaken by local squatters.

Whatever the case, they've both come to the same end: they aren't going back anytime soon. And Jordan, like the other Arab states surrounding Israel, does not fully integrate them into its society. The first refugees who came in the forties were offered citizenship, but arrivals since then must remain "refugees" until the issue of a Palestinian state is settled. As a result, fourth-generation Jordanian-Palestinian kids, who were born and might live their entire lives in Jordan, are stuck in a political limbo. They aren't really wanted in the country of their birth, and they're unable to go to what they believe is their "homeland."

Throughout the school I could see that adults were educating—or maybe the word is *indoctrinating*—these children to think of themselves as Palestinians first and Jordanians second. A sign on a bulletin board exhorted them to keep alive the dream of going "home" someday. Maps of the West Bank, which the kids had drawn in crayon, hung on classroom walls. In the art room, I looked at five student drawings. Four showed scenes of protests and rioting in the streets, with crudely drawn kids throwing rocks at Israeli tanks and soldiers. Only one showed a peaceful scene: a happy couple strolling hand in hand with not a soldier in sight. Four images of violence to one of peace.

Sitting behind her desk in a small office, Khawla al-Balbissi, the principal, had the look of a dedicated educator who had seen her share of hardship. Her face was dominated by large, sad eyes. The pencil-thin eyebrows of a 1930s Hollywood starlet contrasted curiously with her modest white *hijab*.

Principal Balbissi told me that the hardest part of her job was "dealing with the local community," with its old-fashioned, very conservative ways. "For example, we have a program of integrating the sexes, and we face opposition from the community when it comes to teaching girls and boys together." The kids are segregated from the third grade on, because their parents "think that a boy sitting next to a girl affects his behavior, and makes him want to copy the females instead of a male role model. They also think that it's not civilized and it's harming Islam. We're trying to convince them that . . . it's natural to meet females everywhere—in school, in the street. We want to create a generation that doesn't base its opinion on their ancestors'."

Hearing that, I asked Principal Balbissi about her *hijab*. She said she didn't wear it out of choice but because of local pressure. "In an environment where ninety percent of women wear *hijab*s, the majority won't respect me for not wearing it," she said. "Many of the parents used to come to the school in order to ask questions, but when they saw that I was not wearing a *hijab* they left. It got to the point where they started asking to speak to somebody else. They believe it's a sin for them to sit with a woman who is not covered. And I was insulted many times by people while driving in my car on the way to school."

Thinking of those drawings I'd seen, I asked, "Do these kids identify themselves as Palestinians? Even though they're living in a refugee camp and don't really have a country?"

"Of course, everybody has this feeling, even the fetus in his mother's womb," Principal Balbissi said. "They think about their identity, and in fact they feel that they lost all their rights." She believes that "the circumstances of deprivation, poverty, family segregation, and insecurity are influencing them and making them hold on to their Palestinian identity and think more of Palestine as their country. They feel that the ones living in Palestine are better off because they are in their country, even with the war."

One of the things I'd heard people say when they talked about living here was that they felt they had no rights, and I was curious to hear what rights Principal Balbissi thought they were being deprived of.

"The question is, what rights *do* they have?" she corrected me. "They don't have rights to security, housing. They have the minimum rights and education. That's it. They don't have freedom of speech, freedom of clothing, freedom of housing, or a country, nothing. They are living with nothing but their will to live."

It seemed to me that these kids saw Palestine only the way I did—on the TV. Principal Balbissi said, "Everyone who watches TV and sees the violence, destruction, deprivation, killing of kids feels a common identity with these innocent victims. . . . When the kids watch TV, they hear their families, their neighbors, their friends talk about the destruction and killing. So they're all preoccupied about their Palestinian identity and their right to return to a peaceful country."

"What will happen to these kids in the future?" I asked. "Where will they be in ten, fifteen years? Will some of them go off and get great jobs and do great things?"

"A great percentage of these kids, if we care a lot about them, will be successful in society, and play an important role and have a vision of their future," she said. "Even with the suffering that they endure in these harsh circumstances, we have creative, excellent, successful students."

"Do you like your job?"

"I love my job very much, and I am committed to it," Principal Balbissi said. "But sometimes, when you do not get the results that match the effort you put into it, you feel like you want to quit."

"How long do you see yourself staying here?" I asked her.

Her eyes looked sad, as if she were on the verge of tears. She looked down at her desk for a moment and glanced back up at me and said she planned to leave "at the end of this year." She added, "I'm very tired. I have a lot to give, but the pressure on me is bigger than my love for the job."

After I left the school, I went out to look for Osama, or at least signs of Osama, around the camp. In a market on a narrow street, I joined a milling crowd grocery-shopping from carts loaded with grapes, dates, bananas, oranges, limes, peppers, tomatoes, eggplants. Live chickens clucked in little pens, and slabs of meat—goat or lamb, I think—hung by their heels. One booth sold cheap sunglasses. I wasn't just the only blue-eyed, blond-haired person in the crowd but one of the few people whose hair was visible at all; the women were all wrapped in long, dark robes and veils, and many of the men sported the Arafat-style *shemagh* (scarf). Little children stared at me. So did Arafat, the real one, from several posters shopkeepers had hung in their windows. A young boy behind the counter of a falafel stand was listening to Arabic pop music. I busted some of my old-school moves and made him grin.

I met an old man, Muhammad Aissa Taib, who said that he was born in Beit Mahsir, near Jerusalem, but had lived in Jordan since fleeing in 1948—an actual first-generation refugee.

"After sixty years, do you think there is a chance of ever going back?" I asked him.

"Yes, I have hope," he said. "*Insha'Allah*, I have hope. Even if it's not me, my grandson or my great-grandson will go back to Palestine."

"What are the biggest reasons that you weren't able to go back home?"

"America stalled everything, and everything is in America's hands. And the United States at the same time wants to finish off the Palestinian people by any means. They postpone and say today, tomorrow, today, tomorrow, today, tomorrow. And they will say there is a solution, no solution, there is a solution, no solution. And all of it is just a dodge."

Asked what role America could play in solving the conflict, he said, "To take her hand out of Israel." Israel, he said, was "considered a cancer for the Arab countries. The United States created Israel to dominate the whole Arab region."

In every country I'd traveled to so far, there had been people who describe Israel with this same vicious hatred. People in Egypt, Morocco, and France called Israel a cancer. Some said it should be wiped off the map; others said the Israelies had no right to occupy that land, and that the country itself didn't exist to them. It was disconcerting to hear this, especially given the history of abuse and persecution that has followed the Jewish people. I asked Muhammad whether he thought Israel and its people had a right to exist.

"Of course, of course," he said. "They have a right to exist, but not in a land that is not theirs. Me, for example, my ancestors and I were born in Beit Mahsir. What brought me here? Do you think I'm satisfied?"

"Do you consider Jordan home now?" I asked him.

"No, no, no, no, no. No matter what, this is called a camp. This is called a refugee camp."

I asked him if after sixty years he still saw himself as a refugee?

"Yes, yes."

Haithem Sami Abdel Ifattah, twenty-one, and Mahmoud Ziad Mahmoud, twenty, reminded me of two college-age pals anywhere, just hanging out on the street, cracking jokes to each other, talking on their cell phones. I asked them what life in the camp was like.

"Life is kind of hard," Haithem said casually, "and everyone should suffer in life. We live in this camp, and we face some difficulties as struggling Palestinian people. I live in this camp because I'm originally from a poor family, and thank God for all He provides to his Muslim believers."

I asked them if they knew any young people who had joined radical groups.

"In every society, there is a different percentage of these cases," Haithem said. But he added, "Of course, there are large percentages in this camp."

And had many from the camps gone off to fight for Islam in Iraq?

"There are many from the refugee camps," Mahmoud said. "The reason is the injustice."

"How old were the people that went?"

"From fifteen and up."

I couldn't believe it. Fifteen and up! When I was fifteen I was making out with my girlfriend at the movies, playing football, and sneaking shots from my folks' liquor cabinet. The idea of going off to fight anybody was the last thing on my mind. These guys definitely lived in world a million miles from the one I was brought up in. They were aware of global politics and were deeply affected by what was happening around them. I had to know what they thought about 9/11.

"It was of great happiness to me," Haithem said. "Because we feel that an Islamic group or a group of resisters for the Islamic religion are still alive, and there will come a group that holds on to Islam, and Islam will always prevail."

And Osama?

"Osama bin Laden is a hero," Mahmoud said. "Because he fights the holy war."

"What do you think of America?" I asked them.

"When I say America's name, it gives me stomach and chest pains," Haithem said. "Because God forbids this country that doesn't know Muslims, that trespasses the limit of God by cursing the prophet Muhammad—peace and benediction upon him—by stepping on the book of God. They are evildoers, drinking alcohol and gambling. . . . How can we love America? They do what God prohibits and prohibit what God allows. Their lives are to be against Islam. All the countries should unite under Islam."

Another man told me that he thought the Israelis were "Satanic weeds," and America was "the biggest devil" for supporting them. He thought the Jews should all go "back to where they came from," so the Palestinians could return home and live in peace.

Back to where they came from? Where, like Russia, where hundreds of thousands were massacred in the czarist pogroms and during the revolution? Back to Germany, Poland, Lithuania, where *six million* were exterminated during the Holocaust? Back to Iran? Ethiopia? It was sad to me that this man, a refugee himself, had not the slightest empathy for a whole country of refugees, people who had been driven out of their homes all over the world and who had a lot more in common with him than he realized.

I walked down a narrow alley that looked like just the sort of place where Osama might be hiding. I didn't see Osama, but I did see a little boy I could imagine becoming one of his recruits. This kid couldn't have been more than ten years old. He was standing alone, watching me. He had a knife in his hands, and he glared at me as if he thought I were Satan himself. To him, I was the enemy.

Alex was right. It would have been a mistake to wear a red, white, and blue tracksuit for this whole trip.

Just then a short, thick woman wrapped in full-length robes and a *hijab* ran up to me. Her name was Rasmia Abdullah Hassan, and she desperately wanted me to see her house. "My husband is handicapped and my house is burnt and nobody wants to help me," she complained in a torrent of Arabic. "Come, I'll show you." I wondered if she thought I was from a charity or aid organization, as I followed her down one long, narrow alley after another, burrowing deep into the camp.

As I stepped into Rasmia's home, I thought, Is this a trap? No. Whew. But then my relief washed away and my heart sank for a different reason. The place was a wreck. The walls were crumbling plaster. Thin mattresses lay on bare floors. The kitchen was a propane-fed hot plate at the foot of narrow stairs, and the bathroom was a hole in the floor next to where she cooked their food. Her pantry was a battered chest of drawers with a few canned goods in it.

Meanwhile, Rasmia had burst into tears. "Look, here is my kitchen. I don't have a kitchen. The bathroom, we pee and we walk on it. I eat and I drink here. There is nothing. My husband is handicapped. I have nothing. And nobody's helping me."

Her husband, Wael, who was lying on a very narrow bed, raised himself up on one elbow. He had the disoriented, defeated look of someone who's been ill for a long time. Cheap crutches lay beside the bed. He'd worked as some sort of electrician, Rasmia said, but he "fell down and broke his head. Look, there's fifteen stitches in his head." He'd broken his leg as well. Rasmia showed me X rays. She said that she had trouble with her ankles, and feared she had breast cancer.

Behind the house there was a small, junk-strewn courtyard where Rasmia hoped to build a kitchen. "I told them I have nothing—I have no bed, no wardrobe," she said. "They give us charity, they give us steel, and the contractor, but I don't have any cement, plaster, or sand. My kids are all married. And I'm here and I asked my husband to divorce me so that I can collect benefits from the government office, because nobody wants to give me anything."

Rasmia said that the Zakah Committee, Al Bir, and Al Ishan—three Muslim charities—gave her thirty dinars (about $42) a month, but she added, "The development office doesn't give me anything." She couldn't say why. She showed me a clutch of paperwork. "These are my electricity and water bills. I don't have money to pay them. They will cut the water and the electricity."

"And the phone," Wael added, sitting up in his narrow bed. "They cut it. It was eighty dinars."

Rasmia and Wael were distant cousins. Both their families came from the West Bank in the sixties. Wael was eight when his family immigrated. Rasmia was born in a tent in the refugee camp.

Rasmia said she used to clean houses and babysit, but now she couldn't work. "People give me bread and sugar, and my husband brings bread from the mosque," she told me.

They figured they needed five hundred dinars to build a kitchen. I reached into my pocket and gave her all the money I had—about fifty dinars, or seventy bucks. If I'd had more, it would have been hers. She needed it a lot more than I did.

· · ·

Aliyah Ajaj also invited me into her home. By now I was pretty convinced that Osama wasn't in the camp, so I went willingly. It wasn't the wreck Rasmia's house was. It was clean, and bright sunlight filtered through thin, cheap curtains fell on plaster walls painted butter yellow. But it was practically empty. The only pieces of furniture in the living room were some cushions on the floor.

We sat on the floor. Aliyah appeared to be in her forties. She was also wrapped head to toe in the traditional black robes and head scarf. Only her hands and her pretty, round face were visible. Her three sons—two teens and a younger boy—stood in a doorway shyly eyeing us. She also had two daughters.

Aliyah surprised me right at the outset by telling me that she was an Iraqi, from Mosul.

"Aren't you in the wrong camp?" I joked.

She laughed, then turned serious. "I have no choice," she said. "My husband is Palestinian. I'm here against my will, and I am a prisoner. I'm in jail. I don't like my situation. I've been in this situation for many years; I can't come and can't go anywhere. I don't have anybody left from Iraq. No news, nothing. I got some news that the Shiites slaughtered them. My nephew was sending me money, wiring it, and three months ago he disappeared. He was slaughtered by the Shiites. They slaughtered him."

So she was Sunni. Saddam, a Sunni, had favored the Sunni minority over the poor, Shiite majority. When he disappeared, the reprisals began. I knew the flow of Iraqi refugees out of the country had grown to a human tsunami. By this point, it was said, *one million* of them had poured into Jordan and Syria seeking asylum. A report by the Washington-based Refugees International said that more than one hundred thousand people a month are fleeing the country, and estimates that more than two million have sought safety in neighboring countries. And while it may not be the largest refugee crisis in the world, a spokesperson for the agency said, the numbers are "very, very scary."

"I came here at the fall of Saddam," Aliyah explained. "They started killing us, and I was afraid that they might kill my children, so I left and brought them here. They started to kill the children. They were killing boys and girls. They were there, not doing anything anyway. There is nothing there. People can't go out on the streets. There is no security in Iraq. There is no food, there is nothing. There are no committees, no one to give you money. Here they write us checks, fifteen dinars, and the children are taking care of themselves and we're doing okay."

But fifteen dinars was nothing. Her husband had divorced her and left her alone with the kids. Aliyah couldn't buy a uniform for her son Ali to go to school. She depended on food handouts and charity. She said that the Palestinians in the camp received aid from their families, but as an Iraqi she had no family to help her. Only her neighbor, a Palestinian man who was as poor as she was, sometimes gave her a little money, like five dinars, to buy some food for the kids.

"There is no piece of furniture that I have not sold," Aliyah told me. "I sold everything, pots and pans, so I can just spend money on my children. It's Ramadan, and we have nothing."

Life in the camp was "better when it comes to security, especially for the little girls—we have little girls," she went on. "In Iraq, they slaughter people. My niece—I don't know where she is, I don't know what she's doing. I have no news, and there is no security." She said there had been more Iraqi refugees in the camp, but most of them had gone back home. "I stayed because my children are going to school here. Look, I have five children. Where am I going to take them in Iraq? They're little kids."

I asked her what her life was like under Saddam.

"Well, better, it was good. There was food, security, we had land, there was everything. We used to go in freedom. Now this has become a prison—this is a prison for us."

"Do you ever think you're going to be able to go back to Iraq?"

"It's like Palestine," she said. "We are waiting for God's intervention. We, the Iraqis, we're done. There is nothing for us Iraqis, nothing. For me, there is no more Iraq. We forgot our lands, we forgot. We depend on charity now. But don't think about it, only our God will manage. May God have mercy on us.

"What happens in Iraq is injustice, injustice. God won't agree with it. All the Iraqis are being used by America. Who do you think is using them? I mean they're Muslims, and Iran supports the Shiites. The most support is from Iran. The Iranian people pay, and the Iraqis kill each other."

Both Iran and Al Qaeda had picked sides in Iraq's Sunni-Shiite massacres. Iran, predominantly Shia, armed the Shiite militias. Al Qaeda, which was Sunni, regarded the Shiites as *takfir* (nonbelievers), and supported the Sunni death squads. And the United States and Coalition forces, who'd toppled Saddam and left a power vacuum to be filled with bloodshed, were caught in the middle.

"So do you think the Americans should get out?" I asked her.

"Yes, they should get out. If they got out and left the country for everyone to take his part of the land, it would be a normal government."

I don't know if it would be that easy—I think even more people would be killed—but maybe the situation in Iraq has to reach that place of critical mass Martin McGuinness talked about in Ireland, the point when both sides say "The killing has to end." I really wanted to hear how all this had affected Aliyah's view of my country.

"What do you think of America?" I asked her.

"America? May God make America fail," she said. "They humiliated us, killed our relatives, and tore us apart. America left us sitting here, humiliated, asking for charity for the sake of God. What did they do to us? What did Iraq do? I swear, we don't have nuclear [weapons], we don't have nuclear. But they only want to take our oil. They destroyed the youth. They destroyed the people, destroyed the little children. It's a sin what happened to this Arab country."

Aliyah was clearly distressed, and had been affected by her experience in Iraq as well as in the camp. "God, I swear, we are humiliated!" she went on. "Every day I go to the offices and get humiliated, because I have nobody to help me. Any office I go to register in—development office, affairs office—they say, 'You are Iraqi.' This woman comes by and gives me clothes to wear. In Iraq it was never like that. It's not a matter of shame. A woman will come by and give me something to wear. That never happened when I was in Iraq. I didn't take things from people."

I knew that Aliyah was Sunni, but I didn't know anything about her personal or family history. Had her husband been a member of the

Baath Party and among Saddam's supporters? Was her experience typical of other Iraqi refugees, or unique? I hadn't yet met any Iraqis on my trip. I asked Aliyah to tell me how she saw Americans, from her perspective, as a Sunni who had thrived under Saddam.

She said, "They didn't leave an Arab country without destroying it. They made Arabs turn on Arabs. There was no problem between Sunnis and Shiites. The U.S. came in, and with Iran's backing, [set] the Shiites against the Sunnis. Look what has happened. I was in Iraq. I saw the war. I saw American soldiers holding a kid and stepping on his head—on his head! And I saw the Americans with my own eyes grab a girl and tie up her father. And her brothers. And have their way with her. I saw that with my own eyes, and my children saw that, too."

"Right in front of you?" I was incredulous.

"My son saw it, my daughter saw it. On our way out, crossing the border, they would grab a child, give him some kind of toy to play with, and then just step on his head and start beating him. What America? Everything is covered, all of the real images are covered. There is no truth, the truth is covered. The elderly women are beaten. The elderly men are beaten. It's all lies. I saw it with my own eyes, and my son, too. They put a car there with a family in it and killed everyone—children and the whole family. I had an aunt, they shot her while we were standing there. We couldn't speak. That's America."

She pointed to Ali, the oldest boy. "Him, he saw it. She was my aunt. Go ahead and speak. Don't be embarrassed, speak."

"Did you see American soldiers beating and killing Iraqis?" I asked.

"Yes," Ali said.

"Were they family members?"

"Yes, they were related to us."

"What did they do to them?"

"They stepped on them. They shot at them. And killed them."

"Yes, with the gun," Aliyah interjected. "They would hit them on the heads with the gun. I saw all of this."

Like most Americans, I had read and seen reports of some serious abuses in Iraq, but I'd never heard any reports that matched Aliyah's claims. I know war is war and terrible things happen, but I personally had a hard time swallowing this. If it was true, the impact of those kinds of actions will spread like a plague throughout the region, fueling anti-American sentiment. And if it was false did it matter, if everybody believes it anyway?

I wondered what hope Aliyah had for her children.

"By God, there is no hope." She started to cry. "What am I going to do? There is nothing I can do about it."

And then she broke my heart by asking me to stay for *iftar*. Her neighbor had given her five dinars. "Stay and break the fast with us," she said. "There is food—we bought meat. You're welcome to. This is your sister's house."

"Do you really want an American in your house?" I asked. After all she'd told me, I thought I'd be the last person she'd want to eat dinner with.

"Yes, normal Americans are like us," she said. "We are all the same. We're oppressed and they're oppressed, too. We are one people." Aliyah showed me around her house. In a small bedroom there was a TV, and a photo of Saddam taped to the wall, and a child's crayon drawing of Minnie Mouse with words written in Arabic: "God is generous, Iraq."

She showed me snapshots of young men. "These are my nephews who died. And that is my brother, who also died as a martyr." I thought I knew what she meant by *martyr*, but she wouldn't expand on that. And, suddenly, it occurred to me why some of her family might have been targeted. But there was no way to truly know.

I walked out into the sunlight feeling empty. This poor woman was alone in the world, and so sad. And yet suddenly she would smile, and her whole face would change. I told her she had a beautiful smile, and she laughed and said that I was flirting with her. "Tomorrow I will be an American!" she joked. And at that moment I thought this was the real Aliyah, and wondered when was the last time she'd had a chance to do that—to feel happy, the way any person in the world should be able to.

She also reminded me of something else, which is that just because you're a refugee doesn't mean you have to be overcome by a "refugee mentality." Many people talked about this, but I didn't see it until I compared Aliyah's home with Rasmia's up the street. Aliyah's place was sparse, but clean. Things were put away, and she did her best to make it feel like a home. Rasmia, on the other hand, wore her status on her sleeve; garbage lined the halls, and the back alley was a dumping ground. Maybe she'd just lost hope. I can only imagine how hard it must be to take care of herself and her crippled husband, but I couldn't help thinking that maybe she was the type who felt she was owed something. And maybe she was—I didn't know enough to say. But after seeing their homes and the others I'd been invited to throughout my search so far, I thought that no one should ever have to be afraid where they live, no one should have to worry about whether or not their kids can get educated, and no one should ever go hungry.

James Brabazon, a brilliant British journalist I'd hired to help get me through conflict areas safely, came up to me. He'd shot films in the hairiest of hairy locales and he was looking around me, down the alley, and at the windows up above, where countless people were now peering down at us through half-drawn curtains. He was fidgety and obviously ready to leave.

"We need to go," he said.

"What are you talking about?" I asked.

"A lot of people have seen us here. We just need to leave."

"Everything seems fine to me," I said.

"It always is," he responded. "Right up until you get killed."

If anyone outside of Al Qaeda knew where Osama bin Laden was, I thought it would be the Palestinian-Jordanian journalist Fouad Hussein. From Baqa'a I went to his garden apartment in Amman, where we sat out on his beautiful little patio and he shared *iftar* with me.

Fouad's family was originally from Ramallah, on the West Bank. Born in 1956, he graduated from Baghdad University in 1978 "and immediately joined the press," he said. "I worked in the press agencies and the daily newspapers, magazines, radio, and TV. I own a small production company, producing documentaries about the Islamic movement generally and Al Qaeda especially."

In 1996, as editor of the newspaper *Al Aswak*, Fouad wrote an article that was very critical of Jordan's prime minister, who had raised the prices of gas, bread, and other necessities. That was enough to get Fouad thrown in jail, where he stayed for seventy-one days. As it turned out, in the same prison with him were Abu Musab al-Zarqawi and his mentor, the Salafist scholar Muhammad al-Maqdissi. They'd been arrested for plotting terrorist attacks in Jordan.

As a journalist, Fouad said, he felt that he had to meet them. "So I went to them and presented myself and told them, 'I'm not an Islamist, but I heard your story in the media, and I want to hear your side of the story so that people know the truth.' "

Fouad paints a very different portrait of Zarqawi than the one you usually hear. Usually he's described as a small-time thug and gangster, raised in poverty in Jordan, who through sheer ruthlessness became Osama bin Laden's chief enforcer in Iraq after the 2003 invasion; that he was instrumental in whipping up vicious Sunni violence against Shiites in that country; that he personally beheaded the young American businessman Nicholas Berg—who had been kidnapped in Iraq in 2004—and had the videotape distributed worldwide; and that he organized the hotel bombings in Amman in 2005. The kind of guy you wanna take home to mom—if mom is Lizzie Borden.

"I thought from the first time that he was quiet, polite, silent," Fouad recalled of his meetings with Zarqawi. He later realized "that his silence wasn't out of ignorance. Instead, he was preparing himself and thinking about what to do after getting out of jail."

Zarqawi told Fouad that he'd been in solitary confinement for eight months, and had frequently been tortured. Soon after they met, Zarqawi was returned to solitary. Other inmates rioted to show support, and Fouad became the mediator between them and the prison authorities. It earned him tremendous respect among his fellow inmates.

Released in the amnesty declared by King Hussein in 1999, Zarqawi went straight to Afghanistan, where he set up a terrorist training camp. Fouad said that it was the invasion of Iraq in 2003 that made Zarqawi a superstar of global jihad. When the American media kept trumpeting Zarqawi's name as a major organizer of the resurgence against the invasion, it "made him a special personality loved by everyone" in the Muslim world.

Fouad's early contact with Zarqawi has afforded him extraordinary journalistic access to the Al Qaeda network during the decade since. He has traveled to Afghanistan and Iraq to interview Zarqawi and other Al Qaeda leaders, both for print articles and for documentary films. In 2005, his book *Al-Zarqawi: The Second Generation of Al Qaeda* was published in Arabic. In it he describes how Al Qaeda has actually mapped out a schedule for establishing a new caliphate—a unified, global ummah, free from both outside influence and internal secular governments, and all ruled by Sharia law.

He told me there are seven phases to the plan:

Phase 1: The Awakening (2000–03). By attacking the United States on September 11, Al Qaeda provokes the West to retaliate in Afghanistan and Iraq, triggering the "awakening" of Muslims throughout Islam.

Phase 2: Opening Eyes (2003–06). Al Qaeda expands its network and recruits an "army" of young Muslims around the world. "This period included the preparation for the electronic jihad, which will make the use of the Internet common between the jihad organizations," Fouad said. "For example, before 2003 they had only twenty-four websites. Now they have 1,480 websites."

Phase 3: Arising and Standing Up (2007–10). Attacks in Syria, Turkey, Jordan, and Israel destabilize the Middle East and further strengthen Al Qaeda's reputation and recruiting abilities.

Phase 4: (2010–13). Continued attacks both in the Middle Eastern states, especially Israel, and against Western clients for Middle East oil bring about the collapse of various Arabic secular governments in the region.

Phase 5: (2013–16). "The grip of the West will weaken in the region as a result of its defeat in Iraq, and its exhaustion in places like Sudan, Somalia, and Eritrea," Fouad said. "Therefore the Western power will weaken, leading to the weakness of Arab regimes and Israel."

Phase 6: Total Confrontation (2016–20). "A final, sweeping confrontation between the Arabic and Islamic forces of liberation and the forces of the colonialist West."

Phase 7: Definitive Victory (2020). Islam defeats the nonbelievers and the new caliphate is established.

If this script sounds incredible, Fouad countered that it was already well under way.

"If you think about what has happened from 2000 until now, you'll find that they've done exactly what they decided to do," he told me. "I am not Islamist, but I'm sure this movement will be the leader of all this region before 2020."

Fouad went on to tell me that the greatest mistake the United States made in the entire War on Terror was to invade Iraq after routing Al Qaeda from Afghanistan.

"After Afghanistan, Al Qaeda didn't have anywhere to operate," he said. But when we entered Iraq we created a holy cause for jihadists around the world. Basically, we gave Al Qaeda the excuse to reorganize. "If the United States hadn't entered Iraq, Al Qaeda wouldn't be what it is now. It would have ended with the end in Afghanistan."

Iraq, he went on, is now "the new base for Al Qaeda. In the first years of occupation, Al Qaeda became the center of attraction for holy fighters against the American forces. But now Al Qaeda in Iraq has a lot of Iraqi members. Therefore they don't need volunteers from outside the country. And the volunteers who come from outside Iraq receive the military training, the political and legal expertise, then go back to their countries to create new branches for Al Qaeda."

"How many Al Qaeda operatives are in Iraq right now?" I asked him.

"Not less than thirty thousand."

"And in the rest of the world?"

"You can never count them," he said, "because Al Qaeda is now two Al Qaedas—the Al Qaeda as an organization that follows the central command in Iraq or bin Laden, and the stream of Al Qaeda represented by all the young people who believe in the Al Qaeda example and work the same way as Al Qaeda, without having a direct contact with the leadership. And the last kind are of a larger number, and more dangerous."

"So if bin Laden was caught or killed, would it make any difference?"

"None whatsoever. Zarqawi was killed and nothing happened. And if bin Laden and Zawahiri got killed, nothing will happen. Because Al Qaeda became an intercontinental idea, the same as globalization."

First Starbucks, now Al Qaeda. Great.

I asked Fouad where I should go to find Osama bin Laden.

"You can't find him," he simply said.

"No?"

"No. But if he would like to find you, he can."

CHAPTER 9

OLIVE BRANCHES

————————

We are in a strong and brutal battle, between us and the Jews, with Israel being the spearhead, and its backers among the Zionists and Crusaders. So we have not hesitated to kill the Jews who conquered the sanctuary of our Prophet. And those who kill our children, women, and brothers night and day, and whoever stands in the aggressors' ranks, has only himself to blame.

Osama bin Laden, October 2001

Our terrorism against America is a praiseworthy terrorism in defense against the oppressor, in order that America will stop supporting Israel, who kills our sons. Can you not understand this? It is very clear.

Osama bin Laden, November 2001

The sun had been up for only a couple of hours, but already the morning was hot and dry under the hazy blue sky. About thirty of us tramped single file up a low hillside, following a narrow track through long brown grasses flanked by scraggly little trees and bushes hanging their leaves out like parched tongues in the heat. A few insects whirred and rang, but otherwise the air was perfectly still and silent.

Someone said, "Watch where you step. There's a snake in the grass to your left."

An awfully biblical remark, but this wasn't the Garden of Eden. It was the West Bank, one of the most troubled places on earth. We'd come to an area just south of the city of Nablus.

Literally every Muslim I'd spoken to had mentioned Israel and Palestine as a major bone of contention between Islam and the West. Since the early 1990s, Osama had rarely opened his mouth without spewing some rant about the Jews, the Zionists, their Crusader friends in the United States, the plight of the Palestinians, and the sacred duty of every Muslim on earth to see that Israel is utterly destroyed.

Which had got me thinking . . . Who would expect Osama to hide in Israel? Disguised as an Orthodox rabbi, maybe—he already had the beard. It was the last place any sane person would look for him.

So I, of course, went to Israel and the West Bank to do just that. Alex had said I was crazy, after all. At the very least, I knew that if I wanted to find reasons—or excuses—that Osama had done what he'd done, I couldn't look in a better place.

STAGE 8: SEARCH ISRAEL AND PALESTINE

At the top of a hill topped by a grove of olive trees, we looked out across a landscape of many more brown hills where people had been farming and tending sheep for thousands of years. We'd come here to harvest the olives. Hard to imagine a more peaceful, bucolic way to spend a morning in the country, right? But, like pretty much everything in this part of the world, this was a political act, laden with the possibility of violence.

Ahmed, a skinny, easy-smiling teen in a baseball cap and khaki work pants, set up a ladder, while his two adolescent brothers spread a tarpaulin under one of the trees. They gave the rest of us a quick lesson in how to pull the hard, dark-green olives off the branches and let them drop onto the tarp. No machinery, nothing complicated. Just gravity and the human hand. People must have been harvesting olives this way for countless generations, back to the time of Jesus, David, and Moses.

Ahmed and his brothers lived in the nearby Palestinian village of Kafir Qalil, just off the main highway from Jerusalem to Nablus. Their family's olive grove was spread over about fifteen acres of the hillside. Ahmed didn't know how many trees that included; it's considered unlucky to count them, just as it's traditionally unlucky for a shepherd to count his sheep, but the oldest trees had been planted about thirty years ago.

The boys set to work quickly and efficiently. The rest of us, all volunteers, fumbled around. The boys didn't really need our help harvesting—we were there for another reason. A Jewish settlement lay just over the ridge, and throughout the Occupied Territories the fall harvest had been a time of tensions and confrontations between Palestinians working their family land and settlers who were trying to force them off that land. Settlers stole the olives, burned trees, and shot at, beat, or otherwise harassed the harvesters. There had been a few murders over the years, and the Israeli government had recently dispatched soldiers of the Israeli Defense Forces (IDF) to keep the settlers and the harvesters separated, but they weren't always very zealous about it, and reportedly often refused to let the harvesters onto their family land, saying it was for their own safety.

In 2000, a group called Rabbis for Human Rights began the Olive Tree Campaign. The rabbis of RHR were progressive humanitarians and activists who believed it was their duty to work for human and civil rights in the region, speak out against the mistreatment of Palestinians, and promote peace and tolerance. Among other things, they organize international, interfaith groups of volunteers—Israelis, Europeans, Americans, you name it, of the Jewish, Christian, and Muslim faiths—to go out with Palestinian harvesters and, in effect, act as human shields to protect them from the settlers. Today, I was one of those volunteers.

We got to work, and the olives plopped onto the tarps and began to pile up. Through Arnon Regular, an Arabic-speaking Israeli journalist and my interpreter, Ahmed explained that six or seven trees should yield enough olives to make about twenty kiloliters of olive oil. They'd take the olives home and wash them, then bring them to the olive-oil plant. He expected to get about seventeen shekels, or four dollars, per kiloliter—maybe eighty dollars for the day. They would collect more in a day if they had the machinery, but they couldn't afford it. Harvesting the grove was just a supplemental source of income for the family.

Which was just as well, because for the previous three years the harassment had been so intense that they couldn't do the harvest. The year before, Ahmed said, his grandmother and his uncle were beaten by settlers in the very spot where we were working. The settlers stole all the olives, and chopped and burned some of the trees.

We fell silent as we concentrated on the work, and I reviewed what people had told me about the history of Israel and Palestine that had brought things to such a pass that simple farmers couldn't work their land without armed guards and human shields.

At the end of the war that followed the creation of Israel, Israel ended up holding more than three-fourths of colonial Palestine, and half a million to a million Palestinian Arabs fled. During the next decade, huge numbers of Jews emigrated to Israel from all over the world, taking possession of the lands the Palestinian refugees had left behind. Over the years, and through a series of wars begun by their Arab neighbors, Israel made the Occupied Territories (the West Bank, Gaza, and the Golan Heights) permanent parts of its territory, and continued to seed them with Jewish settlers.

Palestinians still living in Gaza and the West Bank were similar to Catholics in Northern Ireland. They received the barest minimum of government services, unemployment was extremely high, and dire poverty was rife. Their travel within Israel was severely restricted. They couldn't even travel easily within what had been their own lands, let alone visit family and relatives in the refugee camps. Today, there are hundreds of armed checkpoints in the West Bank alone.

In 1987, Palestinians rose up in street demonstrations, strikes, and skirmishes known as the First Intifada (Arabic for "shaking off," as in rebellion). In the early 1990s, the escalating violence—and the force of world opinion—brought Israel, Jordan, and Yasser Arafat's PLO to the bargaining table. In 1993, Israel and the PLO signed a Declaration of Principles, commonly known as the Oslo Accords, creating a semi-autonomous Palestinian Authority to govern the West Bank and Gaza, and Israel withdrew its troops from the territories.

In 2000, U.S.-mediated talks aimed at finally creating a truly independent Palestinian state faltered. Extremists on both the Israeli and the Palestinian side used the loss of momentum as an excuse to step up their own agendas. Palestinians rose up in the Second Intifada, which proved to be much bloodier than the first. Waves of suicide bombings in Israel drew brutal reprisals. Between September 2000 and the spring of 2006, close to four thousand Palestinians and about eleven hundred Israelis were killed. Nearly a thousand of those, from both sides, were children.

Arafat died in November 2004. His successor as president of the Palestinian Authority, Mahmoud Abbas, represented Arafat's Fatah Party. While Abbas struggled to assert control over the many political and paramilitary factions among the Palestinians—including his major rival, Hamas—Israel's prime minister, Ariel Sharon, oversaw the start of a process of unilateral "disengagement," which included removing Jewish settlers from the West Bank and Gaza. So the settlers who had displaced the Palestinians were now themselves being displaced—by their own government, often at the point of Israeli Defense Forces guns, which created a lot of bitterness and anger.

Meanwhile, Israel continued construction of a highly controversial border wall separating the West Bank from Israeli land. Former President Jimmy Carter charged that Sharon was trying to wash his hands of the whole Palestinian issue by turning the West Bank and Gaza into walled-off Bantustans (a reference to South Africa's Apartheid-era "homelands" for black Africans). In January 2006, Sharon suffered a massive stroke but his successor, Ehud Olmert, continued on the same course.

That was pretty much the state of things that morning as we picked olives. There were still plenty of Jewish settlers living in the hills all around us—as we soon found out. Mahmoud, Ahmed's younger brother, called out something in Arabic, and suddenly everyone grew watchful.

Mahmoud had spotted a figure under a tree at the top of the hill. Squinting, I could just barely make out the dark silhouette seated on the ground. We couldn't tell if it was a settler or a soldier. Probably the former, from the settlement just over the hill. He must have seen us all looking at him, but he didn't move.

"What is he watching for?" I asked.

Ahmed, at the top of his stepladder, said something in Arabic that made his brothers laugh.

"He is joking that he will just watch you and then beat you and then go away," Arnon translated.

Ahmed added that if we outsiders hadn't been there the settler would probably have shot at them.

I wondered if we should confront him, but everyone said that might spark an incident. We went back to work, but we could all feel the man's eyes on our backs. The comfortable mood of the morning had shifted to one of tension, and we uneasily continued talking about life in Kafir Qalil.

"Every day the army is coming and entering. . . . There are clashes with stones and everything during the day, but at night it's the exchange of gunfire," Mahmoud said. "There's a lot of gunmen in Kafir Qalil, so it's a very busy place. Since the beginning of the Intifada, sixteen people from the village have been killed. With the exchange of fire and the demolition of two Palestinian houses, it's always tense."

The boys said that the army never entered the Jewish settlement, and their houses were never demolished. "Over there the streets are clean, the water is clean, if somebody is sick there is always somebody that will take care of him," Ahmed told me. "We are not even close to that. Don't forget that they are living on our land." Wherever there was open land, he said, it had filled up with settlers.

I asked Ahmed what he thought of the Israelis who had come to help him harvest. "They are human people," Arnon translated. "But he says with or without them we have rights here and we should get our rights."

We talked about politics in the Palestinian Authority, and the boys had surprising and sophisticated opinions. In January 2006, Hamas had won a landslide victory, 76 of 132 seats in the Palestinian Authority parliament. At that point, declaring Hamas to be a terrorist organization, the United States, Israel, and the European Union all cut off funding to the Palestinian Authority, some of which had been used to pay the salaries of civil servants ranging from politicians to policemen and schoolteachers. Here it was, ten months later, and there was still no funding. Ahmed and his brothers couldn't go to school, because the schools had all been shut down. (In 2006, even though the United States had cut off direct funding to the Palestinian government, it still sent about $150 million in humanitarian aid to Palestinian refugees, mostly through private charities, making it the largest donor after the European Union—though this was less than 6 percent of the total U.S. aid given to Israel.)

Tensions between Abbas and his Hamas-dominated parliament were high. Militants from the two sides had recently clashed violently in Gaza.

Ahmed said that even when aid money had been coming in the politicians pocketed it, and very little reached the average Palestinian. "We voted for Hamas for change," he said, but because of the economic blockade nothing had happened. He also noted that no Arab nations had rushed to fill the funding gap. The Fatah prime minister, Ismail Haniyeh, had declared that if necessary the Palestinian people would live on olive oil and *za'atar*, an herb that grows wild in the region. That was fine for him to say, Ahmed observed dismissively, but he doubted that this was all the prime minister ate.

Just then a crash startled us. I practically jumped out of my skin, thinking we were under attack. But everyone started to laugh. Mahmoud had fallen off his ladder, breaking a branch in the process. He was laughing, too.

"Well, it'll be a lot easier to pick now," I said.

We'd just gotten back to work when an IDF soldier came strolling through the trees. He had the casual swagger of a beat cop. But the sudden appearance of his fatigues, with his shiny black rifle slung in front of him, upped the tension yet again.

His name was Ovit. He told me that he was just patrolling, making sure we weren't harassed. I asked if there had been a lot of problems here in the past.

"No," he said. "There are no problems. We are making sure there are no problems. Occasionally there are land disputes, and each side claims to have ownership of the land. We check the papers, and according to that we define who owns the land."

"Who does own the land around here?" I asked him.

He pointed at the boys. "This land is for them," he said. "This is theirs."

Ovit said there were sometimes problems near another settlement, where the settlers were more extreme and aggressive, "but here there are no problems." I told him what the boys had told me. Yes, he conceded, but the violence they'd described had not happened in this area.

We shook hands, said "Shalom," and he strolled off into the trees, vanishing as quietly as he'd appeared.

We finished the harvest. Mounds of olives covered the tarps. We scooped them into large burlap sacks, one of which was stamped WHEAT FLOUR WORLD FOOD PROGRAM. Ahmed and his brothers dragged them away. For them it had been a productive, and more or less uneventful, day. *Baruch Hashem.* ("Thank God" in Hebrew.)

. . .

I met another IDF soldier that day in the olive grove. Or, rather, a former soldier. Like every young Israeli, Elik Elhanan did the required three-year turn in the military. (It's two years for women.) He came away from that experience utterly convinced that change was necessary and he had to be a part of it. Now twenty-nine, he was a founding member of Combatants for Peace, a group of former Israeli and Palestinian soldiers who believe violence is futile. He was also a volunteer for the rabbis' Olive Tree Campaign.

"Why are you here today?" I asked him.

"I really believe the solution to this conflict will come through a solidarity movement, a joint Israeli-Palestinian resistance to the occupation," he told me.

"You're in the minority," I said.

"Yes."

"Why?"

"I think because many people have lost hope, because many interested parties are playing on myths that are implanted not only in Israel but in both sides, in order to create a real dichotomy, a real polarized vision of the conflict."

Elik had been a soldier from age eighteen to twenty-one. I asked him about that time.

"Long," he said. "I learned a lot. . . . For me it was, in a way, a wake-up call, a way to see the difference, the distance between the mythology and the reality on the ground."

He'd served in Lebanon, fighting against Hezbollah. "It was a very difficult experience," he told me. "Through this experience I actually came to realize the cynicism and the hypocrisy that stand behind the discourse of the army and the Israeli government."

Rather than doing something noble, like defending Israel against its enemies, he felt that he was just part of an occupying army, defending itself.

"I saw that all we are serving are political ends, and we are covering for political cowardice, and actually we are treated as pawns in some game that is played elsewhere."

Elik said he was very grateful that he hadn't found himself in a situation where he had to hurt anyone. "But, on the other hand, we really tried," he told me. "We laid down ambushes, we planted charges, things like that. The Hezbollah militants never came, so we never killed anybody."

While Elik was in the army, something occurred back home in Jerusalem, he said, that was "a turning point, a rupture that made me say, well, now things must change. On the fifth of September 1997, two suicide bombers from the Hamas movement blew themselves up in the center of Jerusalem. Killed five people, injured about fifty. And one of those who were killed was my sister. She was fourteen years old at the time. It was the first or second day of school, and she went downtown with two friends to buy books and things for school. They had the misfortune to be very close to one of the suicide bombers. She died instantly, as did her friend, and the third one was critically injured, an injury she never recovered from."

Elik was in Lebanon, he went on, "and then this message came. And in a way it changes everything. Everything stops." But, he added, "The problem is that, well, actually *nothing* stops, and everything goes on. Life doesn't have much consideration for small problems." He said he remembered his army commander saying "that I mustn't sink into sorrow and bereavement. I should get back to activities as quickly as possible. 'Look, I put you on the point of an operation that is being planned. I want you to go out there. I want you to get back on track.' And then he told me, 'I mean, who knows? Maybe we'll even encounter some terrorist and you can even the score.' "

Being asked to kill someone in Lebanon to make up for his sister's death in Jerusalem convinced Elik that he had to try to change the cycle of hatred and violence. And change was coming slowly, he said, but he did see it happening.

"I see organizations that are coming to life, and many ideas that ten years ago were unthinkable and five years ago were extremely radical, and now many people take part in them," he explained.

And so here he was, picking olives on the West Bank.

"Me, as an Israeli who has a responsibility for what's happening here, I must come here and tell them that I'm willing to work with them for peace," he said.

. . .

On the highway running north from Jerusalem into the West Bank, I saw one of the big obstacles to Elik's attempts to bring Israelis and Palestinians together.

I'm speaking literally. It was that "security" border that Israel began constructing in 2002 to wall off the West Bank. It's a brutally, surrealistically grim cross between the Berlin Wall and a prison wall, complete with guard towers, built of monstrously tall, eight-meter slabs of concrete, with armed checkpoints where highways and roads penetrate it.

One Palestinian told me that he feels like "an animal in a zoo that isn't allowed to roam free." Another said, "I feel like a prisoner. Only, my home is my jail and I am trapped inside."

You can tell someone's stance on the barrier by the way he describes it. If he's for it, he calls it a "security fence." If he's against it, it's called "the wall" or the "security wall." I saw how much Palestinians like the idea when we drove through the checkpoint and the base of the guard tower was blackened from the smoke of Molotov cocktails that had been thrown at it. It's a pretty depressing thing just to drive past. I couldn't even imagine having to live next to it, to wake up and see it every day.

"It is sort of a magic solution which will create a situation where we are here and they are there," Arnon explained. Among Palestinians, he said, there was now "a whole new generation who have never seen Jews. Everything they know about Jews and Israelis comes from the websites or the news or the army, or from false images of what is on the other side of the wall."

I knew that was true, because I was meeting many younger Palestinians who had never even met an Israeli. The wall didn't just separate Palestinians from Israelis, Arnon told me. It cut through the West Bank, separating Palestinians from other Palestinians. And, on top of that, it separated Palestinians from potential jobs in Israel, because the government had enforced "a regime of permissions and permits that one has to get in order to overcome this wall."

Arnon argued that Israel was actually compromising its security with the barrier. Before, he said, maybe 90 percent of Palestinians interacted with Israelis. They might not have liked one another particularly, but at least they knew and had some understanding of one another. Now they were strangers on either side of this wall—and it's a lot easier to hate and kill strangers than people you know and work alongside.

Ostensibly, the wall was built to prevent terrorist attacks in Israel launched from within Palestinian land; Israel has built a similar boundary around the Gaza Strip, over on the Mediterranean coast. But when you look at a map or at aerial views you can see what the Palestinians mean when they call it a "land grab." That thing zigs and zags and veers all over the topography to ensure that the best parts—green farmland, freshwater lakes, and the like—are all on the Israeli side. In some places, sections of Palestinian towns and villages were bulldozed into rubble to make way for the wall running right through them. It's gerrymandering on a grand and amazingly ugly scale.

Just south of Jerusalem, the barrier completely encircles Bethlehem—the birthplace of Jesus, which is now home to about 170,000 Palestinians. Stenciled on the concrete was graffiti for bethlehemghetto .blogspot.com, a website put up by bloggers in the city in an effort to let the outside world know what is going on.

Inside the wall, Jimmy Carter writes in his book *Palestine: Peace not Apartheid*, "every Palestinian over the age of twelve living in the closed area has to obtain a 'permanent resident permit' from the civil administration to enable them to continue to live in their own homes. They are considered to be aliens, without the rights of Israeli citizens." Needless to say, getting a pass to leave and enter Israeli territory is no easy task. But Israel also makes it very difficult for Palestinians living in Israel to get passes to visit family and loved ones on the other side of the barrier.

Like the Berlin Wall—or the one President Bush and a lot of Americans want to build along the U.S.-Mexico border—this thing struck me as a colossal monument to paranoia. But, as I found, in Israel and Palestine paranoia is an everyday state of mind.

I thought I should talk to the man behind the construction of this security barrier. In Jerusalem, I met Meir Sheetrit, the minister of construction. He's a stocky man with a no-nonsense manner. From the minute I walked into his office, he was on point, on message, and enthusiastically engaged. He oversees not only the construction of the wall but the construction of Jewish settlements in the Occupied Territories.

Mr. Sheetrit wanted me to understand that Jews have a *very* long history in Israel—and that if he had anything to do with it they'll have a very long future there, too. He noted that Jews have been in Israel since Moses led his people there almost five thousand years ago. But for two millennia, from Roman times to the end of World War II, Jews had no country of their own, in Israel or anywhere else.

"Now, after two thousand years of being in diaspora, we are united," he said. "And after the Holocaust we have at last the possibility to create again our sovereign state, and not be a minority all over the world. Does anybody expect us now to leave here? We are here to stay. And I'm telling you no one will ever shake our will to stay here."

CHAPTER 10

THE BOOM-BOOM ROOM

– – – – – – – –

Hair. That's the first thing I'd noticed setting foot in Israel. I came in by way of Jordan: I had just walked across the Sheikh Hussein Bridge from Jordan and arrived at the Jordan River Crossing terminal in all its air-conditioned glory. When I made my way into the border-control building, the first thing that caught my eye was all the Israeli girls who worked there. All in their mid-twenties, all happy and smiling, and *all* of them with their hair down. After traveling in Muslim countries for four weeks, this was a welcome sight to my Western eyes. Not only that, many of them were wearing short-sleeved shirts, and some were in tank tops. *Tank tops!* I can honestly say that I had never before been so enamored of women's bare shoulders and long, flowing hair.

What I'd also seen at the border was my first taste of Israeli civil defense: almost everyone who worked there was strapped with a sidearm. But their shiny, tangle-free curls were just as likely to stop enemies in their tracks.

Where Egypt felt like a police state, Israel was more like a completely militarized zone. Everywhere you go—city, country, or seaside—you're in the presence of uniformed soldiers carrying machine guns and automatic rifles, rolling by in armored vehicles, or lumbering overhead in helicopters. On every road there's a military checkpoint, and then another one a few kilometers farther along, and then another and another. If you're carrying a bag, there's always a soldier or a cop wanting to look inside it. Concrete walls and steel fences topped with barbed wire subdivide the landscape, even the cityscapes, into an arcane puzzle of security zones. Let me put it this way: *Grand Theft Auto: Israel* would be the hardest video game in history.

Being in Israel really drove home my sense that we Americans have no idea how lucky we are. In America, terrorist violence is an extreme rarity, and yet it has thrown our entire nation into a state of panic. For Israelis, living every single day under the threat of terrorism is the price they pay for their very existence. In Israel, every time you take a bus, every time you go shopping, every time you go out to dinner, every day on your way to work or school may be the day you die. Every day, the person sitting beside you on that bus, or riding by you on a bicycle, or standing in line behind you in a shop could be a kamikaze. It's just the way things are, and have been for more than half a century.

Just east of Gaza is the small town of Sderot. Nearly every day for the past seven years, this town has been targeted by homemade Qassam rockets falling from the sky, launched by Hamas militants in Gaza just a few kilometers away. At any time during the day, loudspeakers in the town will crackle to life with a booming voice, warning, "*Tseva Adom! Tseva Adom!*" (Red alert! Red alert!) From the time the alarm sounds to the moment the rocket hits the ground, locals have five to twenty-five seconds to find cover. Not a lot of time, especially since they have no idea where the weapon will land. Named for a 1930s Palestinian Islamist, Izz al-Din al-Qassam, the unguided rockets are highly inaccurate yet incredibly destructive. Basically flying pipe bombs, they have a range of up to ten kilometers, giving Hamas the ability to attack and torment Israeli citizens from a safe distance.

A school in town had been hit the day I visited Sderot. Luckily, the children were on a field trip; their teacher returned to find a classroom demolished. The rocket had struck a nearby tree, but the blast still ripped through the roof, throwing chunks of steel and debris across the floor. Shards of glass from the blown-out windows crunched under my boots as I walked among the toppled desks. Looking up through the hole in the ceiling, I could see the tree's burned and blackened limbs. Had the rocket struck the classroom directly, I was told, the floor might well have collapsed into the classroom below.

So it could have been much worse—something I bet people in Sderot say a lot. Although thousands of rockets had been fired over the years, only a dozen people in Sderot had been killed. The inaccuracy of the homemade weapons has been their best protection. Not surprisingly, many people have fled Sderot, moving out of range to the homes of families and friends. But others refuse to be driven out, their defiance a graphic illustration of Meir Sheetrit's words.

I approached a group of people hanging out in the afternoon sun in front of the town's lottery shop. One was an older man who moved to Israel when he was a child.

"I arrived in the fifties," he said. "There was nothing in Sderot. Nothing, *neit*, absolutely nothing. Only the sky and the land. And snakes. And scorpions. And there were always Arabic terror units. Even then, same thing. They used to come with bombs on them, so that every person going by will explode."

I was amazed when, just as so many Muslims I'd met blamed the United States for supporting Israel, this man blamed us for supporting the Palestinians! He said that we perpetuate terrorism because we don't let Israel "attack them with full force, to finish business, to mow them down to the ground," and he added, "Do you know what clean ground means? We have enough contractors, bulldozers, that can clean up the ground real nice. No problems, nothing. You take all the people, transport them across the border. Palestine is in Jordan, not here. That's where they should be."

I also spoke to those with more moderate voices. "There are the real Palestinians, and we can coexist with them," the woman who owned the shop said. "They used to work with us, we worked with them, they invited us over, we bought from them, everything. But lately, since Hamas came into the picture, and the other militant groups and all the sects, everything has changed. Everyone wants to rule their side, and we are the ones who suffer from it. . . . We would like peace, we are willing to live in peace, we offer our hand in peace."

She also believed that the United States "controls us. It dictates everything to us."

A man with a long black mullet, who had been quietly smoking and listening, pointed his finger at me. "I want to ask a question that bothers me," he said. "If what is happening in Sderot right now happened in America, would they tolerate it? Would they show restraint? They would erase that country in one hour. . . . I don't know why we don't."

I had to admit that there was some justification in what he said. These people were frustrated, angry, and tired of being afraid. They wanted this to end. I wondered aloud if they thought peace was a possibility.

The old man literally jumped out of his chair. "There will never be peace," he said angrily. "It's war. From the moment they are born, they plant the idea in their head of destroying the Jewish state."

"We gave them the territories," the shop owner said. "What else do they want? There is no limit to what they want."

The sun was setting in my eyes as I drove the short distance from Sderot to the fence that separates Gaza from Israel. About eight feet tall and electrified, it ran as far as I could see. Just beyond it were giant rolls of barbed wire, another deterrent in the event the electric fence, guard towers, and armed patrols weren't enough to keep Palestinians on their side.

And, just beyond that, six Israeli tanks had rolled into Gaza to begin an assault in retaliation for the day's rocket attack. The tank nearest me fired a deafening shot, and I instinctively hit the ground. (I hadn't taken that survival course for nothing, you know.) I had wandered into the middle of a conflict that had been going on for decades, and I was scared. Afraid that I was in the wrong place at the wrong time. Afraid that I might not make it back to see my child born.

An IDF security vehicle roared up, and four soldiers leaped out.

"You must get out of here!" one shouted. "They are firing mortars! You will be killed! You must leave *now!*"

Driving away at top speed, I thought, At least you get to leave. You can go home. What about all the people who can't leave, or who choose to stay because *this* is their home? They face this every day.

I couldn't even imagine what that was like.

I met Nisim Levi, the commander of the bomb squad of the Israeli Police, in a small town on the outskirts of Jerusalem. Probably no one on earth has more experience dealing with suicide bombers, car bombs, land mines, and the like. Nisim was my guide to one of the strangest and spookiest museums I've ever seen—a museum of explosive devices. Call it the Boom-Boom Room.

It was a simple white room lined with shelves, and on those shelves were hundreds and hundreds of things that blow up real good. If someone lit a match in there, he could launch that building to Uranus. Some of the devices I recognized: shoulder-fired RPG rockets, conventional hand grenades, rifle-fired grenades, military-issue land mines. But a lot of them were specifically designed *not* to be recognizable for what they were—IEDs, aka improvised explosive devices, aka booby traps.

Nisim explained that everything I was seeing had been confiscated from would-be attackers and collected here to educate bomb-squad personnel. "We have to recognize each one, because from our point of view each one can contain a bomb, or each one can be combined with a bomb," he explained.

Since the Second Intifada began in September 2000, Nisim estimated, there had been around 320 successful suicide-bombing attacks in Israel (just over one every four months), and maybe 100 more attempts where "our secret service stopped them before it started to blow up." More than 1,000 people had been killed, and "something like 5,000, maybe more," wounded. In that same period, Nisim figured, 1,000 IEDs had been discovered and safely detonated.

Which means that just under 80 percent of all bombing attempts are thwarted in Israel. Pretty amazing odds. With a success rate like that, it's no wonder people from military and police forces all over the world come here to train with the Israelis. They are the best at what they do.

The IEDs Nisim showed me came in all sorts of disguises. One roadside bomb was sculpted to look like a rock. Nisim said it had been filled with "about fifty kilograms of explosives." Powerful enough to rip straight through an armored vehicle.

"They use C-4, they use TNT, they use RDX—and, mostly, they use homemade explosives," he explained. "They are very common right now, because it's very difficult to create factory-made explosives. . . . Basically, they use civilian materials which are used in agriculture, things like ammonium nitrate. They combine it with some specific material, and it's very easy to create a huge amount of explosive material. And in most cases it has exactly the same impact, and it's powerful like factory-made explosives."

Nisim showed me smaller IEDS, including a fire extinguisher that had been filled with explosives and—much scarier, somehow, to the redneck in me—a beer-can bomb. The bomber "put that beer can in a supermarket in Jerusalem," he said. "And suddenly it explodes. It's not meant to cause a lot of damage. It's meant to cause panic. Try to think of the mother that sent her child to the supermarket for milk. She's in a panic."

Another booby trap was a Kleenex box that would explode if you touched it or pulled out a tissue, sending shrapnel through you. Shrapnel might be anything from bullets, which fragment and fly in all directions when the bomb detonates, to nails, ball bearings, and even glass marbles. Those might be the worst, Nisim said, because inside your body they don't show up on X rays, so doctors have to dig around to find them.

Nisim showed me a large plastic paint can that "contained about fifteen kilograms of explosives," he said. "They placed it near an urban commercial center. It causes a lot of damage. We found two of them. One we caught and dismantled, and learned about the firing system. The other one exploded."

One of the IEDs I found most hateful was a birdcage. A booby-trapped birdcage. "In 2002, in the center of Israel, a terrorist took that cage with two live birds in it and set it right in the front of the pet shop and walked away," Nisim told me. "Luckily, the owner of the shop realized it wasn't one of his and called the bomb squad. After we attacked it from a safe distance with our robot, we found that the bottom of the cage contained huge amounts of explosives. The ideas are endless. Endless."

"Anything could be a bomb," I said.

"Anything in the world."

I thought back to how I used to scoff at bra bombs and banana bombs and realized that I might have to revise my opinions.

Suicide bombers also use a variety of devices, Nisim told me. As a case in point, he mentioned two guys who sat outside a Sbarro in Jerusalem with a guitar in a case. "The guitar was filled with explosives," he said. "They just sat near Sbarro restaurant and ignited the bomb. . . . It was a very bad incident. About twenty people got killed in that one."

Backpacks are more popular. You can stuff twenty kilos of explosives and shrapnel into one. Exploded in a café or on a bus, the damage it can do is terrible. But probably the best-known device is the simple suicide vest. Nisim let me try one on, and even though it had been disarmed and was no longer packed with real explosives, it made my heart race. It consisted of just two shoulder straps that went down the back and front and connected to long, narrow pockets stitched around the waist, each one able to hold up to two kilos of explosives and shrapnel fragments.

"With a lot of fragments, that suicide belt can weigh from five to twenty kilograms," Nisim explained. "It's a huge amount."

The triggering mechanism couldn't be simpler: a couple of batteries wired to an on/off switch the terrorist holds in his hand. The terrorist throws a coat on over the vest to hide it and he's good to go—or good to go *boom!* "When he gets to the site, he just presses the button and that's it," Nisim said.

"How do you dismantle a live suicide bomber?" I asked him.

He said it's extremely difficult, adding that these are real "smart bombs"—walking, thinking bombs that can make decisions on the spot, move wherever they want, and detonate on command.

"It can be very dangerous, because if you cut a wire you can just explode yourself away. So you have to know which wire to cut off."

"Do you have a lot of guys on the bomb squad named Lefty?" I joked. Nisim grinned and said they have their own brand of black humor, but he didn't elaborate.

Nisim said the bomb squad gets calls about suspicious packages literally every day. And not just one or two a day. "If we're talking about all of Israel, and if you're talking about average per year, it's, like, eighty-five thousand a year," he said.

Holy cow. "How many of those are legitimate?" I asked.

"Most of them are hoaxes. I'd say twenty-five to thirty-five [a year] are real bombs."

"If I were going to some countries where there's the potential for suicide bombs or IEDs," I asked, "what advice would you give me to stay safe?"

Nisim gave me a look. "Don't go there," he said flatly.

"That's the same advice my wife gave me. What a coincidence."

If I was determined to go, his advice was: "Take care and be aware of everything. It's very difficult to teach somebody who doesn't have the right kind of orientation to that kind of stuff. It takes about six months to [train] a civilian bomb-disposal [officer]. After six months, he has just started to understand the threat that he has to face. So it's very difficult to explain it to a citizen. . . . We have a few signs—don't touch, don't move, call the police immediately. If you keep on that, you will probably stay alive."

While he was saying this, all I kept hearing in my head was that line from *Monty Python and the Holy Grail:* "Run away!"

I kept the Lefty jokes to myself around Amir, the police officer who drove me around Tel Aviv in a bomb-squad van. With his shaved head and muscles, Amir looked like Vin Diesel. He dismantled bombs for a living. He was a really nice guy, but I didn't want to rile him and have him dismantle me.

Amir said nine crews were always ready to respond to calls in Tel Aviv. While I was with him, a call came in about a suspicious suitcase that had been left in a square, in a shopping area along Tel Aviv's beachfront. With Amir at the wheel and me hanging on in the back, we wove through and around Tel Aviv's afternoon traffic.

"How many calls like this do you answer in a day?" I asked him, as modern, gleaming Tel Aviv buildings slid by.

"In one shift I can get, on a regular day, about eight to ten calls. This is a regular day. Some days there can be up to eighteen. In one shift. One shift, one crew." During the first couple of years of the Second Intifada, he said, it had been more like twenty-five to thirty calls a shift. And one a day would turn out to be the real deal.

"Do you ever get nervous when the calls come?"

"Not nervous," he said. That comes "when I see an explosive device. And it happens. It happened seven months ago in a stolen car. Started to check the car, and under the driver's seat I found an explosive device. And it was working. The lights were working."

We pulled up alongside a very nice-looking shopping plaza, with stores facing a busy open pedestrian square. A fountain bubbled in the center. Beyond it, a fringe of palm trees lined the beach, and I could see ocean swells glittering red in the late-afternoon sun. It looked like Miami Beach. Just another day of surf and sun . . . with a bomb scare.

Amir thought he could see a small package near the fountain. He got on the van's loudspeaker and made an announcement in Hebrew. First he asked if anyone had left a package by the fountain. Then he gave orders for the area to be evacuated. A cluster of teenage girls who'd been hanging out in front of one shop dashed around the corner. Most people were pretty nonchalant about the whole thing and just walked away, glancing over their shoulders as they left. No big deal. Apparently, this comes with the territory.

Other cops showed up and blocked off the square. I watched as Amir quickly but calmly strapped on his Kevlar bomb suit—chest armor, leggings, helmet. Other cops opened the back door of the van and lowered a ramp. With whirrs and clicks, a shiny silver robot emerged. It looked like a lunar rover, rolling on small tank treads. I recognized something in its robot arm, an instrument known for its subtlety and precision.

"Is that a shotgun?" I asked one of the cops.

"Yes, it's a shotgun, exactly," he said. "We try to open the object. And with the cameras we can see what we have in it. Inside. And that's how we decide afterwards what to do. But that happens ten times a day in a shift." Then he said, "You stay here."

He didn't have to tell me twice.

I climbed inside the van, where Amir sat at a control panel in front of a small screen, guiding the robot. Through the windshield, I could see Johnny 5 rolling happily across the empty plaza. It looked like one of those Japanese science-fiction toys, but playing an unusually dangerous game of fetch. When it pulled up near the fountain, I could see a small orange plastic case on Amir's screen. Amir worked the controls and the robot extended its arm, grabbed the case, and lifted it. Things had gotten tense and quiet. All the traffic had been diverted and the shoppers evacuated. It was just us, the robot, and that suitcase. And this happened every day in Tel Aviv, ten times a shift. I tried to picture living in a New York City where this kind of activity was a regular feature of every day. Instead, we have Scientologists giving stress tests in the subway. Scary, but for completely different reasons.

Amir aimed the robot's shotgun at the case. Over his shoulder, he explained that if there were explosives inside, the shot wouldn't necessarily detonate them. "Depends on what kind of explosive, how sensitive it is," he said.

A shot echoed around the deserted plaza. Amir wasn't satisfied, and shot again. This time the case flopped open, and we could see its contents on the screen.

A green bikini.

I realized I'd been holding my breath. My heart was pounding.

Amir crossed the plaza and unloaded the shotgun before anyone else was allowed to approach. As I walked up to the fountain, a cop declared, "Here is the bomb." He gestured to the bikini, sprawled on the paving stones next to the ruptured suitcase.

I looked at the sun setting out over the ocean, wondering where the bikini's owner was. All sorts of lame jokes about how she must really be da bomb went through my head.

It was dusk by the time everything was packed up and Amir and I drove away. On the streets around the plaza, life was back to normal: traffic, people strolling to restaurants. As if nothing had happened. Just another day in paradise.

I asked Amir if he was relieved when a call turned out not to be a bomb.

"Truthfully? My job is bomb technician, so I disarm bombs and explosive devices," he said. "So of course I thank God it's not a bomb. No one died, no one got hurt, no one injured. Everyone got home safely. But of course from time to time if there is an explosive device and I have to disarm it, without any casualties, I'm happy. I'm doing my job."

"Have you seen a lot of people get killed in your years as bomb technician?"

"Unfortunately, yes," he told me. "Most of them are from the suicide bombers. Some are from the explosive devices that were put in bags, buses, inside central stations, inside coffee shops. . . . When I'm standing near a bus full of people, I'm scared it will blow up. And the suicide bomber will be happy."

"Have you ever had a bomb detonate while you were trying to disarm it?" I asked Amir.

"No, thank God," he said. But he knew technicians who had.

"Do you think there will ever be a time when we won't need to have bomb technicians on the police force?"

"I'm afraid not. Because even if the world would be good someday, there would be someone who would want to revenge something."

"When you hear certain radicals say that we must wipe Israel off the face of the earth and all Jews must die, how does that make you feel?"

"It makes me feel very bad, of course. I don't want to wipe them off. I'm saying it truly—live and let live. Live however you want, do whatever you want, believe in what God you want to believe in. I don't say how to live. But leave me in peace."

Amir told me he had a son, two and a half years old. "Quality time with your kid, that's most important," he said. "Doing my job, when I go home I just want to recharge my batteries with my son. Play with him. Quality time."

He spoke fondly of reading bedtime stories to his son, of giving him a bath, and of how every time he smiled at the child it reminded him of "the important need of safety, the importance of life." And he went on, "What are we doing here in this world? Why are we living where we live? I live in Israel, you live in New York, but danger can be everywhere. . . . So we all share the same thing, the same happiness, the same families. Also the terrorists, also Islam, the radicals. They also have families. Their families want peace, to be happy, to travel, to go to theaters, go with their children to playgrounds. No one wants wars. Our leaders, they're sometimes doing foolish stuff."

I agreed. I shook Amir's hand and hoped in my heart that he and his son would have many decades of quality time together. I wondered what it would be like to have a son that I could share things with, and my eyes welled up with tears as I climbed out of the van.

In Jerusalem, even your tour guide might be a bomb-planting terrorist. Or at least a reformed, former bomb-planting terrorist, like Ali Jiddah, who took me on a walking tour of Old Jerusalem.

Ali is a very special character, and very well known in Old Jerusalem. A black man with a shiny bald head and a deep, rolling voice, he calls himself an "Afro-Palestinian." His father was a Muslim from Chad who settled in the Old City. Ali was born there in 1950. Today, he gives what he calls "alternative tours," laced with lots of sharp, streetwise political commentary you won't read in any guidebook.

Ali took my elbow—he moved stiffly for a man in his mid-fifties, the result of diabetes—and we strolled the narrow stone paths and alleys that serve as streets in the Old City. Within its walls, incredible layers of history and culture are packed inside a space of only a square kilometer. The Temple Mount, the Western Wall, the Dome of the Rock, the al-Aqsa Mosque, the Church of the Holy Sepulchre and the Via Dolorosa, with the original Stations of the Cross, are all there. The Old City's traditional four quarters—Jewish, Muslim, Armenian, and Christian—only begin to hint at the wealth of cultures, ethnicities, religions, and sects drawn over the millennia to this most sacred square kilometer of real estate on the planet.

Ali showed all that tourist history to me, but he was clearly more interested in relating recent history and current events. As we walked the historic path Christ took, he showered me with stories, both modern and historical, relative in both concept and theme. His passion and enthusiasm were contagious. He perked up even more when we entered the souk, a kind of shopping tunnel burrowing into the heart of the Muslim Quarter, where crowds mill past tiny stalls as shopkeepers hawk everything from CDs, disposable cameras, and T-shirts (including one that said "Israeli Defense Forces Intelligence: My job is so secret, I don't even know what I'm doing") to hummus, religious souvenirs, and candy. Ali enjoyed the noise and bustle, and nearly every shopkeeper called out a greeting to him.

Before the creation of the state of Israel in 1948, Ali claimed, Jews, Muslims, and Christians all lived together peacefully in the Old City. That much seems true enough. Jews, who had been the largest group in Jerusalem since the 1840s, lived, worked, and played in relative mutual tolerance with their Muslim and Christian neighbors. Then, in the fighting and land-grabbing that accompanied the birth of Israel in 1946–48, Jerusalem became a divided city, with Jordan taking control of East Jerusalem and the Old City, and Israel claiming West Jerusalem, also known as the New City. In the process, a lot of Jews fled or were displaced from the Jordanian-held half of the city, and a lot of Palestinians from the Western half fled or were displaced.

In the Six-Day War of 1967, Israeli troops occupied East Jerusalem, taking it out of Jordan's control. Since then, Ali said, a process of "Israelification" has been under way in East Jerusalem and the Old City, squeezing the Palestinians out. Over the decades, more and more Jewish housing settlements have been seeded in the Old City.

"I don't have a problem with Jews living together with Christians [and Muslims]," he said. "But I'm not okay with the kind of Jews we have living in the Old City now. I'm talking about the settlers. They are the most dangerous elements inside the Israeli society. They are unhealthy elements. They are not the neighbors who will be the bridge between Israelis and Palestinians."

Emerging from the souk into bright daylight, Ali showed me an example of what he meant. In the center of the Muslim Quarter, he pointed to a large residential building that was a Jewish settlement. It did not look like a friendly neighbor. Its roofline was fenced with barbed wire, and an armed security guard sat up there in a little booth. Ali told me resentfully that people from the settlements walked the streets and went shopping with armed bodyguards.

Ali's story reminded me of Martin McGuinness's experience in Ireland. Ali was seventeen when the Israeli army occupied the Old City. He said life completely changed for him then. Soldiers would stop him on the street, "humiliating" him. Jewish civilians who'd once been neighborly now turned "arrogant."

"My feeling at the time was that I lost my personal dignity and my national dignity," he recalled. In his resentment, he joined the Popular Front for the Liberation of Palestine, a leftist political and guerrilla organization.

In 1968, "one night I went with a group of comrades," he told me. "We placed various bombs in the New City of Jerusalem. In my case, nine Israelis were injured."

Ali was arrested, convicted, and spent the next seventeen years in prison. He was released in 1985, as part of a famous exchange of prisoners between Israel and the PLO—1,150 Palestinians for *three* captured Israeli soldiers.

"So what happened when you got out of jail?" I asked.

"I became a journalist at the information center," he said, smiling. "With the Israelis! Unbelievable. I worked with Israelis for five years in the information center. But we are talking about progressive Israelis."

In the early 1990s, he became an "alternative tour guide."

"Alternative tour guide, meaning I bring my clients, for example, to the Old City of Jerusalem. I put an emphasis on the political aspect of the situation of the Old City of Jerusalem. Then I take them to the West Bank, to refugee camps, to villages, give them the opportunity to sit and talk directly with Palestinians. So they can themselves have a real idea about the real situation of the Palestinians. I don't want them to just look at the situation of the Palestinians through the eyes of the Bush media in the USA or through the Europeans. I am, due to the response I get from my clients, more effective than the bomb that I placed in 1968."

"So what do you think about the violent acts that are still happening today?" I asked him.

"Well, I don't justify it. But I tell you, if you are desperate you are capable of doing the most horrible things. Unfortunately, the Israelis together with the Americans together with Europe are pushing us to the corner, are driving my people, the Palestinian people, more desperate and desperate. Which means they are becoming more violent and violent. And you will have a lot of miseries. Don't think I feel okay when I see Israeli mothers crying."

We had come to a high, wide doorway in the stone wall, the ancient Jaffa Gate, the western gate leading from the Old City to the New City. So called because the old road beyond it led across Israel to the port of Jaffa, and now the modern city of Tel Aviv. Ali told me that Muslims call it the Hebron Gate, because "Muslims from Hebron who came each Friday for prayer used to come through this gate."

I noticed police officers standing around.

"Are you allowed to pass through this gate?" I asked Ali.

"Well, I have no problem. I can go with my ID card. No problem."

"But other people can't?"

"West Bankers can't go—no way, no way. Even to the Old City, to the Palestinian side, they can't come. Unless they get a permission. If you want to have a permission, they look in your file. If you have a political background, if you have been under detention for one night, there is no way you are going. You are registered in the computer. Which means no Palestinians can come, because you can't find one Palestinian in the West Bank or the Gaza Strip who hasn't passed through that experience. At least one night in detention. Even if afterward they find out that you are innocent, not guilty. No way."

I asked Ali what message he would send to the Americans.

"I say to the Americans, it's time to wake up. Okay, you are supporting Israel. But don't forget, at the same time, that you are creating enemies and hostility in the whole world."

And to the Israelis?

"I say to the Israelis, you don't want suiciders? Give my people hope. Don't make my people desperate. More desperation among Palestinians, more suiciders. More hope for Palestinians, less violence."

I left Ali and walked into the Church of the Holy Sepulchre. At the entrance to this holy place, people were kneeling and kissing the marble slab, the Stone of the Anointing, where Christ's body was prepared for burial. I made my way to Christ's tomb, where I lit a candle and stood in silence for what seemed like an hour. And then I made my way upstairs, where you kneel below an altar, reach through a hole in the floor, and touch Calvary—the rock on which Jesus was crucified. For the first time in weeks, I felt as though I were in a place that was safe. Maybe that's just because I wanted to feel that way—I was looking and hoping for it . . . but at this point, I'll take it wherever I can.

From here I made my way to the holiest of places in Judaism, the Western Wall, aka the Kotel, aka the Wailing Wall. We were here during Sukkoth, the Feast of Booths (aka the Feast of Tabernacles), when each family builds an outdoor shelter (a *sukkah*) where they pray and eat for seven days. Some people even live there during this time to symbolize the forty-year period during which the children of Israel wandered in the desert, living in temporary shelters. It also has agricultural significance as a festival of the harvest, so all along the Western Wall I saw men and women doing the blessing for Arba Minim with the "four species" they are supposed to use to "rejoice before the Lord." These are an etrog (which looks like a lemon), a palm branch, two willow branches, and three myrtle branches. Some say they represent different parts of the body, while others say that they represent different kinds of Jews.

I walked through the crowds of thousands of Jews to the Western Wall. Cracks in the wall are stuffed with thousands of small pieces of paper, each with a prayer (a *Tzetel*) and a request to God written by visitors. I sat down in a nearby chair and wrote mine—a desire to be kept safe, to be watched over, to soothe and comfort my wife thousands of miles away, and a hope to get back for the birth of our child. I was overcome with emotion, as I stood up and inserted the rolled-up slip of paper into one of the cracks where thousands before me had made the same kinds of prayers. I leaned my head against the wall, the sound of thousands of people davening all around me.

I went to West Jerusalem to have Sukkoth dinner with Jai-Jai Max, his wife, Hagit, and their three children. The *sukkah* was a little tentlike thing in the small courtyard behind their house. The kids had festooned it with party decorations and paper rainbows. We ate backyard-barbecue style, with paper plates and Styrofoam cups, which made me feel right at home. So did the little cocktail wieners.

"Pigs in a blanket!" I said. "But it's not a pig."

In Israel, Jai-Jai told me, they represent baby Moses in his *tevah*, his basket. There was also eggplant pie, stuffed grape leaves, homemade pickles, and olives . . . mmmmm. After Jai-Jai said traditional blessings over the food and wine (and Coke), we dug in.

Jai-Jai was born in the United States, but when he was six, he said, his "family, for Zionist reasons, made *aliya*—they immigrated to Israel for ideological reasons. Now I am thirty-six. Actually, most of my life has been in this neighborhood."

"Is it hard raising kids here?" I asked.

"It's a meaningless question," he said. "Most of the men you see, including myself, we're all soldiers in reserve. We've all gone through it at certain times in our lives. There's no fear in the streets because of people walking with M-16s. It's just a part of the life, and it's not threatening."

Hagit was less nonchalant about things. She talked about a bomb that was found in a school near their daughter's, and about how the security personnel checking her bags and purse everywhere didn't always make her feel so secure.

"Yeah, you have to always show your cell phone and your keys, thirty times a day. It really is a pain in the neck," Jai-Jai agreed. "It's definitely a part of life. A bad part of life . . . But we're not living in a state-of-war kind of mentality."

When I asked if it felt as if things were getting better or worse, Jai-Jai said there had been a period in the 1990s, after Israel and the PLO signed the Oslo Accords in 1993, when "there was a real hope that things were changing. [Then] we went through the frustrations of the end of the nineties, when everything was exploding in our face, and all around. We still held hope. But slowly, over the past, I don't know, three or four years, it's just becoming more and more obvious . . . that there's no real hope for a real reconciliation of the cultures that are involved in our area."

"We've done a lot of traveling in Muslim lands over the past few weeks," I said. "And a lot of people have said that they think one of the problems is that the United States has supported Israel unconditionally for so long. Do you think that has been a mistake at times, or do you think it's the right thing to do all the time?"

"Thank God they did!" Jai-Jai exclaimed. "Thank God they did. I don't think anybody else in the world has any commitment to helping us survive as a people. . . . In a world where you really need a patron, it's good that we have the big bully."

"But is it good for America?" I asked.

"All in all, if America is a country that wants to promote freedom, individual rights, human rights, democracy, and technology development, then I don't think that there's anything to lose by supporting a state like Israel," he said.

"What's going to happen here in this region, in this country, over the next ten, fifteen years?"

"Life is going to go on." He laughed. "As usual."

"If Osama bin Laden were to be captured tomorrow, do you think that would change anything?"

"It would mean that a very charismatic and resourceful terrorist would have been taken down, but there are others around. Lots . . . So if Osama bin Laden is taken down—"

"Who's next?"

"Who's next? Somebody else is going to come up. The truth of the matter is it's really a hydra. You take off one head, nine others come up. That's what it's been for the past fifty years. And it will continue being that."

"What do you hope for your kids?" I asked him.

"To have a normal life. . . . Just that things will continue the way they are."

I didn't say so, but the fact that he considered the current situation "normal" seemed stunning to me. Dinner was over, the kids were getting bored and sleepy, and night was falling. I didn't want to overstay my welcome.

"Last question," I said. "I'm going to be a father for the first time. Give me some fatherly advice."

"The only thing I'd say is go with your intuition," Jai-Jai replied. "You have to read, you have to learn, you have to think, but then let it roll."

The more time I spent with Israelis and Palestinians, the more it seemed to me that the traditional politics-as-usual approach might never break the seemingly endless cycle of violence and misunderstanding. I wondered if there were any new ideas or new visions for bringing the two sides together.

Turns out there are, and I met the man who's promoting them: Shimon Peres, the former prime minister of Israel, who was awarded the Nobel Peace Prize in 1994, along with Yitzhak Rabin and Yasser Arafat, for bringing about the Oslo Accords. When we met, he was serving as Israel's vice premier, which is equivalent to the vice president in the United States, and contemplating running for prime minister again.

Despite having spent fifty years in the Israeli government, Mr. Peres told me flat out that he didn't believe peace between Israel and Palestine could be brought about through politics alone. He believes the whole world is moving into a new era, one in which government and politics will be obsolete and the real solutions will be the ones that bring economic equality and prosperity.

"The world is pregnant with a new baby, and the parents are old-fashioned," he said. "We all the time have handled the situation through strategies and diplomacy. They are useless. What introduces the new age is a modern economy. Not tanks. What changed China, what changed India, what changed Europe is the economy."

There will never be peace so long as the Palestinians "live on donations," he went on. "The Arabs are a proud people. They don't want to appear as beggars. So what we have to do is help them to build industrial zones."

To that end, he had recently proposed to "take the whole border between us and Jordan and the Palestinians, which is 520 kilometers long, and convert it into a modern economic zone. Over the last few months, the king [of Jordan] agreed, the Palestinian president agreed, and the Israeli prime minister agreed. And we start to work."

He also got all three sides to start working toward curing the pollution of the Red Sea. "Nature is impatient with the politicians," he told me. "The Red Sea is dying, and we have to save it. We cannot save it in three ways—a Jordanian way, a Palestinian way, an Israeli way. We have to save it one way."

It was interesting to learn that he was making Jordan an integral partner in all this. It seemed he was leaping right over the "two-state solution" everyone else had spoken to me about.

"Because the greatest problem in life is couples," Mr. Peres said. It was a lesson he'd learned from Henry Kissinger. When two groups argue, he told me, they can be like an old married couple, going over and over the same grievances and never agreeing. You need to bring in a third partner to break the logjam.

I tucked that away for possible use in my own marriage. "What do you say to people who tell you you're a dreamer, a cockeyed optimist?" I asked him.

"My record is that most of my dreams came true," he said with a smile. "Nobody can deny it. To dream is to see the new things coming in, without fear, with sober eyes."

. . .

I sincerely hoped Mr. Peres's dreams came true. I had seen that a lot of people on all sides were playing off what Prince Hassan called the "no war, no peace" situation for their own political or financial benefit. And there were literally millions of people caught in the middle. It wasn't just the Palestinians and the Israelis who were in a siege mentality from the conflict. The conflict and bad feelings had spilled over into the whole world.

At least one of the people who benefited from the situation was Osama bin Laden. People across the Muslim world used the Israeli-Palestinian issue to justify the violent actions of bin Laden and his followers.

It was time to continue the hunt. The more I learned, the more questions I had for that guy.

My last stop was Ramallah. Assuming he wasn't undercover in Israel, I figured my best shot was at the headquarters of the Palestinian movement.

From Jerusalem, the heart of Israel, to Ramallah, the heart of the West Bank, is a journey of, oh, about eight miles. Eight miles! I think that's how far I travel between my Brooklyn apartment and my Manhattan office! But I don't have to drive through military checkpoints and a monstrous "security wall," as I did driving from Jerusalem to Ramallah.

Ramallah was quiet the day I visited, but it wasn't a peaceful quiet. It felt more like a tense pause between fits of violence. This impression was driven home to me as I approached the nice, new offices of Hamas, and saw the blackened husks of two bombed-out cars parked at the entrance.

Like the IRA, Hamas has both a political and a paramilitary side. Since the early 1990s, Hamas suicide bombers have killed hundreds of civilians, including women and children, in Israel. That's the reason the United States, the European Union, and Israel all renounced the January 2006 parliamentary elections. Then, just to make it even harder for them to run the government, Israel arrested sixty-four Hamas MPs and cabinet ministers in June. Fatah politicians weren't arrested, because Fatah, as Yasser Arafat's old party, was a signatory to the Oslo Accords, which Hamas rejected.

So you had Hamas politicians in jail and Fatah politicians walking free, which led to a lot of resentment and anger between followers of the two parties. By the time I was in the region, things had turned bloody, with militants of both parties attacking one another. Those two burned-out cars in front of Hamas's offices were "memorials," I was told, of a Fatah attack that happened a few weeks earlier.

Wasfi Kabaha was the Hamas minister of Prisoner Affairs. We met in his office, where he sat under a large portrait of Yasser Arafat. He answered my questions in a mixture of Arabic and English.

Wasfi said that 10,500 Palestinians were currently in Israeli prisons. (Elsewhere, I'd heard the number was 8,500.)

"We have Palestinians who spent twenty-eight and thirty years in prison," he added.

"Thirty years?"

"Mandela spent only twenty-two years," he said. "And all the capitals of the world were open for him! Why are the Palestinian freedom fighters still there, behind bars? It's immoral. . . ."

Wasfi himself had been in prison for six years. He said he was held without charges, just for being "an activist." He had a friend who was held for five years without ever being charged, and joked that when he died and went to heaven he would ask God if he could see the secret file on him.

I asked Wasfi flat out, "Are you a terrorist?"

"No, to the contrary," he said. "I have never been a terrorist, not for one single day. Not a single Palestinian was ever a terrorist. We are a people, a Palestinian people who love peace and struggle for peace—a peace that is just, comprehensive, and encompasses the entire region. Peace and stability to all the peoples of the region."

Evidently, for Wasfi *suicide bomber* and *terrorist* aren't necessarily synonymous. "What is the difference between a terrorist and a freedom fighter?" I asked him.

"The terrorist is the one who transgresses the freedoms, and kills for the sake of wanting to kill," he said. "But the warrior or the person who strives for liberation, and who works according to the international law by using his right to self-defense, that's the freedom fighter."

I asked him if Hamas would ever be ready to recognize Israel's right to exist.

"Why is it always demanded of the victim to recognize the executioner?" he shot back. "Give people their rights, their freedom, and their independence. . . . Then we can talk."

It's one thing to say you're defending your homeland against an occupying force, I noted. "But what does Hamas achieve by killing innocent civilians in Jerusalem or Tel Aviv? Kids who are on their way to school, sitting in a café. . . . What does that achieve?"

"What does Israel achieve when they kill Palestinian children?" he retorted. "How many cars were bombed from Apache [helicopters] and F-16 fighters? How many civilian Palestinians were killed? Make a comparison between that. Palestinian children, the Palestinian kids—the civilians are a hundred times more than what was killed on the Israeli side." Then he added, "At the same time, we feel sorry for every drop of blood that is shed. . . ."

"Where is Osama bin Laden?" I asked him. What the hell—he's on a terrorist watch list, after all.

He laughed. "Osama bin Laden! Ask the CIA."

Ask the CIA. What a good idea! I did just that. I sent them an e-mail:

Central Intelligence Agency
Washington, DC 20505

RE: Osama bin Laden coordinates

Dear Director of Counterterrorism, Whoever You Are (or General Michael Hayden, Director, or Mark Mansfield, Director of Public Affairs),

Hello. My name is Morgan Spurlock. I was recently in the West Bank speaking with a Hamas leader, and I asked him if he knew where Osama bin Laden is. He said he didn't but that you do. Is that true? If so, would you please tell me where he is? I'd really like to talk to him.

Thanks in advance,

MORGAN SPURLOCK

Funny, I still haven't heard back.

But on a happy note for my stomach, Ramadan ended while I was in Israel. But the truth is, I'd fallen off the fasting wagon a week short of the goal line. Yes, I'm a bad Muslim. But I promise I'll make up the final eight days I missed sometime this year . . . or the next.

CHAPTER 11

SAUDI AMERICA

— — — — — — — —

The greatest disaster to befall the Muslims since the death of the Prophet Muhammad is the occupation of Saudi Arabia. . . .

Osama bin Laden, August 1996

STAGE 9: GET BACK TO WHERE IT ALL BEGAN

When I arrived in Saudi Arabia, my mind was filled with visions of a Bedouin camp in the desert at night, bright stars flickering overhead, people sitting around the campfire wrapped in long, flowing robes, eating lamb, and watching belly dancers. You know, all the great cliché stuff we grew up watching in movies and expecting to be real. I wanted to live the dream, Warren Beatty–Dustin Hoffman style.

Now, here I was, about forty-five miles east of downtown Riyadh, sitting in a large tent that was open on one side to let in the soft night breezes. Some of the men were dressed in gleaming white *thawbs* (the long, floor-length robes) and *kaffiyeh* (the red-and-white head scarves with the black tube), and they knelt and touched their foreheads to beautiful red prayer rugs spread on the sand. Others were straight out of the J. Crew catalog, dressed in jeans and sweatshirts; one guy actually had on a Lakers hoodie. They were all saying their evening prayers, facing Mecca, which was not too far across the desert. When the prayers were done, they left the tent and reclined on more rugs thrown on the sand around a small campfire, smoking *shishas* and having quiet conversations under the stars.

This is everyone's dream of Bedouin life. Everyone from T. E. Lawrence to Osama bin Laden has seen this as the true, pure image of Arabian Islam. I knew that before he exiled himself from the country Osama used to come out to the desert—maybe this very patch of desert—on nights just like this. I didn't really expect to see him out here, but you never knew. Maybe he got homesick and sneaked back for a good, old-fashioned evening under the stars with his Bedouin compadres. Wouldn't hurt to look.

But the men reclining around the campfire were no more real desert Bedouin than I was, though I must say I looked really schmancy in my heartthrob *thawb*. The guys kicking it around me were from the city, and they didn't cross the desert on camels and horses. They drove out from the suburbs in brand-new SUVs, some of them pulling up on four-wheelers, roaring out into the rolling dunes for an evening of "dune-bashing." As the sun sets in the desert, Arab locals do what my hillbilly homies do every weekend—go four-wheelin'. As I sat there looking around, I thought that these were my kinda people: guys who like to drive trucks, hunt animals, ride four-wheelers, and sit around campfires. There are rednecks everywhere, and wouldn't you know that I'd find 'em. Only difference with these guys tonight was they were hunting with falcons, and there was no Miller High Life in sight—or ladies, for that matter.

Next to the campfire was a young three-year-old falcon with a leather mask strapped to its head.

"The mask calms him down," the owner told me. A noisy electric generator powering the lights strung inside the tent provided a constant background to our conversation.

These urban Saudis had come to the desert to get in touch with their inner Bedouin, as they do every Thursday night during the winter months from October to March. They're like the American guys who went out to the woods and did drum circles in the 1990s to search for their inner Iron John—modern men trying to connect with their more primitive, traditional roots. When the evening's over they'll drive their SUVs back to their mansions, slip the latest outlawed DVD into the ultra-high-tech home-entertainment system, and kick back with a black-market Black Label scotch and a Cuban cigar. Well, maybe not all of them have the scotch or the Cuban, but some of them do.

I think Saudi Arabia was the most schizophrenic Muslim country I visited. The tensions between rampant Westernization and extreme Islamic fundamentalism—the same tensions that produced Osama's reactionary evangelism—were painfully obvious. On the one hand, Saudi

Arabia, at least in the cities, is the most Americanized society in the Muslim world. Not just Westernized but Americanized. Riyadh looks like Miami with mosques and a drought. There are Pizza Huts, Starbucks, McDonald's, and shopping malls everywhere. Young urban Saudis dress like American college kids, listen to hip-hop and rock, pimp out their rides, get the latest DVDs before you and I do, go to America to study if they can, and speak English with American accents, not the highfalutin, Britishy version I heard everywhere else. They live in suburbs and text one another on brand-new cells and rehearse with their rock bands in their parents' giant dens, blog on the Internet (check out saudiblogs.blogspot.com), and host massive underground parties with booze, sex, drugs, and rock and roll. It may sound like just another Tuesday for Lindsay Lohan, but in Saudi Arabia this is revolutionary.

But you don't read about that, mainly because a lot of it—in fact, almost all of it—has to be done in private and on the supersecret "down low." In public, Saudi Arabia enforces a very strict, Wahhabist version of Sharia.

All I heard when I was there was "how lenient" things had become, yet there are no movie theaters, no rock clubs or discos, basically nowhere for young Saudis to hang out. And even if there were, boys and girls couldn't hang out there together: separation of the sexes in public is fiercely observed and enforced. They can't even meet up at the mall, where security guards bar any young person not accompanied by a parent. Groups of males aren't allowed in, period, because they're all seen as "singles," and they might harass women. Single girls can go in only as part of a family, with their mothers or brothers. Restaurants also have separate sections for "Families" and "Singles," and *singles* means groups of men. Groups of women can sit in the family section, but if they try to sit in the singles section, where the men are, they're often refused service. Just driving in a car with someone of the opposite sex who's not a relative (or a hired chauffeur if you're a female) can get you flogged in public. The penalty for adultery is a public beheading. And, despite the extremes, hard-line Wahhabis always want stricter rules.

Of course, hardly anyone is actually killed for adultery, because to charge someone the act must be substantiated by four witnesses, who, needless to say, are usually scarce.

Still, like Americans, the Saudis have their fair share of executions—

only they do them in public. The day before I got there, a young woman's head was lopped off in Deera Square, where the public executions take place. Nicknamed Chop Chop Square, Deera is a courtyard in the center of Riyadh, not far from the religious courts and directly in front of the "White House," HQ for the religious police. She was charged with drug smuggling, a crime that will get you killed very quickly in Saudi Arabia. Someone nearby told me she was the thirty-fifth person to be beheaded in 2006. Her head was cut off in the morning, over a drainage grate in the center of the square, in front of hundreds of people; by the afternoon, kids were once again playing soccer in the square. Crazy.

Women's rights are severely restricted in Saudi Arabia. Women can't vote or get a driver's license. They can't walk out the door without making sure their hair, arms, and legs are covered. It was one thing to see women in burkas in rural Afghanistan, and something else again to see a lot of them just as covered up in their black *abayas* in hyper-modern Riyadh. Some of them are covered head to toe, so that not even their hands are exposed; and while some women have slits through which to see, others wear black veils that shield even a glimpse of the eyes. It's a bit discomfiting to see this at first, because it isn't just a few women who dress this way; it's *all* women. They're jokingly referred to by urban professional men as BMOs—black moving objects. But it's no joke that the religious police, called the *Mutawa*, patrol the streets to make sure they comply.

Men can have multiple wives. (Not just in Saudi Arabia but in many Muslim countries.) There are countless reports that men beat their wives and divorce them pretty much on a whim, too. But the biggest problem is that women there have little recourse for such actions. It's almost impossible for them to successfully prosecute their husbands for abuse, and even harder for them to initiate a divorce. I look at the statistics in the United States, where nearly half of all first marriages end in divorce and one in four women is affected by domestic violence, and while we may not have much room to crow, at least we can call Ponch and Jon to haul that jerk downtown!

Women use separate entrances to many public facilities, as well as the rear doors of buses. Girls can go to school and college, but in segregated classrooms from the first grade on, and only with female teachers. When they graduate, they'll represent only 5 percent of the workforce. That is, *if* they survive until graduation. In one horrible incident in 2002, fifteen students in a girls' school in Mecca died in a fire when the local *mutaween* prevented them from leaving the building, *because they weren't wearing their head scarves!* Think about the insanity of that for a second. We'd rather you burn to death than be seen in public with your hair uncovered. Maybe someday Saudi Arabia will get its own Rosa Parks, Harriet Tubman, and Betty Friedan, but that day still looks pretty far off.

At the hotel where I stayed in Riyadh, there was some sort of an investment conference taking place in one of the meeting rooms on the second floor. I happened to walk past the room during a break, and all the men were outside hobnobbing in the lobby, smoking cigarettes and drinking coffee. I glanced in the room as I walked past and saw that they all sat around a giant U-shaped table and a PowerPoint presentation was being projected onto a sliding wall that was at the top of the U, dividing it from the other side. I thought this had been done to separate the room from another conference next door, but when I walked past the second set of doors I saw a woman sitting at a table alone, staring at a small screen that had the same PowerPoint slide show on it. She was dressed from head to toe in a black *abaya*, her face covered. As the sole female attendant of this conference, she had been banished to this side of the room, away from the men, behind the screen, unable to talk to anyone or do anything during their breaks. I couldn't believe it.

Why these insane restrictions, especially in a society that shows so many obvious Western and American influences? It goes back to the pact between the House of Saud and the Wahhabis and a three-decade resurgence of fundamentalism. In return for helping them keep a tight control on society, the royals have allowed Saudi Arabia's archconservative mullahs, imams, and religious teachers to become some of the most powerful figures in the world. They've been arguing with the royals over the corrupting influence and "cultural attack" of modernization and Westernization since the first American oil prospectors and wireless radios showed up in the 1920s and 1930s.

But since the big oil boom of the 1970s, as the gazillionaire royal family and the high-rolling business elite fast-tracked modernization and sidetracked thoughts of spreading the wealth a little, the religious leaders have shrieked much louder. And they were able to spread their influence throughout Saudi society, from the mosques and madrassas to the public schools and universities and the TV stations—where they've been known to appear regularly to teach their audiences wonderful religious precepts, like how "throats must be slit and skulls must be shattered" in the fight against "the brothers of apes and pigs, the murderers of the prophets"—aka the Jews, and sometimes the Christians, depending on who's doing the spewing.

As with most of the countries I visited, I found this outlook to be far from the majority opinion. Still, these ranting mullahs have enormous sway over the millions of Saudis who are *not* wealthy, high-living "Saudi Americans." Many Saudis never cashed in on the oil boom, and the unemployment rate is a whopping 30 percent. These poorer Saudis live outside the big cities, in places like the vast desert at the southern end of the Arabian Peninsula. Some of them really do live the traditional, nomadic Bedouin life. Others are farmers and laborers. Poor and uneducated, deeply conservative by nature, they're easily converted to jihadism. Many of the Saudi hijackers on September 11 were from the poor south, and bin Laden is said to have a whole lot of sympathizers there.

Osama was a teenager in Jeddah during the 1970s, when the sky-rocketing price of Saudi oil brought the tensions between Westernization and fundamentalism to full boil. He watched many of his older siblings become Westernized jet-setters. But he was pulled in the opposite direction. Like the Wahhabist mullahs, he believed that Western influences were defiling and polluting Saudi Arabia, the holy land of the Prophet. He saw the House of Saud encouraging sin and corruption everywhere, and leading the people away from true Islam.

And when King Fahd allowed U.S. troops on Saudi soil in 1990, Osama saw it as an all-out military occupation by infidels, a new Crusade that would turn Saudi Arabia into "an American colony." He condemned the royal family for permitting it. In an open letter to King Fahd, issued in 1995 through his Advice and Reform Committee, he put it bluntly:

"It is proven, O King, that your regime has committed the forbidden things in Islam which nullify its validity before God. The devastating failure and the dishonorable corruption which have been proven against your regime are enough reasons to overthrow it. By legislating the positive[ly] blasphemous laws and obligating people to seek judgment by them, by pledging your allegiance and support to the infidels against the Muslims, you have committed many of the things which are contrary to the teachings of Islam and which demand that you be revolted against and removed."

And that's why Al Qaeda, and various jihadists inspired by Al Qaeda, struck inside Saudi Arabia. The attacks began as early as 1979, when the extremists staged the bloody seizure of the Grand Mosque in Mecca. Things kicked up a notch in the 1990s, after the arrival of the U.S. troops.

Then the U.S.-led invasion of Iraq in 2003 set off a new rash of retaliatory attacks against the Americans' friend and ally, with dozens of suicide car and truck bombings, kidnappings, armed ambushes, and targeted assassinations of both Saudi officials and Americans working in the country. Although I moved around freely there and never felt threatened, many Westerners in Saudi Arabia, whether military personnel or corporate contractors, live in giant walled-in fortresses with extensive security, and rarely travel without armed escorts. In 2003, Al Qaeda operative Yusef al-Ayeri (alias Swift Sword), who had been arrested and then released by the Saudis, made two attempts to overthrow the government. He was killed, and in a shirt pocket officials found a six-month-old handwritten note from bin Laden, congratulating him on the outstanding job he was doing.

Before I left on my quest, I spoke to Prince Turki al-Faisal, former head of the Saudi intelligence service (1977 to 2001), who was currently the Saudi ambassador to the United States. He told me that he believed even 9/11 was a roundabout attack against Saudi Arabia. Osama "wanted to create a rift between the United States and Saudi Arabia," he said. "His main target, of course, as leader of Al Qaeda, is Saudi Arabia. . . . The U.S. is an enemy because it supports Saudi Arabia, not because it's the United States."

The royal family walks a very fine line with the mullahs, and takes great pains to appease them. Sharia is law, and Wahhabism, as the state religion, is taught in every school. Over the past few decades, the House of Saud has spent billions of dollars opening and funding Wahhabist madrassas literally all over the world. Even more problematic, certain well-off Saudis give tons of money to Saudi religious charities, some of which—at least before 9/11—are known to have funneled support to jihadist groups like Al Qaeda. Since September 11, the government has moved to shut down these charities, but no one I spoke to was convinced that it was anywhere close to completely cutting off the flow of funds from Saudi donors to extremists in the West Bank, Gaza, Afghanistan, Pakistan, or to Osama and Al Qaeda themselves. So there's still a weird daisy chain of Saudis made rich by American oil money giving donations to fund ultraconservative religious schools and terrorist organizations that strike against Americans and rich Saudis. Lunacy.

Officially, representatives of the Saudi government often downplay or even deny that there's much extremism or anti-American sentiment in the country. Prince Bandar, who was Prince Turki's predecessor as ambassador to the United States, famously said, in a post-9/11 *Frontline* interview, that claims of widespread celebrations from the Saudi people when the twin towers fell were, and I quote, "bullshit."

Khalil al-Khalil, Ph.D., told me differently when I met with him in Riyadh. He's a member of the Shura Council, a group of 150 scholars, businessmen, and religious and professional leaders appointed by the king to advise him and his ministers on political and social matters.

"Within the country," I said to him, "there are still a lot of imams who preach against Israel and America in very vicious terms. How do you address that?"

"It's unfortunate, but these ideas in fact are in our textbooks, delivered in the mosques, and in our public media we have been hearing some of these terrible, extreme ideas," he said. "And coming from no really planned groups, but coming because they are never being challenged."

"Are there still radicals within the country?"

"We still have a lot," he said. "And they are dangerous. We should not think for a minute that they are going to disappear in a few years.

We should work very hard together at all levels to eliminate their leaders from the effective positions in education, in media, in religious institutions, and the society."

"How many people in your country would you say are sympathetic toward those types of ideologies?"

"My concern is not about individual acts," he said. "They happen everywhere. My concern is about organized groups, and unfortunately we have in the Kingdom of Saudi Arabia some secret, organized, extreme groups that are working underground to undermine the society and governmental institutions. . . . Those groups are sick people. And we have to work together against those guys."

As I drove back to my hotel that night, past the packed U.S. fast-food chains, past the kids all decked out in hip-hop gear, past the parked *Fast and the Furious* ripoff cars with undercarriage neon kits and booming sound systems, I couldn't get over how intense the Saudi love-hate relationship with America and Westernization was. It's an entire society with a split personality. Some people embrace it in public, but others hide their dark side. Sheikh Jekyll, the public face, is an observant, very conservative Muslim, who's helping to spread fundamentalist and jihadist ideals around the globe. Sheikh Hyde is a jet-setting party animal behind closed doors or out of the country—in Bahrain, for instance, just off the coast in the Persian Gulf, where the liquor and the prostitutes are plentiful, making it the horny Saudi man's version of Tijuana or Las Vegas.

Back in Morocco, Aboubakr Jamai had talked to me about this hypocrisy within Islam. It struck me as the same hypocrisy we see in the United States, where religious leaders are caught with drugs, prostitutes, or having extramarital affairs. Islam hasn't cornered the market on hypocrisy.

Sitting around the Bedouin-style campfire that evening in the desert, I met a young Saudi guy who personified the divide. In his jeans, sneakers, sweatshirt, and wool cap, Saud would fit right in with hipster twenty-somethings anywhere in America. And he *loved* America. He went there in the winter of 2005, as part of an international military training program. Saud was in Saudi Arabia's National Guard, which is nothing like the National Guard in the United States. The Saudi National Guard is the king's private army, separate from the country's regular armed forces, pledging allegiance directly to the House of Saud, not to the government. Its primary mission is to guard the royal family against attack or rebellion from any source, including the regular army.

Saud told me the other guys in the training program were from Azerbaijan, Ethiopia, Mongolia, Nepal—there was even one from Jamaica named Captain Morgan. (Sounds like a handsome genius.)

When he flew into the post-9/11 JFK from Jeddah, Saud was taken aside by security, ordered to strip down to his boxers, and all of his ID and paperwork were closely scrutinized. After clearing that hurdle, though, he was free to roam the country and experience America—and he took full advantage of the opportunity. In San Antonio, Texas, where his training took place, the Saudi government paid for him to have a private apartment off the army base, in a complex with a swimming pool. This made the other international officers jealous at first, because they had to live on the base, but Saud solved that little problem by having them over for parties—good, Saudi, Muslim-style parties, with coffee, tea, and lamb instead of beer, whiskey, and hot dogs. He said the lamb gave some of them stomachaches at first because they'd never eaten it. They were all swine lovers, like me.

Saud got himself a Mexican girlfriend in San Antonio. He also got AAA, rented cars, and drove all over the Southwest. On one drive from Texas to Arizona, he saw Mexican immigrants scurrying across the highway at night. The American officers had warned him not to pick any of them up, "because maybe some of these people have a pistol, or maybe a knife." All he saw, though, was "an old woman, and she had a small daughter or a small baby, in the middle of night."

Saud went to New York City for New Year's. He told me, "I celebrated in Times Square, with a live show with Mary J. Blige and Beyoncé. . . . There were a lot of Japanese people, and Chinese. And it was so cold. It was amazing. . . . New York City. It's, like, crazy. I love Times Square. It's so crazy. I love the shows. I went to Broadway Street. And Fifth Avenue." He got pictures of himself at the Statue of Liberty.

And then the Saudi split personality surfaced. As much as he enjoyed the freewheeling lifestyle in America, he didn't seem to have any problems with living in a locked-down fundamentalist society back home in Saudi Arabia, where his mother had to cover her hair before leaving the house, and he didn't want his little brother looking at girls. "I cannot let my sister get a boyfriend," he told me. "No. We have, like, a religion, we have a system. It is good for me, and it is good for every family."

So he thought it was okay for women to be segregated from men like that? And be completely subservient to them?

"Here? Yeah. Our religion, our system, in the government, it is coming from the Holy Koran."

I was confused. "So what did you think when you were in the United States, when you saw girls who weren't covered?" I asked him. "Girls in miniskirts?"

"It's good. I saw a lot at the San Diego beach. Yeah, but it's okay. What should I do? Because I am an open-minded person." But at home "I protect my family. I have to make my family in a good shape. I cannot let my sister hang out with someone outside, and she went to the party and she is coming back to the home so drunk. No. This cannot happen. She have to stay home, she have to stay with her mother, until someone come up to the home and say, 'I want to get your sister for marriage.' I say okay, we make a procedure to make a wedding, and everything is going right. He can see her. . . . But they cannot live together before wedding. No. It's *haram*. It's prohibited. That's good for us. That's good for everybody here."

I told Saud I'd been to Chop Chop Square, where thieves get their hands lopped off, and drug dealers, murderers, rapists, and adulterers are beheaded.

Well, he said, "Everybody, they all know, this guy who was killed in the morning, he was naughty. He deserve to be killed. Because he killed someone with no reason."

"But you can also get killed for adultery," I pointed out.

That was okay with him, too. It was the law, and maybe it was strict, but it made society peaceful and safe, "because everybody have to watch out what's going on."

Yep, in Saudi Arabia you sure have to keep your head on straight; and if you don't, they have a nice public street you can keep it on.

. . .

The Man didn't show up anywhere I'd been, so I went looking for him in other places. I also wanted to hear more about this Saudi love-hate relationship with America. Why did a Saudi like bin Laden pick up on only the hate side? Where is the love, Osama?

In Riyadh, I met a couple of guys I figured could help me get a better understanding of the man I was hunting. They were also avid Internet bloggers. I was hoping that if anybody could help me get a fix on Osama's present whereabouts, it was a pair of Net-savvy Saudis.

Omar and Ahmed (not their real names) would have made my campfire buddy Saud really jealous—they were so Americanized it was incredible. Twenty-year-old Omar and his friend Ahmed, forty-two, dressed, acted, and spoke totally like Americans. If I hadn't met them in a coffeehouse in Riyadh, I could just as easily have seen them in any Starbucks in the States.

Starbucks and Starbucks-like coffeehouses have popped up all over Saudi Arabia in the past few years. It's easy to see why. With no movie theaters, clubs, or bars, they're just about the only public space where young Saudis can meet up, hang out, or just sit with their laptops.

Omar actually lived and studied for ten years in Portland, Oregon (go, Trail Blazers!), before moving back to Saudi Arabia in 1998. He said that he thought the rigid segregation of the sexes was "fucking people up."

"Just imagine, you grow up, you have not seen any female besides your sisters, your mother, your aunts, your cousins," he said. "Obviously, you can't do anything with them. And whenever you see them they are covered. You don't even know anything about them. You're not taught in school anything about them, like their bodies, menstruation, anything. You're just clueless. . . . I know guys who are actually scared of meeting with girls. They're, like, 'What do we do? What do you talk about?' "

Ahmed said he'd recently seen a guy actually yank a woman out of her car, "and everybody was just watching." He recalled, "The police were further down the street and they didn't do anything. I didn't stay long enough to see what happened, but she was being, like, abducted in the middle of the street, because this guy liked her. . . . It was, like, at eight o'clock at night, and I was, like, what the fuck?"

Omar and Ahmed—who also wrote for a newspaper—told me that in the few years since the Internet had become available, as many as a thousand blogs had been started in Saudi Arabia. It was one way that young Saudi males and females could talk to each other and meet up. They'd connect online, then arrange to meet secretly in person.

"We do all the normal things that teenagers would do in America," Omar said. "I go to parties. I have girlfriends. But it's all underground."

"Yeah, you just need to have your own circle of friends," Ahmed agreed. "And then anything is possible."

They said there was even—avert your eyes and cover your ears, little children—premarital sex. This applies to Saudi society in general, they said. Drinking, drugs, and prostitution all go on, behind closed doors and on the black market. People make their own moonshine, called *siddiqui*, which means "my friend" in Arabic. If they're rich, they can buy Absolut on the black market—for $225 a bottle.

"Being rich here is license to do whatever you want," Ahmed said. "Just live in your own world and say fuck the system, fuck the rules."

The government, not surprisingly, tries to restrict Internet access just like everything else. All ISPs are routed through a main server in Riyadh, and the government blocks not only porn sites but things like MySpace, Friendster, and YouTube. "I think next to China we are the second country in the world that blocks the Internet the most," Omar said.

Ahmed said he thought it was a lot of wasted money and effort. "I have a satellite Internet connection at home, so the server is in Australia," he told me. "It just bypasses the Saudi censors completely."

I asked Omar why so many Saudi youths were sent to study in the United States. His answer was blunt.

"It's the education system here," he said. "It's not up to grade like it is in the U.S. When you have a U.S. degree in your hand, you can get a job here easily. It will be more accepted." He said that a recent international survey had ranked Saudi universities among the very lowest worldwide. And there were so many majors—political science, journalism, law—that simply weren't offered to female students.

I told them I'd heard that Wahhabist ideas—anti-Christian, anti-

Jewish, anti-Western—had permeated the teaching in Saudi public schools. Was it true?

Well, Omar grinned, contradicting what I'd heard from Khalil al-Khalil, "It's not in the textbooks," he said. "It's not like we have 'Chapter 13: Hate America.'" It was more the teachers passing along their attitudes and opinions. "For example, if they are teaching us about religion, they say if you pray five times a day you're going to be closer to God—unlike the Christians, who don't." He also said kids hear it from their parents. "Their parents will tell them, 'You are better. You were born a Muslim.'"

"We are the chosen people," Ahmed said, smiling.

"I thought the Jews were the chosen people."

"Well, no, not according to Muslims."

Ahmed added that kids aren't taught an officially anti-Israel or anti-Jewish line in the schools, but then again Saudi Arabia had become home to a lot of Palestinian exiles, and many of them are teachers. "I had a teacher who was Palestinian-British, and he used to sit down and tell us these horrible stories about how his grandfather died and how they were kicked out of the country," he recalled. "And when you hear this it does affect you, definitely." Especially since Saudi kids grow up not knowing anyone Jewish. "So they just think Jews are all devils, evil. They just don't look at them as human beings."

"We've been taught that, no matter what, you can never be friends with a Jew," Omar agreed. "They're always money-hungry, they're gonna steal from you, stay away from them, they are not your friend." That is, until you need a *really* good lawyer.

I loved the insights into Saudi youth culture that I got from Omar and Ahmed. Unfortunately, they weren't much help to me in my Hunt for Red Osama. They didn't even seem all that interested. Omar thought he was in Afghanistan; Ahmed said Pakistan. Like I hadn't heard that before. But Ahmed did pass along a rumor he'd heard from a friend of the bin Laden family that until the previous August Osama had been calling his relatives in Jeddah, using a satellite phone and multiple relays so the calls couldn't be traced.

"Until this past August?" I repeated. That was two months ago! *Verrrrry interrrrresting!* It was the following month that rumors of his death began to circulate.

Ahmed had also heard that the family had continued to send Osama money from his share of his multibillionaire father's estate. That, at least, seemed totally plausible, despite U.S. efforts to limit the money being funneled to Al Qaeda. It was an open secret that wealthy Saudis—wealthy Muslims in a lot of countries—admired Osama and supported jihadism. Why shouldn't his own family? True, they publicly disowned him back in 1996, but in Saudi Arabia, I was learning, what you do and say in public can be very different from what you do and think in private.

I kept looking for signs of Osama in Riyadh. I went back to the street I'd passed earlier, a place where young guys hung out, and thought I might spot him there, cruising for new recruits for his jihad. I was blown away when I got there. It looked like Anytown, USA. The street was lined with strip malls, and they were packed with American fast-food joints. In this one strip alone, maybe a block long, I saw Starbucks, Applebee's, Chili's, Häagen-Dazs, Baskin-Robbins, Dunkin' Donuts, Domino's, Quiznos, Subway . . . and a GNC, where you could get herbal remedies for the tummy ache you got from eating in all those places. The only un-American thing about these places was that the seating was segregated into sections for "Families" and "Singles," like all restaurants in the country.

I sat with a quartet of hip-looking young guys—Mohamad, Ahmed (popular name), Mansour, and Faisal—who were hanging out in front of Quiznos, smoking cigarettes, sipping Pepsi and Lipton iced tea, shooting the breeze. Their ages ranged from eighteen to twenty-two, and they looked fully Americanized—from Mohamad, with his long rock hair and black Metallica T-shirt, to the more hipster Ahmed, who had short, chopped hair and wore little designer glasses. A couple of them had visited the States, and they all had friends or family there.

"I'm looking for Osama bin Laden," I told them.

They all laughed.

"He orders a lot from Domino's Pizza," Mohamad joked, pointing at the nearby store.

"So Quiznos is the wrong place to look?" I asked. "He's a Domino's man? No wonder I didn't see him at the Pizza Hut. Well, if I'm not going to find him, what do you guys do for fun around here?"

"Mostly, we hang out at anyone's house," Mansour said.

"Just cruise up and down the street," Mohamad said. "You can find people hanging out at cafés and just talking. They don't give us much to do, which is a problem. Personally, I just stay home. There are no recreation centers you can go hang out at. Malls are strictly for families—they won't let bachelors in. They have a specific day for bachelors, and it's only in the morning."

"There's nothing else to do," Ahmed agreed. "They complain about the youth, saying the youth are wasting their time on the streets doing nothing. Well, you didn't leave us much choice, did you?"

We shot the breeze about how hard it was for them to date girls, about their favorite bands, movies, and TV shows ("*South Park* is probably the greatest American literature that ever came out," Mohamad declared), and about how, like a lot of young dudes everywhere, you basically had to drag them to the mosque to get them to pray. Somehow I wasn't surprised to hear that there's a branch of the religious police that does just that, cruising the streets in SUVs in search of rebellious youths to haul off to prayer.

These were four young Muslim males that I couldn't see getting attracted to radical, extremist movements anytime soon. Extremist heavy metal, sure. Radical partying, uh-huh. But Al Qaeda? Mohamad claimed that he didn't even know what it was.

The faculty at King Abdul Aziz University had a lot to do with turning the young Osama's mind toward jihad. I wondered if he was still in contact with anyone there—someone who might help me get a bead on where to find him. But after everything I'd heard about the Muslim Brotherhood and radical Islamists at the university, Dr. Omar S. Elmershedi totally broke the mold. He's a professor of economics, and about as far from being a radical Islamist as anyone I could meet in the Arab world. He had studied in America in the 1980s, at Michigan State University—"a Saudi in the Snow Belt," he joked. He fondly recalled getting to shake Magic Johnson's hand when Magic was a mind-boggling point guard for the MSU Spartans. Omar was a big fan of both American-style democracy *and* American-style coffee, so we also met at Starbucks. Hey, I'm always up for more caffeine.

After a few cheers of "Go, Spartans!" we got down to talking about Saudi-U.S. relations. Omar smiled and said he would probably be giving me minority opinions, "because I've been contaminated, so to speak, by my education in the United States."

"Do other people think you're too 'Americanized'?" I asked. "Is that an insult here?"

"I'm not ashamed of being Americanized," he said. "Thank God, and thanks for the beautiful golden opportunity I got to be educated in one of the finest schools and rub shoulders with the finest kids in the United States. It's a beautiful opportunity. So if it's insulting to be Americanized, thanks, I'll take it."

"It seems to me there are two Saudi Arabias fighting each other," I observed.

"I think all the advancement you see in Saudi Arabia, and the amount of wealth from oil revenue, has enabled us to improve *structures*," he explained. But "it's extremely difficult when it comes to *cultural* changes. We have changed so much materialistically, but under the *thawb*, so to speak, we're still conservatives, we're still deeply religious people."

"Do Saudis love freedom?"

"A good number of Saudis are scared when it comes to freedom. We like the notion of freedom, but it's also scary, because it means rapid change. And we Saudis by nature don't like rapid changes."

"In almost every country we've gone to, everyone has said that the reason there is so much hatred and so many problems in the world is because of the Israeli-Palestinian conflict," I said to him. "Why is there is so much hatred toward the Jewish people?"

"Because a good number of the political systems in the Arab world and in the Muslim world based their legitimacy on fighting the Jews," he replied. "I don't think any Arab political system is truly honest and sincere about Palestinian independence. They all use the Palestinian issue for their own self-interest. To cover up for their inefficiencies."

"And it's easy to blame it on America."

"Precisely," he agreed. But "as much as we like to blame the United States for taking on the Israeli position, we also have to blame ourselves for not presenting ourselves, Arab countries, as reliable friends and partners in the entire process."

"What do you think Saudi Arabia's role should be in solving the problem?"

First, he said, Saudi Arabia should join Egypt and Jordan in formally acknowledging that the Israelis "have as much right as everybody else to exist and operate and live in this part of the world." But he didn't think that would happen anytime soon.

"What's the role of the United States in the conflict?" I asked.

"I truly believe that the United States has taken on a divine responsibility," he said—a very surprising thing to hear in the Arab world, even from a Spartans fan. He went on, "For a nation to believe that principles such as freedom, democracy, and the right of each one of us to express his views, to pursue happiness, to take that and place it on a global level—goddammit, it is such a divine responsibility that I bow my head to it. I know this view doesn't fit well with many of my friends and students and colleagues."

I was really interested in hearing Omar's opinions about Osama. "How has he affected Saudi Arabia?" I asked.

"In so many unfortunate ways. He's a product of the religious establishment in Saudi Arabia, there's no denying it. We have to accept that. And, with it, a moral and a spiritual responsibility to ourselves and the rest of the Islamic world."

"Do people in Saudi Arabia still see him as a hero?"

"Not very many. At least not the people I have contact with, the kids at university level that I've been teaching for the last twenty years. No, I think it's fading out rapidly. Because they have discovered that they have been tricked in so many ways. They have been tricked intellectually. They have been sold some cheap propaganda on what Islam is, and they found out that propaganda wasn't true and Islam is not that Islam that Osama bin Laden claims. The change won't happen overnight. But the reverse trend has begun."

"Where is he?"

"You guys should know better than us!" Omar said. Then he added,

"The physical presence of bin Laden isn't of importance. And I think his era is on the way out."

And the Saudi government is doing its best to make sure it stays out. Realizing that Saudi Arabia is as much a target as Western countries, Saudi government and intelligence officials have been doing all they can to curb extremism within the country. In the spring of 2006, they arrested 173 individuals for allegedly being linked to a massive terrorist plot to blow up oil fields in the country. Almost all of those arrested were Saudi, confirming the fear that the biggest threat in the years ahead will be from homegrown jihadists.

I flew from Riyadh to Jeddah, and I have to say, nothing is scarier than hearing your pilot drop "*Insha'Allah*" into every announcement he makes. This "God willing" phrase had become one of my favorites in Arabic, and is used as a response to nearly everything.

I would say to someone, "I hope to see you again soon."

"*Insha'Allah*," he'd respond.

"I just hope my baby is healthy."

"*Insha'Allah*."

"I will find Osama."

"*Insha'Allah*."

But when you're thirty thousand feet in the air it's pretty unsettling when the pilot is talking about when you'll land, "*Insha'Allah*," saying that the plane is in great condition and running fine, "*Insha'Allah*," and that we shouldn't hit any bad weather, "*Insha'Allah*." I, personally, like to keep any praying that's to be done on a plane all to myself.

In the desert outside Jeddah is a farm where Osama and his family lived before his self-exile. It seemed like a good place to look for him. Maybe he got homesick. So I drove out there with Mamdouh, my Saudi fixer. He kept the music pumping the whole ride. Deep Purple, Tori Amos, Yes, Supertramp. He had stuffed the glove compartment full of this stuff—as well as at least ten CDs of people reading the Koran.

Snooping around Osama's farm could also be a good way to get into trouble. I was told there were extremists in the area who were fans of his and didn't take kindly to foreign journos poking around with cameras. So I went incognito, in my full Lawrence of Arabia white robes and *kaffiyeh*.

Wouldn't you know it, the first guys I met, when we stopped at an old-fashioned gas station out in the middle of flat, khaki-colored nowhere, were all wearing T-shirts, shorts, and flip-flops. So much for fitting in. I looked like Lawrence of Arabia, they looked Mamdouh of Milwaukee, lounging around on a pair of old sofas outside the station. It didn't make me any more at ease that the sofas had an army-green camouflage design.

"I was hoping you guys could help me," I told them. "I'm looking for Osama bin Laden."

Like everyone else, they just laughed. "Like he would come see us here?" one guy scoffed.

It turned out that they weren't locals, anyway. They'd just arrived from Yemen. Then a man drove up in a brand-new SUV and rolled his window down. He was an older man, gray-bearded. I was happy to see that he was dressed Bedouin style, like me. He, however, did not look very happy to see me. Suspiciously, he asked who I was, where I was from, what I was doing, and whether I had permits to do it.

When we got that over with, though, Mohsin Saud al-Slaymi al-Miytani al-Huthali—yep, that's all one guy—relaxed and became friendly. He had a farm nearby.

"I'm traveling around the world looking for Osama bin Laden," I told him.

He chuckled and said, *"Wallah!"* Which means "Really!" Then he joked, "If I know where he is, I will take the $100 million."

"Maybe you and I can go and look for him together," I said. "We could split it."

Mr. Huthali wanted me to know that the Saudis didn't create Osama. "United States of America made him. So it's USA-made? A trademark of yours. You know this. You plant, you harvest, yes?"

"You reap what you sow?"

"Yes. You are planting these people, so now you're hunting them. It's not our mistake."

He invited me to see his farm. This was a little dicey. A few months after I was there, four French journalists would be kidnapped and killed along this very road while looking around for Osama's old farm. But Mr. Huthali seemed all right to me, so we followed him along a dusty track out to his land. The sun was hot, the land flat and sandy. We parked on the road, and he and I opened the back hatch of his SUV and sat in the shade of some small trees, our feet dangling.

Mr. Huthali said that the long friendship between the United States and Saudi Arabia was a good thing for both sides, but he couldn't get over some of the bad and crazy things our presidents had done.

For example, he said, "Clinton was telling us be good, go to church—for us go to mosque—and he is using cigar! Cuban cigar!" He laughed and shook his head. And then there was Bush. "I hear from your people on discussions on CNN or NBC, or something like this, that your president is talking to Allah! God talking to him! You hear about this?"

"Yeah, I heard he said God told him that he should invade Iraq."

"Isn't this impossible now? We are in the twenty-first century! Don't tell me that God now talks to people. He doesn't anymore talk to anybody."

Jeddah, Saudi Arabia's big port city on the Red Sea, is the gateway to Mecca. Muslims from all over the world coming for the hajj pass through Jeddah. There, I felt I was getting really close to Osama, at least in spirit. All the reactionary, anti-Western, antimodern ideas behind everything he's done as an adult he first soaked up in and around Jeddah. In that sense, it's not only his birthplace but the birthplace of the whole post-9/11 world as we know it.

I looked for Osama all over Jeddah. Who knew? Maybe he got tired of living in caves in Pakistan and Afghanistan and sneaked home to the family compound, wanted to walk along the sandy beaches of his youth, which I'm sure would be a helluva lot more comfortable than Econo-Cave.

I asked a lot of people on the street and in shops if they knew where he was. Most of them just said no, but I got a few funny answers. One man told me Osama was with Bush in the White House. Jeez, I hadn't even thought to look there!

Another guy said, "On the moon." (Not in my budget, in case you're wondering.)

Jeddah felt a bit more culturally relaxed than Riyadh. After all, it's an international port, open to outside influences, whereas Riyadh is the royal family's center of power, out in the middle of the desert. Jeddah is filled with statues and artwork; massive sculptures line the coastal King's Road and dot roundabouts all the way up the shoreline. It was impressive, especially after ultraconservative Riyadh, where I didn't see a single monument, and where questionable pictures were torn out or blacked out of magazines and newspapers before they hit the newsstands. I picked up one paper that showed Posh Spice with a big black-ink bar across her back—God forbid anyone should see her tempting shoulder—and another with six whole pages ripped out. In Jeddah, the magazines were sold as is, though I still didn't see anything like *Maxim* or *FHM* anywhere.

Also, not every single woman I saw in Jeddah was cloaked in a black *abaya* and hiding her face behind a *niqab*. In fact, Manal Soliman Fakeeh was wearing stylish, casual Western clothes, with just a lacy black scarf worn loosely over her hair as an "Islamic" touch. But then Manal didn't fit anyone's stereotypes. She was an attractive, divorced, single mother, she was on the board of the Dr. Soliman Fakeeh Hospital in Jeddah, which her father started, and had just been nominated vice president of the National Women's Council for Employment and Training, *and* was getting a Ph.D. at the University of Glasgow in Scotland.

"You look nothing like the other Muslim women I've come into contact with," I told her.

"I don't know if I should take that as a compliment or not," she said. "I'd like to think that I'm a great Muslim. . . . I'm not going about advertising an alternative way of life. I'm just living it peacefully."

"Do women have rights in Saudi Arabia?" I asked her.

"They have plenty of rights," she said. "Our problem is, we don't know how many rights we have."

It isn't the religion of Islam that restricts women's rights, she argued; it's social and cultural conservatism using religion as a justification. Women in Saudi Arabia used to be more free to work and to dress as they liked. The gradually increasing restrictions began in the 1980s, as part of the same conservative movement that swept up the young bin Laden.

"When I went into offices to do interviews in Riyadh, I never saw a single woman there," I said. "It was all men. Do you think more women would have jobs and careers if they could?"

Absolutely, Manal said, "provided the road is paved for them. It is not easy. We are not a culture that actually fights for change. We fear change. On a deeper level, we fear for our beliefs, we fear for the family, we fear imitating the West. That's *you* guys."

"Will there be a women's liberation movement in Saudi Arabia," I asked her, "where women rip off their face veils and burn them in a bonfire and cheer?"

"Dream on," she said with a laugh. "No, I don't think there are enough of us that want that. And definitely the men don't want that to happen."

While I never saw Osama in Jeddah, I did meet two guys who had tragic personal connections to him. One was Abdullah Thabit, a cerebral, hip-looking thirty-three-year-old school administrator with prematurely gray hair and casual Western clothes. I soon found out what might have turned his hair gray: Thabit could have been *The 20th Terrorist*. That's the title of his bestselling novel, published in Syria in 2006. It's a somewhat fictionalized account of how he was recruited at age fifteen and trained for jihad, along with hundreds of other boys, by a shadowy extremist organization led by teachers in his own public high school, in the southern Saudi town of Abha. That blew my mind. When I was in school, extracurricular activities meant going out for the football team, not the terrorist squad. Abdullah broke away from the group after a few years, but another guy from his town, Ahmed Alnami, ended up being one of the fifteen Saudi hijackers on September 11.

Abdullah told me that he grew up on a farm, like a lot of kids around Abha, working the fields and herding the cattle with his eleven siblings. Local society was conservative and religious, but he said it only gradually became the death-cult jihadist extremism that we know now. It was the 1979 seizure of the Grand Mosque in Mecca that began to inspire the underground jihadist movement in his area—the same act of glorious martyrdom that had also inspired the twenty-two-year-old Osama in Jeddah.

Abdullah had just started high school and, like any teenager, he was full of questions about himself, his identity, what his role in life should be. The organization lured him and other boys with easy, ready-made answers to their questions, supposedly straight from God and the Koran. On top of all the usual youth group activities like camping and field trips, they used bizarre indoctrination techniques. One night they took the boys to a cemetery and had them lie in open graves while they recited verses about hell and damnation from the Koran. Sort of like a *Scared Straight* tactic, only these kids were being scared straight into terrorism.

Abdullah came to his senses and left the group. Years later, he said, it came as "a very violent shock" to learn that one of the boys from Abha had grown up to be among the 9/11 jihadikazes. "I felt extremely sad," he went on. "Sadness about those who were killed and died in a violent and horrendous way, and sadness about this person, Ahmed Alnami. . . . He deserved love, music, and life. He had the right to live a normal life. Ahmed Alnami was a victim, just like other victims of 9/11."

When I asked Abdullah what he thought we needed to do in the world to keep young people from being easy prey for violent fanatics, he said, "To put life, art, and beauty first, not bullets, aircrafts, and weapons." He said he believed that when people saw that they could live in peace and with justice, only the completely mad ones would turn to violence and death instead.

In Jeddah I also met Othman, thirty-three years old, who ran a local real-estate agency. No, I wasn't interested in buying a condo in Mecca with a view of the Kaaba. (Which I couldn't do, anyway, since non-Muslims like myself aren't allowed anywhere near it. As you drive up the highway toward Mecca, there's a roadblock with a turnoff and a giant sign overhead that says "Muslims/Non-Muslims." The Muslims can stay on the yellow brick road all the way to Mecca, but people like me have to take the turnoff and head back to Jeddah.) I wanted to speak with Othman because one of the fifteen Saudis on 9/11 was a relative of his. For the sake of his family, Othman asked me not to be more specific than that.

"What were your thoughts when September 11 happened?" I asked him.

"September 11 was an international shock," he said, though "not a shock to some." When I asked what that meant, he said he believed there was still "a missing link," and went into the same conspiracy-theory talk I'd heard before, citing "movies made by the sons of America, like *Fahrenheit 9/11*," in which "you'll find a lot of questions being posed that the average person cannot answer." He insisted that the United States had never produced any real evidence that either Osama or Al Qaeda was behind the attacks, and the families of the fifteen Saudi hijackers "are not entirely convinced that their sons were behind the events. They are not entirely convinced, because they did not ever belong to Al Qaeda."

"So even the statements several of them videotaped before the event, the ones that circulated everywhere on the Internet, didn't convince you?" I said.

"I don't believe that it's solid proof," he insisted. "Americans can make unbelievable things in cinema. We've seen science-fiction films, horror films. . . . We've seen the lion, the dog, and the pig in many movies talking like humans. It's easy to make anybody make a speech saying I'll do this or do that."

This was the first time I'd ever heard a conspiracy theory linking Al Qaeda, *The Chronicles of Narnia*, and *Babe*.

I asked Othman how his family felt when they were told that one of the hijackers was a relative.

"We were very much shocked. . . . We couldn't believe it was true. To this day, if you were to ask me about my personal opinion, I'd say that I can't believe it."

"But if your relative didn't die on 9/11, where is he?" I asked him.

"He could be anywhere," Othman said. "He could have died in war, or been imprisoned. We don't have a real list, or access to American detention centers. Neither do we know anything about how many detainees [America has] from the Arab and Muslim world."

"Yeah, but could all nineteen of them simply have disappeared on the same day?"

"They are missing," he said. "The missing are either imprisoned or dead."

Okay, so Denial *really* isn't just a river in Egypt. I asked Othman how many people he knew had gone to wage jihad in Afghanistan and Iraq.

"A lot."

"And how many have come back?"

"Unfortunately, nobody came back."

"Did you think what they did was worth it?

"The young folk don't think like you and I," he said. "They are driven by ambition and passion more than by reason."

"Why didn't you go?" I asked him.

"Well, maybe because I'm not convinced one hundred percent by jihad now. . . . We still have hope that America will change its policy in the region."

Othman described a friend who went off to fight jihad, "a normal guy who graduated from the university, got a good job." About a year after the United States invaded Iraq, this friend became convinced that the country had done so for its own economic interests, and he became outraged by all the deaths of "civilians and innocents." He and four young friends went to fight in Iraq, he said, and within a week "we got the news that they'd become martyrs. They were killed by American planes. When I heard the news, I was very sad for them. I felt that Saudi youth at this historical juncture have become cannon fodder for the wars in the region. He could have been a good citizen and an asset to society. I don't blame him or think it's wrong that he went off to jihad, but he could have been great for his country if he were to live."

When I asked Othman where he thought Osama bin Laden was, he gave me one of the most interesting answers I'd heard from anyone on my trip.

"Osama bin Laden is now in many young people's hearts, in Muslims' hearts," he said. Then he added, "And who opened the door for him? America."

What Othman said haunted me as I sat in my hotel room that night: Osama lives in many young Muslims' hearts, and you Americans put him there. I don't fully subscribe to this idea, but I knew where he was coming from. As with Saddam Hussein, we originally supported Osama and his pals, back in the 1980s, when it suited our purpose. They were the enemies of our enemies—Khomeini in Saddam's case, the Soviets in

Osama's—and so, for the time being, they were our friends. Then, when they got out of our control and turned on us, we responded in the time-honored American way: we invaded their countries. We toppled the governments, captured Saddam, sent Osama into hiding . . . and created bloody chaos in the aftermath, then found ourselves mired in two new Vietnam-like situations.

We'd also made lots of enemies throughout the Muslim world, people who saw what we did in those countries as attacks against *them*, against Islam, against the ummah. And though Osama was in hiding, that sure hadn't stopped him from continuing to inspire at least some of those Muslims around the world to acts of violence against us and anyone else they thought was on our side against them. I'd seen evidence of that in every country I'd visited so far.

Way to win hearts and minds, Uncle Sam. . . .

With those gloomy thoughts bumming me out, I switched on the radio in my room, hoping to find some music. I forgot for a second that popular music is officially *haram* in Saudi Arabia. There was only one real music radio station in Jeddah, a remnant from when the U.S. base was there, scandalizing Osama and the mullahs by its very presence. You could sometimes catch some rock and roll on it, but tonight all I could find on the dial was a station with people reading from or preaching about the Koran. At that moment, I would have given anything to hear a little Metallica.

I thought about going out for a movie or a drink, but that was, obviously, not an option. I switched on the TV, hoping to at least veg out to some movie—any movie—even if I didn't understand a word that was being said. But the first thing I saw was a mullah preaching, and I switched it off.

Oh man, I was really beginning to miss home. See, it's all those things, all those little freedoms, that we take for granted in America. And then you go to a place like Saudi Arabia, which looks so American on the surface, so modern, so up-to-the-minute . . . and the people can't do *any* of those things, at least not in public or legally.

And that's just in the past thirty years. Thirty years ago, there were movie theaters in Saudi Arabia, and women could walk down the street in the latest Paris fashions without being accosted, and the country was moving toward becoming—in its own Arabic, Islamic way, of course— a fully modern society, fully integrated with the rest of the world. And yet it was that very movement toward modernity that sped up the reactionary, conservative backlash, which has so locked the society down over the past three decades.

I said the heck with thinking about this anymore right now—I had a flight to catch the next morning and I had to catch some sleep. My edumacation was now complete. I'd gotten all the background I needed. It was time to head for where everyone said Osama bin Hidin'.

CHAPTER 12

WELCOME TO HELL, MAN

-- -- -- -- -- -- -- --

I miss my country greatly, and have been long absent from it; but this is easy to endure because it is for the sake of God. . . . In Afghanistan I have a home and friends, and God gives great provision.

Message from Osama bin Laden, December 16, 2004

Someone was pounding on the door. I awoke with a start, under a mosquito net, in a room I didn't recognize. I'd been dreaming about Alex. The room was tiny, bathed in a blue glow of moonlight from the window.

Someone banged on the door again. I remembered where I was. . . .

When a stranger comes knocking in the middle of the night in Afghanistan, you react much as I did—heart pounding, instantly awake and sweating, breathing heavily and a little freaked out. I was in Kabul to find bin Laden, but what if that knock meant he had found me first? Just that evening, I'd heard a story about gunmen kicking in a foreign journalist's hotel-room door. His local fixer had saved his life by groveling on the floor, kissing the gunmen's feet, and begging them not to hurt his employer. The gunmen relented—and broke into the next room, where they killed the occupants.

Whoever was outside my door knocked louder.

"Who is it?" I called out from inside the mosquito netting. And instantly regretted it. Now they knew for sure that a foreigner was inside. Not smart of me.

I tried to radio to AJ, my security adviser, but my walkie was dead. My mind raced as I tried to remember the safety precautions AJ had taught us. If I heard small-arms fire or the thud of mortars outside, I had to resist the urge to run to the window to look out—it could be the last sight of my life if a bullet or even the shock wave from a blast shattered the glass. In case of fire, I shouldn't stop to grab my bags. Just take my passport and press credentials and get out quick. . . . But if he'd told me what to do when a stranger knocked on my door, I couldn't remember it.

The door was locked, people were sleeping right next door, and all I could do was sit inside, be quiet, and hope whoever it was went away. My heart was banging against my rib cage, trying to jump out of my chest. I grabbed a flashlight, the closest thing to a weapon in the room, and stood against the wall so that I'd be behind the door if it was kicked in. *Boom boom boom*, my heart pounded in unison with the knocking.

After about ten minutes, my visitor went away. The next day, the owner questioned everyone at the guesthouse where I was staying, but no one fessed up; no one knew who it was, and, lucky for, me he never came back.

Welcome to Afghanistan.

STAGE 10: KNOCK, KNOCK, KNOCKIN' ON THE CAVEMAN'S DOOR

Kabul felt like a garrison city besieged on all sides by enemies—which, in many respects, it was. Driving its streets, I passed barricade after barricade, all with armed security guards. President Hamid Karzai's palace looked like a fortress, standing well back from the street behind gates and surrounded by security forces. When I went to speak to his staff to request an interview, I passed through *seven* checkpoints before I even got to the palace. You have to ask why the president of the country must hide behind so much security. . . . And I did. They declined to be interviewed. *C'est la vie. C'est la guerre.*

It wasn't just Karzai's offices that were armed to the teeth; the entire city was a fortress. The streets themselves weren't safe. Suicide bombers had come to Kabul in the previous year or so. Their latest tactic was to ride up beside a car on a bike and blow themselves up. A scout would radio if he saw you stuck in traffic, and the kamikaze would weave his way through the stalled cars on his bike. I was told that a few weeks before I arrived some Canadian soldiers were standing on the street handing out candy to kids when a suicide bomber rode up and detonated. More than a dozen soldiers were killed, along with a bunch of innocent children. That's low, even for a suicide bomber.

AJ had established very careful security procedures for getting around the city. We wore body armor under our clothes at all times when we were out and about. It wouldn't just stop a bullet, but also anyone who tried to stab you in the back. Man, I longed for the day when the most dangerous thing I did was go on an all-burgers-and-fries diet.

We traveled in two cars, and always positioned them so that in case of trouble we could use at least one of them to get away fast. And the rule of thumb was to spend no more than fifteen or twenty minutes in any one place. Get out of the car, walk around, talk to some folks, do your business, but be back in the car and gone in twenty minutes. Because when you got out of the car somebody might spot the Westerner, make a cell-phone call, and within minutes a suicide bomber or would-be kidnapper or killer would show up.

As James Brabazon put it, "You won't know the difference between someone who comes up to you because they want to tell you about Karzai and someone who wants to shoot you in the chest. Which is exactly what happened to a friend of mine a couple of months ago. Filming in a crowd, quite friendly event. Someone in the crowd just walked straight up to him, while he was reloading [his camera], shot him at point-blank range in the back, and walked back into the crowd. He had just been on the ground for half an hour."

I went for a walk one day with a dozen young British (well, one South African) Royal Marine Commandos. They were baby-faced teens—eighteen, nineteen—led by a twenty-five-year-old captain. They'd been in-country for a month, and I got the sense that they hadn't yet strayed far from their walled-in, razor-wired compound in a deserted industrial area on the outskirts of Kabul. I watched them suit up, layering an awful lot of equipment over their camouflage fatigues—Kevlar vests, backpacks, radio headgear, knives, grenades, automatic rifles, futuristic machine guns. That's what it took for them to go walking even in a relatively empty and quiet part of the city. One guy showed me the scar in his scalp where a bullet had gone through his NODs (night-vision goggles) and ricocheted off his skull. All he got was two stitches. "Very lucky," he said, grinning. This happened days after he arrived.

We tromped down dusty dirt roads between warehouses, homes, and locked gates with barking dogs behind them. Occasionally, a turbaned man would go by on a bicycle or a small motorcycle and we'd all tense up briefly. Three little kids in the middle of a dirt road, trying to fly kites on a day of no wind, smiled shyly at us. The strangest moment was marching past a gas station. Men in turbans and traditional Afghan clothes filled the tanks of their Japanese cars while futuristic soldiers armed to the teeth filed by. The Afghan men smiled and waved at the soldiers, which is exactly what I would do if a dozen or so men walked past with submachine guns.

I stayed at one of the safest and most secure places in Kabul—Gandamak Lodge, a guesthouse founded by the famous British news cameraman Peter Jouvenal. With bleak but appropriate humor, he named it for the spot where, in 1842, Afghan warriors surrounded and massacred British and Indian troops retreating from a crushing rout in Kabul. From the outside it looks like a prison for supervillains, with its double-gated and razor-wired perimeter and guards toting automatic weapons. But inside it's luxurious by local standards, with tiny but clean rooms, hot water, hearty meals, and a peaceful courtyard with little birds twittering in the trees and views of blue mountain peaks in the distance. Marred only by the occasional snap, crackle, and pop of gunfire somewhere.

Jouvenal told me that he had lived in Afghanistan and Pakistan for twenty-seven years, and had reported on the fighting there as well as in places like Somalia, Bosnia, Chechnya, Liberia, and the western Sahara.

"Places with a lot of bang-bang," I observed. "I'm trying to find Osama bin Laden."

He laughed. "Right. Okay. Good luck. I don't know where he is. I don't even know if he's alive, actually."

"Have a lot of people staying at the Gandamak been looking for him?" I asked.

"No. I think a lot of people decided, 'If the CIA can't get him, then we can't get him.' "

"I don't give up that easy," I said.

"Good on you," he replied. "But how to find him is a good question."

Gandamak Lodge is the unofficial information nerve center of

Kabul. Everyone stays there or comes there to eat and drink—journalists and film crews from around the world, military and government people, workers from the United Nations and international aid organizations. It's even said that Osama kept his fourth wife in the first Gandamak Lodge, long before Peter moved in and turned it into a halfway house for wayward journalists—and before Osama had to flee to the mountains.

I drove over and took a walk through Osama's old digs, the original Gandamak Lodge. You could rent OBL's old house for $8,000 per month, and I was there scouting it out as the "rep of a big U.S. NGO."

"Eight grand? A little rich for my blood," I told the landlord, who was looking at me with dollar signs in his eyes. As I stood in the center of the most wanted man in the world's old living room, I wondered if this was as close to him as I was going to get.

There's an old joke term in the military, FUBAR. It stands for "fucked up beyond all repair." By the time I entered Afghanistan, the situation there, as one soldier put it, was "teetering on the brink of becoming permanently FUBAR." The United States and its allies had invaded Afghanistan in an effort to neutralize some of the world's baddest bad guys, to liberate the people from an extremely repressive regime, and, most important, to capture or kill the man who had planned the 9/11 attacks against the United States. Instead, we had created a completely destabilized environment and were mired in a mess with no end or exit strategy in sight.

During my time in the country, I talked to lots of people who filled me in on how things had gotten to that point, and what part Osama had played in it. It goes something like this:

At the end of the 1980s, when the Soviets pulled out of Afghanistan and Osama and his Arab Afghans went home, local factions were left to fight for control. On one side were the warlords and the mujahideen of what was called the Northern Alliance. On the other were the Taliban, which means "seekers of knowledge" or "students." Under the guidance of the reclusive Mullah Omar, they came roaring out of the madrassas in eastern Afghanistan and Pakistan in the early 1990s, determined to impose their ultraconservative, Wahhabi-style version of Islam on the country. With the Soviets gone, the United States took little interest in this civil war.

By 1996, the Taliban were in control of most of the country. They established Sharia as law. They banned music, sports, and television, forced women to wear the burka, and kept girls out of school. Men had to wear beards of a specific length. They used former sports stadiums for public floggings, amputations, and beheadings. On the plus side, I suppose, they almost completely cut off the poppy production, Afghanistan's number one cash crop and the source of more than 85 percent of the world's opium/heroin. (Clearly, these guys don't know how to party.)

It was in 1996 that the Taliban welcomed Osama bin Laden back after his expulsion from Sudan. He praised Afghanistan as "a land in which I could breathe a pure, free air to perform my duty in enjoining what is right and forbidding what is wrong." He set up compounds, training camps, and homes from Kandahar in the south, to Kabul farther north, to Tora Bora in the mountains bordering Pakistan. He swore allegiance to Mullah Omar as "the ruler and rightful commander who rules by God's law in this age."

That year, Osama issued one of his infamous fatwas, this one against "the Zionist-Crusaders alliance and their collaborators." Among the "collaborators," he named the Saudi monarchy, Jordan, and Egypt. "My Muslim Brothers of the World: Your brothers in Palestine and in the land of the two Holy Places [Saudi Arabia] are calling upon your help and asking you to take part in fighting against the enemy—your enemy and their enemy—the Americans and the Israelis. They are asking you to do whatever you can, with one's own means and ability, to expel the enemy, humiliated and defeated, out of the sanctities of Islam."

For the next five years, Osama had the run of Taliban-controlled Afghanistan. Al Qaeda's training camps really *were* "terrorist assembly lines." In 1998, Osama, Zawahiri, and a few others, calling themselves the World Islamic Front, declared a global jihad, stating that "to kill the Americans and their allies—civilians and military—is an individual duty for every Muslim who can do it in any country in which it is possible to do it." A few months later, John Miller interviewed Osama in

Afghanistan for ABC News. "We believe that the worst thieves in the world today and the worst terrorists are the Americans," bin Laden told Miller. "Nothing could stop you except perhaps retaliation in kind. We do not have to differentiate between military or civilian. As far as we are concerned, they are all targets, and this is what the fatwa says." Unless American policy was drastically changed, he predicted, "it will inevitably move the battle to American soil."

Three months after that, the U.S. embassies in Kenya and Tanzania were bombed, killing 258 people and injuring more than 5,000. President Clinton responded with cruise-missile attacks against an Al Qaeda training camp in Afghanistan and a supposed chemical-weapons facility in Sudan said to be funded by bin Laden. Osama himself began to move from place to place in Afghanistan, making himself increasingly hard to trace. The CIA developed several plans to assassinate him, using the Northern Alliance hero Ahmad Shah Massoud, but they were never carried out.

On September 9, 2001, two Al Qaeda suicide bombers posing as television reporters assassinated Massoud. You know what happened two days later. On September 14, President Bush declared bin Laden "wanted dead or alive." U.S.-led allied forces invaded Afghanistan the following month. Within hours of the first bombs being dropped, bin Laden taunted the United States in a video broadcast on Al Jazeera. He praised the 9/11 attacks without (yet) claiming responsibility. The tape showed him seated in a cave with Zawahiri. Bin Laden insisted, "Every Muslim must rise to defend his religion. The wind of faith is blowing."

The Coalition invasion, with Northern Alliance help, rolled straight through Afghanistan. Taliban forces and Al Qaeda's leadership abandoned Kabul in November 2001. Osama withdrew to his mountain stronghold of Tora Bora on the Afghanistan-Pakistan border. Coalition air strikes pounded the system of caves and tunnels, but instead of Coalition troops being sent in, Northern Alliance warlords were recruited for the ground assault, and bin Laden escaped. In December, a videotape broadcast worldwide showed bin Laden rejoicing over the events of September 11. He even joked that some of the hijackers thought they were assisting in a non-suicide operation.

Though Osama slipped through our fingers, we brought down the Taliban regime of Mullah Omar and replaced it with what many locals say is our own puppet government . . . er, a democratically elected national government, led by President Karzai.

There was a tremendous groundswell of hope among the Afghans when Coalition forces arrived in 2001. They welcomed both the troops and the promise of a new, democratic government. But by the time I got there, the joke in Afghanistan was to refer to Karzai as the Mayor of Kabul, because his power and influence barely extended beyond the capital. The rest of Afghanistan had fallen back into the hands of a resurgent Taliban and Al Qaeda in the south and east, and to regional warlords of various tribes throughout most of the north and west.

With resources siphoned off to fight the simultaneous war in Iraq, the roughly forty thousand U.S. and NATO troops in Afghanistan— officially, the International Security Assistance Force (ISAF)—found themselves in their own little version of a new Vietnam. Our efforts to train and "mentor" a homegrown Afghan National Army (ANA) so that our troops could eventually withdraw weren't progressing very quickly.

In fact, pretty much the only thing going well was the poppy production, which had bounced back to record highs after the Taliban were removed from power in 2001. According to the Associated Press, in 2005–06 Afghan farmers harvested enough poppies "to make 610 tons of heroin—more than all the world's addicts consume in a year." It was the driving force of the national economy; the Afghan government itself estimated that it accounted for about $3 billion a year, roughly 60 percent of the gross national product. The whole country—and much of the fighting—seemed to be run on drug money.

Meanwhile, everywhere I went I was stunned by the number of beggars. Those drug profits—not to mention billions of dollars of U.S. and international aid—obviously did not trickle down to the people who need it most. Driving down any street in Kabul, you could guarantee that a woman in a burka would pop up six inches from your window as you raced past, holding her hands up in a gesture that cried out,

"Please, please—anything!" Sometimes she'd lift a baby up to the window. It was heart-wrenching.

I got several earfuls about the current, grim state of affairs sitting out on the veranda of the Gandamak Lodge courtyard with three veteran British war correspondents: cameraman Jim Foster, documentary film producer Sam Kiley, and producer-director Sean Langen.

Sean had just returned from the northern province of Konar. "It was a very isolated outpost, where the guys are literally up there for a year, not rotated out," he told us. "I saw one guy who had been shot the week before. He went down to Jalalabad for a week's leave, came back, and still had a bullet in his arm. It was amazing."

American soldiers in Konar told him the fighting there was worse than they'd seen in Iraq. "But when they go back on leave friends and family say, 'Have you been to Iraq?' And they say, 'No, Afghanistan.' And the reaction is always 'Oh, I thought we finished with Afghanistan. I thought that was all done.' Which makes it harder for them to come back into the fight."

Sean showed me a bandage on his lower back.

"I got the shrapnel with the British down south," he said. "I was on a twenty-four-hour operation." Seventeen British soldiers were mentoring an ANA team. They thought they were going up against maybe fifty Taliban fighters, "and it turned out there were three to five hundred Taliban, and we found ourselves in a weeklong battle." The Taliban were very well organized, "being re-supplied at night from across the border with Pakistan, our great ally in the War on Terror," he said sarcastically. At one point three days into the battle, "I remembered—sitting there as the bullets were literally flying, the British breaking records with how many rounds they were firing—the words of our then defense secretary John Reid, who, when asked what he hoped to achieve in Afghanistan, said 'hoped to achieve the reconstruction without firing a single shot.' "

He continued, dryly, "Of course, there isn't a war here in Afghanistan. It's a *reconstruction*. It's peaceful. Because we actually defeated the Taliban and routed Al Qaeda five years ago. So I don't know who these people are who are fighting, but they certainly can't be the Taliban."

The fight was in the south-central province of Helmand, where the

Taliban resurgence was particularly strong. "As the Americans said when they handed it over to the British, 'Welcome to hell, man.' It's been a summer of rolling, intense battles in various parts, and across into Kandahar. The Canadians have been fighting in weeklong battles, rolling battles, counterattacks."

"It's all going swimmingly," Sam joked. "This is a roaring success for NATO, and will likely produce peace and stability right across the region. Sir. Your Honor."

"And what about Osama bin Laden?" I asked. "Where's he in all this?"

"I reckon he's working for a neocon think tank," Sam said. "I mean, there are no greater recruiters than the senior elements of the American administration."

Hmm. I remembered the guy in Saudi Arabia who said Osama was hiding in the White House. Maybe, I thought, I really should go back to D.C. and have another look around.

Jim noted that the tactic of suicide bombing, which had never been a feature of Afghanistan fighting, was being imported from Iraq. "It's not a natural Afghan thing to be a suicide bomber," he said. "It's not in their nature. They're not that sort of people. That's changed certainly in the last year. . . ."

"I met a suicide bomber," Sean said.

"Before or after the event?" Sam deadpanned.

"*Before* the event. He was wearing a suicide belt. His brother had already blown himself up, killed some Americans. He was from Pakistan. Sent over by a mullah."

If Sean had spoken to a suicide bomber, I wondered how hard it would be for me to get someone from Al Qaeda to talk to me.

"He wasn't Al Qaeda," Sean said. "He was Taliban. He said he was doing it for love of Islam, not hatred of foreigners." As for finding Al Qaeda, he said, "they're not meeting media. They don't need to. They've got their own media wing who put out videos."

I asked these gents where they thought I should go in Afghanistan, and what I should do or not do.

"Don't get shot," Sam drawled.

I made a note of that: Don't get shot.

Sean said I should go to Pakistan, then added, "Just don't end up like Daniel Pearl. No kidding."

More good advice: Don't get kidnapped and beheaded.

"I met the Taliban a few times," Sean went on. "And one of them, a Taliban commander, pulled me aside, and he said, 'You really shouldn't do this kind of thing too often.' Which was an odd thing for him to say. And then I asked why. He said, 'Well, every time before you've come down we had a *shura*.' A gathering. 'We voted whether to kill you, kidnap you, or let you interview us. And you won't know which way we voted until you come down.'"

Sean said that the War on Terror has been real boom times for war correspondents.

"But the fun's gone out of it," Sam interjected. "Now we're the targets. I'm sick of that. In the old days, you could move between the front lines and there was a sort of understanding—we're the media, we're not on anybody's side. But now that our democracies and elected leaders have decided to do this the insurgents turn around and say, 'Well you bastards elected him, it's your fault.'"

"I've never come across so much hate just for being American or British," Jim agreed. "Before it was, you know, your government. Now it's you are British, we hate you, you support Israel, and all that. I've never come across that in the Middle East. That you are, just for being British or American, not taken as an individual, you're lumped together. To me, that's the saddest part."

"That's why we'll never win the War on Terror," Sam said.

Sean sighed and shrugged. "I've decided I'm retiring," he said. "I got divorced this year. I'm going to become a fishing correspondent."

That afternoon I was invited to tea at the home of a man named Abdul Haji, along with his adult sons and other men from his family. We sat cross-legged on the floor around a tablecloth covered with dishes of cookies, candies, chocolates, cakes, and fruit. Abdul and his second son, Mohammed, poured tea from thermoses.

Abdul was a gray-bearded man with kindly eyes, wearing a turban and a traditional Afghan outfit. He was a large man, not fat but thick and strong. He reminded me of Santa, if Santa was a few years younger and a boxer. He was the Buzkashi champion of his village for years. Buzkashi is sort of the Rambo version of polo, played on horseback with two teams of up to hundreds of players. Each team has a circle within which it scores points. The goal is to drop the carcass of a dead calf or goat (which weighs anywhere from 100 to 250 pounds) in that circle as many times as possible. While you're doing this, the players on the other team beat the crap out of you with their fists and switches, trying to get you to drop the carcass before you reach their circle. The team with the most drops wins. Games usually end when the sun sets or the horses are exhausted.

So a champion Buzkashi player is the kind of guy you'd want on your side in a bar fight—if there were bars in Afghanistan.

Abdul's older son also sported the traditional look, while Mohammed was clean-shaven and wore Western slacks and a dress shirt. I wasn't surprised to see only men in the room; the women here are also kept separate from the men.

Mohammed ran a private security company, and he had arranged to have a guard stand outside. Just in case any bad guys saw the Westerner go into the house.

Through Naji, my interpreter, I thanked them for sharing their home with me and asked them how things had changed in the country over the past five years.

"At that time it was very tight, under the Taliban regime," Mohammed said. "Now everybody can go everywhere and enjoy, listen to music. At that time, you couldn't go out without a beard. Religious police were on the roads, on the street. They put you in jail until you grew a long beard."

They all laughed at the memory.

I asked Abdul, "How is it, being an elder in Afghanistan? In the United States, when people start to get old we put them in old-folks homes."

When Naji translated, Abdul exploded into laughter and shook my hand. He told me that in his country the older you become, the more respect you get. "It's very wrong what you do there, putting your parents in an old-folks house," he said. "When you didn't exist, these were your parents, they brought you up. Your mother was pregnant with you, and then they raised you, they fed you. Now, when you're in a place that you can help them out and be looking after them, you give them to the old-folks home? It's not good. You shouldn't do that."

Abdul noted proudly that he had ten sons and five daughters by two wives. He grinned and offered to arm-wrestle to show me how strong he still was. He had a crushing grip.

As I looked around at Abdul's sons and his young grandson, who would quietly sneak a cookie from the tray on the floor when no one was looking, I thought about Alex at home, pregnant, and the future of my own family. I asked Abdul for some fatherly advice.

With Naji translating, he said, "When your child is two years old, send him to kindergarten, and when he's six years old send him to school, and give him all the necessary notebooks and pens and stuff, and give him a proper education and training, and get him to behave, character-wise, and when he gets a job tell him goodbye and good luck."

I laughed. It was the most practical advice I'd heard yet. Abdul added that I should send the kid to Afghanistan for a few years, so he'd learn how to treat his elders and not throw me in an old-folks home when the time came.

Abdul went on to tell me that conditions had changed in Afghanistan during his lifetime. He said that before the last king was deposed, in the 1970s, "everybody had a good life, and it was peaceful and secure. But for the last thirty years, since the Russians invaded Afghanistan, and then the Taliban and Karzai, every day you can get killed. It's not safe."

Mohammed and I talked about the Taliban comeback in the southern provinces. He said the United States and the United Kingdom needed to pressure Pakistan to stop supporting the Taliban. Stop them at the source.

"The problem is Pakistan," he said. "The other neighbors—Tajikistan, Iran—they don't train Taliban or Al Qaeda or other terrorists."

Abdul added that the ISAF should be making more use of the Northern Alliance warlords and their fighters. "They are all sitting in their homes waiting for orders," Naji translated. "They are just relaxing, chilling out, getting training. They are ready. They are just waiting to be told to come in. More than a hundred thousand—like two or three hundred thousand."

Mohammed confirmed what I'd heard about the government being in power only in Kabul: south, it was all "Taliban government, terrorist government," and north it was all the warlords' land.

The others discussed this, while Naji translated: "They are saying now they have divided the country. And the power. During the day, Karzai runs the country. During the night, the Taliban run it. During the day, Karzai has the country. During the night, the Northern Alliance has the country."

Abdul told me that one good thing about the Taliban regime was that crime went way down, because the punishments were so harsh. The new government, careful to observe civil rights under the watchful eyes of its international supporters, had abolished capital punishment, and crime had shot back up—housebreaking, carjacking, kidnapping for ransom.

"He's saying one of his friends' sons was kidnapped the other night," Naji translated. "And he was strong and tough and resisted the kidnapper, and the kidnapper started beating him on his head and he was unconscious. They took him to a hideout, and [the family] sent some money. But the guy was injured and bleeding, and the next day he died. The kidnappers called up and said, 'No, we don't want money. Come take your son's body.' "

I asked them where Osama was, which prompted a lot of joking around. He was in the United States, they said. He was a CIA agent.

Turning serious, Mohammed said he thought the hunt was a charade. "If Osama is arrested, there's no other reason for Western countries to stay here, or in Iraq or other countries."

Abdul said, "We were praying that the United States would come to our country and bring peace. But since the U.S. came the peace is gone; insecurity is increasing day by day, criminal activity is everywhere. And, every day, if they kill one American, they kill a hundred of us. So we are losing more than you guys in this war."

As I got up to leave, Abdul and his family invited me to stay for dinner, and also for the night. They wanted me to be with their family so that I could really see what living in their neighborhood was like, what their Afghanistan was like. I was overwhelmed by the generosity of the offer, and I would find this wherever I went in the country. I had heard that there are no better hosts on the planet, that Afghans would open their doors wide for you and give you the shirts off their backs. As long as you were their guest, they would look after you.

But from my point of view, the key to being a good guest is knowing when to leave.

CHAPTER 13

BE MY LITTLE GENERAL

flew to Kandahar Airfield (KAF) packed into the back of a C-130 Hercules being flown by Her Majesty's Royal Air Force. While the accents were posh, the ticket was far from first-class. I was sandwiched between a Royal Marine Commando and a general from the Afghan National Army. Both men were asleep before the four massive propellers roared to life, apparently only a few feet from our heads, judging from the sign on the wall across from me that read "Danger Propeller." (I'm a quick study.)

The crewmen pushed a giant palette down the rollers through the massive rear hatch and strapped it to the floor. As I looked at it, all I could imagine was that strap snapping, the iron slab wheeling down those rollers, and my leg getting crushed into a sloppy mess of bony meat goodness. I looked around, and no one else seemed to be worried; they were either listening to their iPods or reading. Some of the preferred reading on the plane was *The Sea* by John Banville and Mark Hollingsworth's *Thatcher's Fortunes: The Life and Times of Mark Thatcher*, while a guy diagonally across from me was engrossed in Jackie Collins's *The World Is Full of Divorced Women*. Hey, no judgments here—either it was boredom or a future plan, but whatever that guy with the big gun under his seat wanted to read, I was all for.

If you've never flown on a C-130, let me give you some advice: when they offer you earplugs before the plane takes off, *take them*. It was so freakin' loud on that boat. And the thing was huge. There were easily fifty of us on the plane with that giant leg-crushing palette, and there was room for more. When those planes take off, especially in war zones like Afghanistan, they don't ascend nice and easy like a commercial jetliner. Nah, as soon as those wheels leave the ground the pilot rocks that stick back into his chest and you climb, almost straight up, as fast as you can, and then he levels off, hitting zero gravity for a second or two and sending whatever was in your stomach promptly into your throat. It's similar to the ride you get on those astronaut training planes called Vomit Comets.

I looked so out of place among these soldiers. Here I was, this pale, lanky guy in his gray outdoorsman chinos with a green button-down. My helmet was pulled tight over my gigantic head, and my bulletproof vest was churning up the sweat in the one-hundred-degree heat. At least when we gained altitude it cooled down.

The flight was barely an hour, and the behemoth shook and rattled like it was falling apart when it hit the ground and taxied to our parking spot in Kandahar. The airfield and base in Kandahar, KAF, is like its own little town, with eleven thousand–plus people: soldiers from all over the world, plus all the support staff from companies like Halliburton spinoff KBR, which is there to maintain the generators, do laundry, cook food, build housing, build roads, fix cars, clean facilities, and so forth. KBR does just about everything except strap on a flak jacket and go to war. But there are companies here that do that, too—not on the front lines per se, but at the gate of every NGO compound you see men in baseball caps and body armor, usually strapped with sidearms and an M-4. They're from companies like Titan, Blackwater, and DynCorp— and those companies alone have military contracts in excess of $11.9 billion. You see as many, if not more, private contractors on the base as you do people in uniform. It was incredible.

In the center of the town is a boardwalk that was completed just before I got there, something to make everybody think they're anywhere but in the middle of Afghanistan. Around the dusty boardwalk are little shops, places to buy gifts for the folks back home, like traditional Afghan clothing or bowls and cups made from lapis lazuli, the precious electric-blue stone that's found only in the mountains of the region. You can also buy rugs there, handwoven and beautifully made.

Taste, on the other hand, is solely the responsibility of the buyer. One of the rugs featured the Twin Towers with planes crashing into them. The man who owned the store said that it was a rug of peace, a record of history, showing "action what happened to bring Americans to Afghanistan for peace." I got the gist of what he was saying as he pointed to the American and the Afghan flags in the middle, and a flying chicken with a stick in its mouth (a speedy attempt at a dove and an olive branch, I could only assume, unless I missed the press release about the peace chicken).

"I give you good price," he said. "For you $50."

For me, no thanks. But I did buy some rugs that were maps of the country with tanks and AK-47s on them. As I said, taste is in the eye of the buyer.

Scattered around the boardwalk were fast-food restaurants, more reminders of home. Pizza Hut, Subway, and Burger King all operated out of converted shipping containers or tractor-trailers, and each had lines down the boardwalk. Now *this* is the front line of the War on Terror. My favorite was the Tim Hortons, which is like the Canadian version of Dunkin' Donuts, only with better doughnuts and worse coffee. Outside their little love shack, the proprietors had built a monument to all Canadians who have or will ever serve at KAF: a hockey rink. And every night throngs of people, mostly Canadians, but also some Norwegians and other cold-weather transplants, would crowd around the rink and cheer on players from their native countries as they knocked the shit out of one another running up and down the "ice." Yeah, there wasn't any ice in the ice rink. Guys had to play in their shoes, but it was still pretty amazing to see people playing hockey in the middle of a dusty valley in Central Asia.

The day I got there, a barbecue was in progress. A couple of soldiers pitched horseshoes that clanged off a gravel-covered courtyard, surrounded by heavy military vehicles and stacks of steel containers. A guy in shorts, with a huge black pistol on his hip, grilled steaks, burgers, and hot dogs. Army helicopters crossed the hard blue sky overhead. It was like a day in the park, except there were no trees, grass, children, or dogs, only dirt, dust, and gravel, and the few females wore the same camo fatigues and field caps as the men.

I was told that at night the rocket attacks were such a regular occurrence that soldiers had learned to distinguish between incoming and outgoing, and slept through the latter. One night, an officer went back to the DFAC (the dining facility) after dinner for some ice cream, and was injured when a rocket hit the building—spawning the popular line "Don't go back for ice cream."

One soldier I spoke to said this was the first time he'd ever traveled outside the United States.

"So where have you gone since you've been here?" I asked him.

"Just here, on the base," he said. "That's it."

"Where will you do most of your time?"

"Right here on the base. That's it." He would be there for ten more months, he said, and then he was going home. "I've seen enough of the world," he added.

So for him this was it. This base was "the world." With the exception of the locals who were hired to work on the base, he would never meet the Afghan people outside its walls, travel into the town of Kandahar, or see any of the country he was there to help liberate. This base *was* "Afghanistan."

The city of Kandahar itself sits in the middle of the resurgent Taliban area of south-central Afghanistan, where the mountains of the north trickle down into the southern desert. The ISAF base is just outside the city, and from there ISAF and ANA forces fan out to try to cover an area that's about the size of Texas. But it looks as sharp, jagged, and bare as the face of the moon. Highways snake for many lonely miles across that harsh landscape, strung with isolated little villages that blend into the monochrome-brown landscape because their walls are all mud brick.

Flying into Kandahar Airfield, you might catch a glimpse of Tarnak Farm a short distance south. That's where Osama built his first compound and training camp in 1996. He kept some of his wives and children there, and did a lot of horseback riding out on the dusty flats. I wondered if Osama was a Clint Eastwood fan. Did he daydream about *High Plains Drifter* as he rode? Or was he more of a *Josey Wales* man?

In war zones, it's always the local civilians who get the worst of it, and the people of southern Afghanistan—Kandahar Province, Helmand Province—have been in a war zone for more than twenty-five years. They're literally caught in the cross fire between the Taliban and the ISAF, and there's a lot of collateral damage. The poverty in the villages is brutal, clean drinking water is scarce, and government services are close to nonexistent. In the city of Kandahar, the locals are lucky to get a couple hours of sporadic electricity a day, and luckier still not to get taken out in the new rash of suicide and car bombings. I got there a few days after Coalition forces had called in CAS (close air support) to assist in a Taliban attack just outside the city. Dozens of innocent civilians had been killed, and people were devastated.

Colonel R. Steven Williams told me about one of those bombings and a lot of other things about life in wartime in southern Afghanistan. Colonel Williams was commander of U.S. forces in Regional Command South, commander of Kandahar Airfield, and deputy commander of NATO forces in Regional Command South. Field officers don't get that many titles or that much responsibility unless their superiors are sure they can handle it, and Colonel Williams seemed like a natural to me. He was like a living recruitment poster for the officer corps. Blond, blue-eyed, and confident, he carried his position with an easy grace. He was smart, had a great sense of humor, and was amazingly straightforward for a military guy talking to "the media."

His office was in a long wooden shed. The walls were plywood, his desk was a folding table, and we sat in folding chairs. My kind of place. Half a dozen laptops surrounded him, and a framed photo of John Wayne stood among them. It seemed almost too appropriate.

I noticed nine or ten cases of Dr Pepper stacked near him when I walked in, so I thought I'd ask him the most important question first.

"Do you know where a guy can get a Dr Pepper?" I asked.

"I can help you out right there," he said, laughing. He reached into the mini-fridge behind him and handed me a frosty one. "That's all I eat and drink is Dr Pepper. Hey, we all have our vices."

"Is this the key to staying happy in Afghanistan?" I asked him.

"Yeah, it's the only way to survive. A little bit of caffeine never hurt."

Colonel Williams was six months into his second tour in Afghanistan.

"Last time I was here it was 2002–03," he said. "There were remaining elements of the Taliban, more in the remote areas. A lot of the fighting was just very sporadic, short-term fighting, long distances. The Taliban really didn't get in close. Now they're a little bit more organized, and some of the fighting is a little bit closer. They like to get in close so they know that we can't put aircraft or indirect fire on them. . . . To me, now, it seems like they're kind of throwing the younger kids—I call them the young-and-dumb kids—that are ideological, from the madrassas in Pakistan. They are not well trained. They kind of just hang right in there, and they get killed. So you kind of get sick of a bunch of young Afghans getting killed because of some stupid ideological thought by the Taliban."

Colonel Williams distinguished between what he called tier-one and tier-two Taliban troops. The tier-one fighters, he said, were "your hard-core guys who have been trained by foreign fighters or are being assisted by foreign fighters." They had "very good command and control, where they know how to do an ambush and they know how to get in close, so they know how to use their weapon system." Tier-two were "very unorganized, and they don't know what they're doing, and they're easier to engage. The tier-two guys are just the guys who kind of got thrown into the mess—here is a weapon, here's how you shoot, go and follow these guys."

That September, ISAF and ANA forces had gotten locked into an incredible twenty-three-day battle, code-named Operation Medusa, against Taliban forces in and around a Kandahar Province village called Pashmul, a fortified stronghold from which they'd been launching attacks against NATO forces for months. "The Taliban had bunkers and trenches, booby traps, IEDs, mines," Colonel Williams said. Canadian forces had closed in from one direction and Colonel Williams's U.S. troops from the other, in a classic pincer operation, clearing the Taliban out one bunker and village building at a time. "It was Normandy invasion–style tactics," Colonel Williams told a British reporter at the time. "Call it World War Pashmul." There was also some *Apocalypse Now* to it: Colonel Williams used loudspeakers blasting rock bands like AC/DC to keep his men fired up. Much of the village was bombed to rubble.

I asked him where the Taliban fighters were coming from.

"You have some of the local fighting groups that are still in Afghanistan," he said. "But you've got a lot of Afghanis that are in Pakistan that are going to the madrassas and, after graduation at the madrassas, are coming over from Pakistan into Afghanistan. The biggest problem is that in the madrassas in Pakistan they're getting radical thoughts, radical schooling." To counter that, he added, "One thought is they are trying to get these more moderate mullahs to open up madrassas in Afghanistan, so people don't have to ship their children off to the ones in Pakistan. They'll get more moderate, normalized teachings, instead of what they're getting in Pakistan."

Given all the talk back home about setting timetables for withdrawing our troops from Iraq and Afghanistan over the next few years, I was amazed by Colonel Williams's assessment of when that might be.

"This is a counterinsurgency operation, and any counterinsurgency takes a long time, mainly when the insurgency has a safe haven to go to," he told me. "So you're probably looking at another ten to fifteen years to get this place to where those of us in the West see it as security, reconstruction, economic development, and you can actually leave it to the Afghan people."

"What would have happened if we'd sent more troops here in 2002?" I asked him.

"I think you would have killed more Taliban, but we are killing a lot of Taliban right now." He added, "In a counterinsurgency, killing the enemy doesn't work. You've got to work on the center of gravity, and to me that's the people. When you start getting the people in Afghanistan saying they're sick of this and [telling] the Taliban to leave, and they see a better outlook with the West, that's when things will start getting better. You're starting to see that in villages, but it's very difficult. The Taliban will come into a village, they will force their way in. We've heard recently stories of people asking the Taliban to leave, and they say, 'No, we are not leaving.' They'll kill a few village elders or family members, they'll take some of the kids and force them into their fighting units."

The Afghan people were sick of war after twenty-five years of it, Colonel Williams said. "They see the West as supporting, rebuilding their country, helping them out, but they'll support whoever they think is the strongest element. . . . So you can go into one area, where they think the strongest is the Taliban, and they support the Taliban just for pure survival."

Just a week before my visit, Colonel Williams said, "we were doing a convoy through Kandahar City, and a SVBIED hit my convoy." (That's a suicide vehicle bomb improvised explosive device.) "When we secured the area right after the blast, we had a suicide bomber come up to the edge and guys had to shoot him. It was the most gruesome thing. I'll never forget it. Burnt bodies on the other side of the road—a family in a taxi, little kids, mom and dad—fried, just steaming bodies. I opened my door to get out and a hunk of brain fell on my leg. I mean, it was gruesome. Bodies all over the place, civilians and wounded people everywhere. It was such a big bomb, on the other side of the road buildings [caught] on fire, on the far side."

Colonel Williams said it was hard on his troops. "I've got eighteen-, nineteen-year-old kids who are in shock. I mean, they went out and did their job, but afterwards I had combat-stress people there in the chapel when we got back."

I asked Colonel Williams if he thought most Afghans saw us as liberators or as occupiers.

"I'd say that over ninety-nine percent of the tribal elders that I meet—and I've met hundreds of them—support us. Because they really feel that we're here for the right reason. I think they see that the West can provide a better quality of life for their children than the Taliban could."

One big problem, he said, was that the elders in the villages had no faith in the central government. They weren't pro-Taliban, but they sure weren't pro-Karzai, either. After Operation Medusa, he met with the elders in Pashmul. "These guys were antigovernment, but they were kind of pro-us," he said. "We had developed a relationship with them for about a month and a half during the fighting. And when I told them I was leaving and we were giving the battle space to the Canadians, some of them cried. They said, 'What can we do to keep you here? You have to stay here ten years.' They were offering us a compound and some grape vineyards."

"Is this the front line in the War on Terror?"

"I think so. If we weren't here fighting these organizations right now, you would see a stronger Al Qaeda, you would see a Taliban supported by Al Qaeda, you'd see insurgent terrorist training around here in Afghanistan. Now, what we've done is interdicted that and affected their training grounds. . . . I think that for the world community it's provided more security by just removing these guys out of this area and removing the insurgent support base that they had here."

"Where is Osama bin Laden?" I asked him.

"He's in Mazatlán right now, on vacation." Colonel Williams smiled, making it very clear that he wasn't going down that road with me. Didn't matter, I was still impressed with the guy.

There's a mnemonic device that new recruits are taught in basic training to help them remember the rankings for generals, the step above colonel: Be My Little General. It stands for Brigadier General (one star), Major General (two stars), Lieutenant General (three stars), General (four and five stars).

I wondered how long it would be before I'd be hearing about Brigadier General Williams.

From Kandahar I headed farther out into the desert, into real Taliban territory, to a Forward Operating Base (FOB) called Fort Apache, and I could easily see why. When I met the commander, Colonel Martin Leppert, he looked like a robo-warrior from the future in full battle gear—camo fatigues, camo helmet, camo gloves, Kevlar vest, wraparound sunglasses, radio headgear, M-16, pistol on his hip. He was pacing the graveled courtyard inside the perimeter wall, having tense, distracted conversations with junior officers.

"This TIC that developed here this morning is kind of an ongoing deal," he explained to me. "I just dropped a bunch of CAS, sounds like we got some pretty good BDA. So we're trying to get back to the TOC and get ahold of the situation."

I had no clue what he was saying. TIC was pronounced "tick," TOC was pronounced "tock." "Colonel Leppert, what's a BDA?" I asked, trailing behind him as he marched toward the steel shed where his command center was.

"Battle damage assessment," he replied. It turned out that he'd just heard over the radio that a patrol of his men had gotten into a fight (TIC, troops in contact) with some Taliban, and one of them was KIA (killed in action). Colonel Leppert was clearly upset.

"They got CAS in there pretty good," he said, more to himself than to me. "We got some ANA and ANP on some good, high ground. Brought the CAS in. Sounds like they had a pretty good roll in there. Sounds like the enemy is trying to work in there to collect the dead. We just wanna get an assessment. We're green right now. Green means everything up on personnel vehicles, equipment, ammunition. Where we just wanna make darn sure. I'm more comfortable when I'm at my TOC and can control a situation than when I'm mobile and out."

"Absolutely." I nodded.

Let me pause here and explain that few of the military people I met spoke as clearly as Colonel Williams had. Most talked more like Colonel Leppert. I did better with Urdu and Pashto than with Army. Here are some of the acronyms, abbreviations, and other terms I wrote down:

ACM: Anti-Coalition Militant
AGE: Anti-Government Elements
ANA: Afghan National Army
ANP: Afghan National Police
BDA: Battle Damage Assessment
BDU: Battle Dress Uniform
BII: Basic Issue Item
CAS: Close Air Support
CCP: Casualty Collection Point
CHU: Containerized Housing Unit
Coms: Communications
Corona: Satellite tracking imagery
DCU: Desert Combat Uniform
DFAC: Dining Facility
Down Range: To be out on a mission
DTT: Dynamic Tactical Targeting
EPW: Enemy Prisoner of War
ETT: Embedded Training Team
FOB: Forward Operating Base
FragO: Fragmentary Orders
Green: Good to go; operational
IO: Information Operations
ISR: Intelligence, Surveillance, and Reconnaissance
ITGA: Interim Transitional Government of Afghanistan
KAF: Kandahar Air Field

LN: Local National (citizen)
METL: Mission Essential Task List
NOD: Night Vision Optical Device
ODA: Operational Detachment Alpha
PERSTAT: Personnel Status Report
PRTs: Provincial Reconstruction Teams
OMF: Opposing Military Force
QRF: Quick Response Force
TIC: Troops in Contact
TOC: Tactical Operations Center
UXO: Unexploded Ordinance

Besides official acronyms, there are slang acronyms, mostly terms of derision. POGs (pronounced "Pogues") are people other than grunts—noncombat, rear-echelon personnel. A variation on that is FOBBITs, meaning noncombat personnel who get to spend all their time safe in an FOB. Another is REMFs—rear-echelon motherfuckers. FNG is fucking new guy. A TDS is a terminal dumb shit. TGF stands for total goat fuck—any operation that goes completely FUBAR is TGF.

Okay, back to Colonel Leppert. Like several of the other mature officers I met, he actually requested to be sent to the war.

"After twenty-eight years, I got in the game—and had to sign up to do it, because I was an active-duty guardsman at the Pentagon," he told me. "When they put the call out for volunteers, a bunch of us just said, 'Hey, put me in, Coach.' So here we are."

He'd been in-country for nine months.

"It's been an interesting nine months," he said. "Truly a life-changing revelation for me. Late in my career, but better late than never. Learned a tremendous amount about soldiering, about leadership, about my spirituality, about being a husband and father—an absentee husband and father. And I think the most important thing that I've learned is just how difficult it is for the spouse back home, but how rock-solid my wife is, and what a great choice I made twenty-five years ago. I got married twenty-five years ago this year."

"For you, what's the hardest part about being here?"

"The hardest part truly is the days when I'm in here and my men are out there, and today is a prime example. Today has been a very challenging day. We've had troops in contact from midmorning, working in a fairly remote village. It's like you can never get enough information. You feel like you can never get enough help to them. So it's very difficult. I've been in these situations multiple times, and it never gets any easier."

Earlier that day, the colonel told me he had discovered something about his spirituality since he'd been in the field. I was curious to learn what that was.

"Just having to reach deep to get through on tough days. Tough days. We've had some. We've lost soldiers."

Colonel Leppert paused, and I was startled to see tears welling up in his eyes. "Today is one of those days," he said. Eventually, he went on. "But you got to pick yourself up by the bootstraps and drive on. One of the most difficult things for me, going back to that, is trying to not do what I'm doing right now, which is show emotion. And it's a tough thing. My guys know when I'm upset and when I'm worried. But they also have to know that I'm in control. Because they are looking to that commander to be that rock. And it's not always an easy thing. That's probably one of the toughest things to deal with. Especially on a day like today."

"In the years you've been in the military, has this been the hardest tour for you?" I asked him.

This was "perhaps the most challenging and the most rewarding all at once," he said. "We were warned before we came here that it's one step forward, two steps back. Three steps forward, two steps back. And you just have to be willing to accept that nothing in Afghanistan is easy. Everything is hard. From getting your point across, to the language barrier, to culturally—what they may want to do and what we see as the right thing to do may be two different things. But slowly, over time, you build that trust factor up between yourself as the mentor and your mentee. Over the last nine months you begin to start thinking like, I understand where he is coming from culturally and what his norms are, and what is acceptable and how far and how much I can push him to see and to make the right decisions with his staff. And I know when to back off. That was something learned, and that just comes with experience."

I said it must be hard knowing that Americans hear about Iraq every day but seem to have forgotten that we're still in Afghanistan.

"You know, I've heard that this is 'the forgotten war,' but we're here," he said. "I don't slight any of my brothers who sacrificed a year of their life trying to help the Iraqi people. To bring about the same thing we're trying to do here. . . . We've had success over the last four or five years. Now ACM forces are coming out of the woodwork, and they're biting hard. They believe in what they believe, and we do, too. So the ANA soldiers that we're working with and helping along, their expectation is that we're going to be here to help them, come what may. So if the folks back home, the folks in Iraq wanna think that life is hard, that's okay. My journal is full of my story and our story here this last year, and that'll be living proof long after I'm gone."

Colonel Leppert told me that his tour of duty would be up in a couple of months. "Do you ever worry that you might not make it home?" I asked him.

"Whatever happens happens, man. I hate to be clichéd, but I've told all my men and myself the same thing. We have a little pact. Nobody surrenders here. Nobody punts. Nobody ends up in the goddam videotape on the Internet, either. We all fight. Period. Bravely, as American soldiers. That's the bottom frickin' line."

"What will be the first thing you do when you get home?"

"The first thing I'll do when I go home, in terms of a big thing, is kneel down and pray for all these guys that are still back here." Tears welled up in his eyes again. "And then I'm gonna sit on my back patio and make a big old jug of wine and fruit juice, and I'm gonna get happy."

"What are your thoughts on the Muslim people that you've come into contact with throughout Afghanistan?"

"It's interesting, because as we journey into this line of questioning, back in training in the United States, we were told to stay away from that area, because it is a sensitive subject. When I first met my counterpart [in the ANA], one of the first things they wanted to know, they wanted to know where I sat with regard to my beliefs. So when they found out I was a 'man of the book,' as they say, they were very happy. They hugged me and shook my hand. And they knew that they could probably trust me. . . . They know, and I want them to know, that I'm not the infidel, but I'm here as a Christian, believing human being trying to just take care of people. . . . Just like I know they're good Muslims, they need to know that I'm a decent Christian human being, not some heathen that has no beliefs or is atheist."

"Is it hard to win hearts and minds when you're walking through a village with a machine gun?" I asked.

Colonel Leppert said he always left the machine gun behind. But he added, "I always carry my sidearm. I even take off my helmet, because I'm trying to show the people that I trust them enough that I'm standing down. Quite honestly, I'm surrounded by a lot of people with guns and stuff, but I want the ANA leadership and the villagers to see that an American soldier is willing to walk around their village unarmed to a point, helmet off, opening up to them. That I am a human being. And I often make fun of myself, I joke about myself, I try to humanize myself, so that I'm not seen as this fancy machine from the West. You know, there is a human side to the American soldier. One of the things I always tell my soldiers is, first and foremost, you're an ambassador of your country. Of the West. Of the United States. So portray yourself accordingly. . . . What kind of visual signal am I sending if I'm standing around, gear down with my weapon and my helmet still on, and I'm trying to talk to elders with my sun shields on?"

"It's a little intimidating."

"Yeah. And you know, take that stuff off and deal with it. I got plenty of other guys to protect me, but at least I try to humanize myself."

Here I was, deep in the mountains of southeast Afghanistan, thousands of miles from home, but probably only hundreds of miles from the Man himself. I figured Colonel Leppert had to have heard some info on where I could find him, right?

"You know, we ask that, just for fun, every time we go out," he said. "We see people on the road and ask, 'Hey! You guys know where Osama's at?' And they always point up to the mountains. So we always figure he's up in the mountains somewhere. Towards Pakistan."

CHAPTER 14

ONE DOWN TALIBAN

- - - - - - - -

What is unfolding now in Afghanistan is one of the great wars of Islamic history. The great powers are united against Muslims, so taking part in this war is something that deserves a reward from God.

Osama bin Laden, November 2001

Colonel Leppert arranged for me to hitch a ride with a convoy of Humvees from Fort Apache to Camp Wolverine, which was even farther out in the desert, out in the mountains. Fort Apache's military intelligence officer, Major Brent Baxter, briefed me on what to expect.

"Here in the country it's no secret—the things we're seeing are your pressure-plate IEDs, your remote-control IEDs, a lot of stuff that's being shown in the media world right now. What's hard is we can't see them coming a lot of the time. We know who's in-country, a lot of what their tactics and procedures are, some of the things being trained on, but the hard thing is trying to figure out where it's going to happen next."

"So who's in-country right now?" I asked him.

"Well, you guys know as well as I do," he said.

This didn't make me feel too comfortable—I would hope the intelligence officer knew *much more* than I did.

"You've got light foreign fighters from Pakistan," he continued. "There's a lot of reports of Chechnyans being here. Arabs. They've all been here since the beginning. From what I'm seeing, I don't think anything's changed. I think their tactics are a lot of the same."

"Where are the weapons that the Taliban are using coming from, and how are they getting into the country?"

"You know what, we're not sure yet. . . . That's what the intelligence side of the world is trying to do—they're trying to figure out that answer right now. They've got their ideas, they've got some plans to try to figure that out, but right now I can't confirm exactly where it's all coming from."

Hmm. I was beginning to think that, however much military intelligence Major Baxter had at his disposal, he wasn't sharing much of it with me.

"Is there stuff coming from Pakistan?" I asked him.

"We do know that a lot of it is being filtered through Pakistan," he said. "The Pakistani border is very porous. But is Pakistan producing it? I don't know. I couldn't tell you for sure."

"Are there Taliban and Al Qaeda training camps in Pakistan?"

"You know, I couldn't tell you if there are or not. That's above my level. It's a need-to-know thing. Even though I am an intelligence officer, some things they figure I don't need to know."

He pointed at a large sign on the wall, above a map of Afghanistan, that said, "Who Needs to Know?" Obviously, I wasn't that person.

"Based on the intelligence you have access to, who is winning the War on Terror?" I persisted.

"Oh, you know what, I think we're still at too early a stage to tell right now. We're making good progress, in my opinion, but we still have a long ways to go."

"How many people in Afghanistan are sympathetic to the Taliban?"

"I don't know," he said. "I've heard all kinds of numbers. And I don't even dare to speculate on that. It's a guessing game from day to day. I've heard numbers anywhere from fifteen to fifty percent. To ninety to ten, eighty to twenty. Depends on who you're talking to and what their opinion is."

"Where is Osama bin Laden?" I asked him.

"Oh jeez, if I knew that I'd be home right now. We wouldn't be here trying to fight this war. Is he alive? We don't know that for sure, either. We've got all kinds of reports and rumors that he is not alive."

"Is he in Afghanistan?"

"Don't know. Really don't."

"What does your gut tell you?"

"Gut tells me no. But that's just a gut feeling, and that's Brent Baxter. I think there's some information out there, but it's way above my pay grade. What they suspect he's doing."

"Lying on a beach somewhere with a margarita?" I asked.

"Exactly. Sunning himself with a turban on."

James Brabazon, who was with me, weighed in. "We've heard reports that the Taliban are attacking in groups of upwards of two hundred," he said. "That suggests there must be a high level of local support, because you can't have large groups operating like that who aren't supported by the community."

"You know, we generally have a concept we live by around here—if they say two hundred to three hundred, we usually drop a zero, because Afghans will tend to exaggerate. I'll admit a lot of the times the fights we've seen, we haven't seen more than maybe thirty to fifty in one attack. Maybe three to five, five to ten—it just depends. But generally we see small engagements where they'll hit and then run."

"How do you identify local areas that support the Taliban?" I asked.

"It's funny. We've gone through some of those areas a little while back. Some of the people will try and wave. The whole idea behind this is to win the hearts and minds of the people. So we'll go through and wave and talk to people and do what we have to. And it's funny, you can see it change. We went through some of these areas and they were waving, and the kids were waving—it was like a parade. And as soon as we hit Taliban country they wouldn't wave, wouldn't smile. Just watched us come through with that glare in their eyes. We could see that mistrust in the eyes of the people, in some of those small villages out there. It was obvious."

That didn't sound like high-level intelligence-gathering to me. If they wave they're on our side, and if they don't, they're not?

By now, I was pretty convinced that Major Baxter was giving me the runaround, because this conversation was going nowhere fast. I didn't know how much intelligence he had at his fingertips, but I was sure it was a helluva lot more than he was offering up. All I knew was that if the ISAF really was as clueless about the enemy as he made it sound, our side was in deep, deep mountain doo-dah. But then again, I did fall into the "Boy, does that guy *not* need to know" category.

The four Humvees lined up outside the barracks were the same dirt-brown color as the monochrome landscape. The soldiers, in their desert camo outfits, blended in as well. In fact, in my gray chinos and blue shirt, I was the only spot of color from horizon to horizon. Great. Maybe that's why Colonel Leppert told me to write my blood type, O POS, on my boots, helmet, Kevlar vest, and goggles strap. Just, you know, in case I became target practice.

The Humvees didn't much resemble the blinged-out rides you see rumbling down the streets of American cities. Maybe it was the big machine-gun turrets on their roofs. The soldiers called them gunships. As we boarded, one gunner slung an old scrap of a fox stole over his shoulder, with the animal's little ratlike face and glittering fake eyes hanging over his chest. He said it was the gunship's mascot.

"This is El Diablo de la Muerte," he said, grinning wildly. "The Devil Weasel of Death."

This is gonna be some ride, I thought.

The convoy pulled out of Fort Apache, and we were heading twenty kilometers across the wilderness to Wolverine. We rolled slowly, as nonthreateningly as possible, through a small shantytown of makeshift shacks that reminded me of Sidi Moumen in Morocco. Turbaned men with long beards stared at us expressionlessly. I wondered if they'd set up camp near the base for protection. We crossed a bridge over a narrow river that was so muddy it looked like chocolate milk.

Beyond that, the landscape was like the surface of the moon, which is why they call all the thick, dusty roads moon dust. The ground was flat, spreading out to the horizon, where rocky peaks shot up to the heavens, sharp mountains biting the hard blue sky. I sat in the rear passenger seat of the last gunship, gazing out a small, bulletproof window at the clouds of dust kicked up by the gunships ahead of us. I felt like a Rebel convoy cruising toward an Imperial Outpost on Tatooine, but I'm a geek.

The turret gunner's legs were at my left shoulder. The driver and another soldier up front, helmeted and wearing wraparound shades, were crammed in among all sorts of communications and satellite tracking gear. Through the narrow windshield, I could see the other gunships ahead of us, and the dusty highway snaking across the brown emptiness of this Afghan moon. We were the only traffic as we rattled along the road.

If and when we did come into contact with vehicles, they were ordered to stand down, to stop, while the convoy rolled past. Every once in a while I would see one of these locals, pulled off into the deeper gravel of the road, and as we passed, the occupants just looked at me. I looked like a soldier in the back, with my helmet and goggles, so it was interesting to see who would respond when I waved. Kids, almost always. Men, about half the time. And women, never. In fact, they never even looked up. We were just as invisible to them as they are supposed to be to all outsiders. (Only a woman's family is allowed to see her without her *hijab* and *abaya*.)

Suddenly, the radio crackled with volleys of terse codespeak. Our guys responded, there was a brief conversation, and our convoy picked up speed, hauling ass up the road in a boiling cloud of dust. Everything inside our gunship bounced and rattled. I asked the guys up front what was going on.

A few klicks (kilometers) up ahead, a convoy of vehicles with the governor of Zabul Province in one of them had been ambushed. Taliban on three motorcycles had ridden up alongside.

My heart sank. I'd just met Governor Arman the day before at his office. I'd asked him, "Do you fear for your life, now that you're working with Coalition forces?" He said, "Yes. Every day." But then he added that the people of Afghanistan needed the help of the Coalition "to make them strong, to give them independence, to give them education, to give them health, to give them strong inner force. Without the Coalition force, the UN, we will have again a very bad tragedy in Afghanistan."

I was relieved when I heard that no one in the convoy was hurt. One motorcycle had been taken, and there was "one down Taliban."

A few miles farther on, the convoy halted in the middle of nowhere. A couple of small pickup trucks were already parked there. Japanese pickups were the ANA's low-tech version of Humvees. I'd see them hauling down roads or bouncing across the moonscape packed with Afghan soldiers, like clown cars at the circus. I guess they always drove so fast because those guys jammed into the back were completely unprotected, literally sitting targets.

We clambered out of the vehicles. The highway was raised above the desert floor atop a low dirt embankment. At the bottom of the embankment, a little Japanese motorcycle lay on its side and about a dozen

ANA soldiers stood in a circle near it. Through their legs I could see the dead body lying in the dust in traditional Afghan clothes and turban, killed by the ANA. One down Taliban. As I watched, soldiers lifted him by the ankles and wrists and hauled him like a dangling slab of meat up the embankment, where he was unceremoniously dumped into the back of a pickup.

We stood under the fierce sun for a long while. Another pickup loaded with ANA came zipping across the desert in a swirl of dust. Otherwise, nothing moved but the heat shimmering off the hard ground. I thought of that corpse lying in the back of the pickup, cooking.

Across the desert, we could just make out a small village lying low against a jagged ridgeline. I was told that the soldiers recognized the dead Taliban as having come from that village. The surviving Taliban had ridden across the desert to hide there, they believed.

We all stood around, not saying a lot, the way people do at the scene of a car wreck after the bodies have been cleared away. The soldiers waited for orders. Roll over to the village to look for the other Taliban, or move on to Wolverine? Eventually, we were told the latter. As the convoy proceeded along the highway, I thought of that pickup behind us, the ANA soldiers crowded into the back with a dead guy sprawled at their feet.

I had just watched them haul off a dead body. The first casualty of war I had ever witnessed. It felt as if I had eaten a box of rocks that were now stacked in the pit of my stomach. At least I didn't actually see him get killed, but I don't know if witnessing this was much better. Later, I would find out that he was an evil character, a Taliban rogue named Throatcutter who got that delightful handle after slitting his own brother's throat to gain advancement within the organization. A classy guy, right? The soldiers said he'd been living on borrowed time anyway.

We rolled on to Wolverine, where I spent the night. The next morning, I rode out to the village with a convoy of American and ANA soldiers. It was another hot, harsh day. Along the way we drove through a small grove of dusty trees, planted along irrigation ditches with the barest trickle of muddy water in them. They were the first green anything I'd seen in the desolation of the region.

The village itself was a cluster of squat mud-brick huts. We rolled up slowly and gently, and parked our vehicles around the village well, a hand-cranked pump. The point was not to alarm anyone. This morning's mission was simply to talk with the elders and confirm that Throatcutter had come from there, if that was indeed who had been killed. As we dismounted our vehicles, people trickled out from the huts. Little girls with astonishingly pretty faces acted coy. Their dresses were the only colors to be seen—vivid greens, purples, and reds that stole your eyes from anything else you tried to look at.

Then the men of the village appeared, all in white or black turbans and long cloaks. The elders were tiny, wizened old men with white, scraggly, billy-goat beards—the sign of an elder who deserves respect—their sunbaked faces deeply creased and wrinkled. They all squatted in a line against one mud-colored wall. One man began to chant a prayer, and the soldiers and I knelt respectfully.

A brief powwow between a couple of the elders and the leading ANA officer followed. Then the men trickled back into their huts. Mission accomplished.

It turned out that one of the elders was the deceased's father. And he was indeed Throatcutter, the troublemaker the soldiers had been chasing for some time. The old man, with tears streaming down his face, told the soldiers that he had disowned his son some time ago, that he was glad he was dead, and that he hoped for peace.

Back at Wolverine, I sat around with some of the soldiers. They were from a National Guard unit that had been sent to Afghanistan six months earlier. Some of them were in their thirties like me, a lot older than many of the soldiers I'd met.

Guardsmen sign contracts guaranteeing to serve for a minimum of three years; most of these guys were now in their fourth, fifth, sixth year of service or more. In the past, guardsmen (and reservists) were sometimes dismissed as weekend warriors, because they kept their regular jobs and family lives and spent only one weekend a month in military training. In peacetime, they're mostly called upon to help in national emergencies and disasters, like Hurricane Katrina. All these guys had been sent there before coming here.

Since 9/11, I was told, the United States has stretched its full-time military to the breaking point in order to maintain a presence in both Iraq and Afghanistan—at a time when the number of young Americans volunteering for regular service has steadily decreased. More and more guardsmen and reservists have been thrown into the widening gap and have seen active duty overseas. *Half a million* have been called up since 9/11 (compared with the Vietnam War, when only about thirty-seven thousand of the two million who served were Guard or Reserve). Back in the day, joining the Guard may have kept your butt in America, but signing up now is a surefire way to get yourself a first-class ticket overseas (and by first-class I mean packed into a C-130 with a company of your closest friends). It's estimated that nearly half the U.S. troops in Iraq and Afghanistan are now guardsmen or reservists.

And they sure aren't weekend warriors anymore. Now they're deployed overseas for months or years—and, through a legal process called stop-loss, the Department of Defense can even force them to stay on active duty after their contracted terms of service run out. Critics call it a "stealth draft," and it can put a terrible strain on marriages and careers.

These guys all had wives and families back in the States, so I asked them what the conversations were like when they called home.

"When I talk to them on the phone, I don't want to talk about what's going on here," Specialist Joseph Trachsel said. "I want to talk about how they're doing, let them know that I'm okay. Other than that, when you start talking about stuff that's going on over here, stuff comes out that shouldn't come out, that you are not supposed to talk about. So you might as well nip it in the bud right then and save it for stories after you're done. When I talk to my dad, the first thing he says is 'Son, it's really good to hear your voice.' You know, that's all I need to hear."

Staff Sergeant Travis Baughman had been in the National Guard for sixteen years. It had never been a strain on the family until recently, he said.

"About six days before Katrina, I had a child," he told me. "Then I got deployed to Katrina, and did that for, what, thirty-five days? And came back and saw him for about forty-five days." Then he got shipped overseas. "So I've seen him for about a total of sixty days, and he's thirteen months now. But my wife has been outstanding. She's handling it. We figure that this is a good time—he's young enough he won't remember it. He knows who Dada is from the photos on the fridge, so that's cool. He can pick me out of other photos, so at least he knows who I am."

"I hear the horror stories about guys who come home and they can't get back into their groove with their family," Specialist Sean Ellis said. "I try not to let that happen. Whenever possible, I talk to my wife every day, which is great that we can do that. I can't imagine what it was like decades ago, when contact with home was a letter and it would take weeks to get there. But, you know, I'm missing birthdays, anniversaries. My boys are old enough now they're starting to wonder, 'Why did Daddy do this? Doesn't he love us?' They don't mean it the way it comes out, but it still kind of gets you."

He'd recently gotten an e-mail from his wife in which she told him that one of their sons asked her, "Is Daddy dead?"

"So it just reminds you of what you've got back home, and to treasure it while you're here and when you get back," he said.

"You know," Trachsel observed, "people don't realize how good they have it until they have been somewhere like here. I mean, I've never been on deployment before—this is my first one—and I'll tell you right now I have one hundred ten percent turned around in my perspective of life in general. How good we've got things. You take five people, like a *Real World* situation on MTV, and you stick them over here, and there is definitely going to be a change of heart. Whether it benefits them, that's their deal, but I definitely have a different perspective on life now."

I asked the men why they had originally volunteered for service.

"Do you want the real reason or a cool reason?" Private Nathan Corbin asked. "My real reason is a buddy of mine. It was actually his idea. I never even thought about joining, ever, and he brought it up. It sounded like a good idea. We went in and checked it out, we looked at a bunch of videotapes, and I joined. He didn't, and there you go."

"Why didn't he join?"

"Oh, a little thing called a felony. He got into a little bit of trouble with a shotgun. When a team of SWAT has to come in and handcuff you and take you to jail, I don't think you're going to be in the military anytime soon, really."

"For me, the military always represented that cool thing," Ellis said. "It was always something I wanted to do. So it was the adventure, and I wanted to get money for school, I wanted to have some fun in a physical environment. I wanted to do something for my country. . . . I guess I wanted to know that I did my part. But what really happened—this is probably the biggest factor—was a midlife crisis. I was thirty-five and running out of time. If I was going to do this, I had to do it now. I was saying to my wife, 'I've been thinking about this,' and she said, 'You should do it.' So I did."

For Trachsel, it was "kind of a family deal." He told me, "My father is a marine, my little brother is active navy. He's actually over here with us. I got to see him for the first time in a year and a half, and I almost broke him, hugging him. I don't know. I've always wanted to do it. I'm what they call a late bloomer. I didn't join until I was twenty-seven years old. I don't think when I was eighteen I was in the right frame of mind and ready for the whole package yet." The full-time soldiers might make fun of the National Guard, he said, "but you know, I can make money on the weekdays and blow stuff up on the weekends and have a blast. I get the best of both worlds. Plus, I want to be able, when I go to the house of God and enter the pearly gates, I want to be able to say I actually did something while I was here. I put in my time for a great country."

Stepping up to the plate and doing something for their country was high on the list for all these guys. Baughman, who had been deployed in Iraq previous to Afghanistan, contrasted their stance with what he called "bumper-sticker patriotism."

"When I came back from Iraq, that made me sick," he said. "It really did. I see it as false patriotism. I see it as something that almost puts what we do out here as trivial. Why join the army when I can throw a yellow magnet on my car and a WE SUPPORT OUR TROOPS flag by my house? I don't have to join the army, I don't have to do my job, I just have to make it *look* like I'm a patriot."

Ellis agreed. "What is it that makes you a patriot? What is it that makes you a good citizen? It's not word, it's deed."

Trachsel quoted the song from *Team America: World Police*—"America, fuck yeah!" Everybody laughed.

"Who here has had to kill somebody in combat?" I asked. "And how do you deal with that?"

"Not to say you're stupid," Trachsel said politely, "but it's one of those stupid questions that people ask you when you get home from war. 'Have you killed anybody?' To this day, I won't answer that question. . . . It's, like, I did what I had to do when I was over there, and I'm back. And that's bottom line right there."

"Those people give us a bad name, the people that brag about that kind of stuff," Baughman complained.

I was really interested in hearing if, after six months there, they thought Afghanistan was a winnable war.

"Just getting rid of the Taliban, getting rid of the terrorists, that's not a problem," Baughman answered. "The problem is getting the people to stand on their feet. . . . I think the more that we are able to do for them—get the wells dug, get them this, that, and the other going so they don't have to concentrate so hard on just making ends meet and making a daily living and getting a meal for their family—then they are going to be able to stand up more and provide more of their time to take care of the security of their areas."

"The secretary of defense said that the U.S. military can win anywhere," Ellis said. "But that's not how you end the conflict. You don't win a war by annihilating every last enemy. You win a war by negotiating terms of surrender or peace or whatever with a lawful government. So the only way to win the war is to get that government legitimized, and I think that's what we are working at. But I think at the final accounting there are going to be those who say, no matter when we leave, we left too soon or we stayed too long. It's going to be debated endlessly, I think. But establishing a government over this country, so it's not a failed state anymore, is the only way to say, 'We won. It's over.'"

Thinking and talking about families—Afghan families, these guys' families, my own future family—got me wondering. . . . What kind of family man was Osama? I hadn't really thought about it a lot. I knew that, chip off the old block that he was, he'd married several times. I figured he had kids. But I didn't really know much. Were his wives and kids holed up in the mountains with him—if that's where he was? Did his wives go shopping at the local mountain 7-Eleven? Did his kids go to cave school? Did any of his sons plan to follow in the old man's footsteps and become the most wanted men on earth themselves someday? I mean really, what was it like to be a wife or a child of the most wanted man alive?

When I had the chance, I did some looking into it. I found out that Osama married for the first time when he was seventeen and still in high school. She was a fourteen-year-old cousin from Syria. He married four more times after that; since Islam permits a maximum of four wives at a time, he had to divorce one in order to marry the fifth. I read his theory on multiple wives: "One is okay, like walking. Two is like riding a bicycle: it's fast but a little unstable. Three is a tricycle, stable but slow. And when we come to four, ah! This is the ideal. Now you can pass everyone!"

I had a funny talk with an ANA general about this multiple-wives thing. He had two wives and an attitude that was very different from Osama's. "With one wife I was happy," he said. "Ever since the second, my life has been miserable." It probably didn't help that he married his wife's sister after her fiancé was killed, but he said that's the tradition. Better you than me, pal.

Osama liked smart women—two of his wives had Ph.D.s. Still, like his dad he kept them pregnant, and among the five of them they had given him at least twenty-four children. Abdullah, his oldest son, was the first of eleven kids with his first wife. Abdullah stayed with his father through the Sudan years, but when Osama left for Afghanistan Abdullah packed it in and went home to Jeddah. Steve Coll told me that he was in his late twenties, ran an advertising and publicity firm, and did not speak in public about his dad.

According to everything I heard or read, Osama was an affectionate father, though strict about religion and things like having music in the house (it's *haram* for Wahhabis). As a young dad in Saudi Arabia, he took the kids to the beach or for nights out in the desert, like that one I spent with Saud and the other men. He taught them how to ride horses and hunt with falcons. In Afghanistan from 1996 on, the extended bin Laden and Zawahiri families made for what sounds like a

Brady Bunch gang, with all the kids growing up and playing together. The Taliban had basically shut down all the schools, so they had a lot of time to kill. The wives lived in separate houses in the compounds, sometimes getting along, sometimes not. At some point, after more than twenty-five years of being on the run with her terrorist husband, Osama's first wife gave up and returned to Syria.

Osama married his daughters off to various Taliban and Al Qaeda members, at least one of whom was killed fighting Coalition troops in Kandahar in 2001. And here's a weird twist: Osama married one of his girls to Mullah Omar, which made him the Taliban leader's father-in-law! Man, I thought my West Virginia peeps were close-knit.

He kept his boys near him at all the compounds and when he was up in Tora Bora. In Kandahar, he once took over a former movie theater (closed by the Taliban) to stage a gala wedding for his seventeen-year-old son Mohammed. The proud dad was videotaped reciting a poem he wrote for the occasion—a happy little ditty about Al Qaeda's suicide-bombing attack on the USS *Cole* in 2000. Everyone at the wedding cheered, "*Allahu Akbar!*" Tell me this guy doesn't know how to par-tay!

Unlike Abdullah, several of the other sons did in fact follow in the old man's footsteps. Osman served as one of his father's bodyguards, and Hamza became an Al Qaeda fighter. The best-known was Saad, who's in his mid-twenties now. He's thought to have helped plan the Casablanca suicide bombings. So I'd been right about there being an Osama connection there. After the fall of Tora Bora, Saad escaped to Iran.

Hearing about Osama's sons, I remembered the tears flowing down the face of Throatcutter's dad, and how it choked me up. I wondered how Osama would feel if he heard that one of his sons had been killed "fighting the infidels"? Would he be glad? Would he be proud? At the funeral, would he recite a poem in his son's honor? Would everybody there cheer? It was one of the times when, despite everything I'd been learning about him, I felt that I would never really understand the way this man looked at the world.

CHAPTER 15

OSAMA BIN GONE

From Wolverine I drove out one morning with some U.S. and ANA soldiers to a village called Bouragai. I wanted to ask the regular people how they felt about all the ISAF troops in their country. I thought they were there doing something positive, but what did the locals think? The older men of the village gathered under the sun, seated together on a large rock, while some of the younger men stood with children at their feet.

One man told me through a translator that they still had bad memories from when the Russians were there. They came, did whatever they wanted, and then left. He said he worried that the ISAF would do the same. He also said that the ISAF had promised to build roads, schools, and clinics, and none of that had happened yet.

"Why do you think that hasn't happened?" I asked.

And right then, on cue, the soldiers interrupted us. We had to leave. An IED had been spotted nearby. Where there's one IED there may be more, and we were ordered to return to Wolverine while the ANA searched and secured the area. As we headed back to the armed gunships, I wondered what the villagers thought, standing there, cut off in mid-conversation while the Americans ran away.

It's got to be intimidating to see these Humvees roll up on you with a guy standing on the roof of the vehicle manning a 70-mm machine gun. I would have to think that it's only when those things drive away that the villagers' heart rates return to normal. As we ran to get back into the trucks, *my* heart was racing. Sergeant Baughman ran beside me to make sure I didn't get shot—at least not from that side.

Later that day, we were able to return to Bouragai and pick up the conversation.

"We do not want to fight anymore in this country," one man told me. "Like what happened today, an IED in the road. We're stopped from going to irrigate our land or cultivate our land. If the Taliban go away, then everyone is going to find a good life for himself. Ever since the Taliban went out of power, we have not supported the Taliban, and we do not want to support them. I don't know why [others] still support the Taliban."

I asked if anyone in the village had joined the Taliban. They all shook their heads. I asked the translator to assure them that they could speak freely, even with soldiers standing around.

"Whoever is standing here, I will tell the truth," one man replied. "This is the truth. I don't like the U.S. *or* the Taliban. I think they all have to go away." He said they'd had no trouble from the Taliban until the ISAF arrived. Now "Taliban is coming here, and they are beating us, and you guys are attracting the Taliban."

I was told that, despite the closeness of the American base, the Taliban had forced the villagers to close their small school just two months before. I couldn't believe it. Another man explained that they were risking being beaten or killed by the Taliban merely by speaking with us now.

I needed to understand their relationship with the ISAF and ANA troops. The rest of the men deferred to the eldest. He told me that when the army drilled the well for Camp Wolverine it disrupted the water supply in the village. They had complained to the American troops, but although an American specialist had come to the village to help fix the problem, the streams had continued to dry up, and they did not have adequate water to irrigate their crops.

They also complained that their homes had been searched repeatedly, day and night. "We had a hard time with that," another man said. "Our children, our women were scared." And, they said, the ANA shot mortars at them if they turned on lights at night.

Before I left, I asked if they had any final thoughts.

"This is what I have to say," one man replied. "The government of the U.S. needs to talk with Karzai and the leader of the Taliban. Talk with him and solve the problem. Not by fighting. I'm sure the Taliban will not agree to talk with the U.S., but then the U.S. guy should step back, let other Islamic countries talk with Karzai and the leader of the Taliban to solve this problem."

It is interesting to note that only six countries with substantial Muslim populations even sent troops to help diffuse the situation in Afghanistan and Iraq, and the numbers they committed were beyond paltry. Albania, Armenia, Bosnia, Kazakhstan, the Philippines, and Singapore *combined* sent fewer than five hundred people to both countries. If these conflicts are the source of such dissent in the Muslim world, why aren't more Muslim countries—like Saudi Arabia, Egypt, Jordan—stepping forward to help solve the problem and end the fighting? If they want U.S. soldiers to leave, why don't they send Muslim peacekeeping soldiers into the regions? It was one of the most frequent comments I heard in Afghanistan: Where are the Muslim nations that could help bridge this gap?

When the Taliban regime in Kabul fell on November 13, 2001, it was General Gul Haider and his Northern Alliance troops who took the city. Then he moved on to the eastern mountains, to help Coalition forces pry remaining Taliban and Al Qaeda fighters out of their caves.

When I met him in Kabul five years later, Gul Haider was just as tough as he was during the Soviet-Afghan War. While I sat with him, countless people who worked at the Gandamak Lodge made it a point to come over and pay their respects to this Afghan legend, a man who had lost his leg from a land mine years earlier, who had been shot countless times but could never be killed, who fought side by side with Ahmad Shah Massoud, and who still represented the undying spirit of the Afghan people. Today, he was a general without an army and was growing increasingly frustrated as he watched the ISAF and ANA struggling to defeat the Taliban and Al Qaeda all over again.

Following the ouster of the Taliban and the formation of a new government in 2002, Northern Alliance leaders were asked to disband their forces and hand in their weapons. And they did. Well, sorta, mostly. The new Afghan National Army would take over the defense of the nation, it was said. In return for their cooperation, several Northern Alliance leaders got nice positions in President Karzai's cabinet. But by the fall of 2006, Karzai had shuffled them all out of power.

"We fought against Al Qaeda and pushed them well back, and everything was going well," General Haider complained to me through our interpreter, Naji. "But in the past three years the situation has changed. I can tell you the Taliban didn't exist two years ago, but because of these problems, and because of these mistakes, they are gaining power day by day."

"What's going wrong?" I asked.

"The Coalition forces have taken the wrong direction in handling the situation," he said. "Instead of sending British or American or French troops to the front line to fight the Taliban and Al Qaeda, they could have sent us, because we know the terrain and we know the country, and we could have done a better job. There would be no loss of life in the foreign troops. But they disarmed us and pushed us to the side in fighting them, and it's going nowhere."

I met a lot of Afghans who agreed. So why were the Northern Alliance leaders removed from power? Partly, it was their own fault. In the 1990s, from the fall of the Soviet-backed government in Kabul to its takeover by the Taliban, the Northern Alliance warlords got to run Afghanistan, and they did a lousy job of it. Corruption and drug trafficking were rife. So were human-rights abuses against women and, as the civil war with the Taliban worsened, against the Pashtuns in the southern and eastern provinces around Kabul, whom the mujahideen accused of supporting the Taliban (who were largely Pashtun themselves). Human Rights Watch reported "killings, indiscriminate aerial bombardment and shelling, direct attacks on civilians, summary executions, rape, persecution on the basis of religion or ethnicity, the recruitment and use of children as soldiers, and the use of antipersonnel land mines."

When the Coalition invaded in 2001, we used the Northern Alliance because we needed their help militarily. But we had no intention of letting them run the country again. We set up a government led by a Pashtun, Karzai. The Pashtuns are, after all, the ethnic majority in Pakistan, the educated elite of Kabul, as opposed to a bunch of tribal warlords from the mountains. General Haider and the others were persuaded to lay down their arms in return for positions in the government. Then Karzai slowly weeded them out anyway.

General Haider, and a lot of Afghans, believed there was another reason the Northern Alliance had been pushed out: Pakistan. I'll get more into Pakistan's murky involvement in Afghanistan's affairs in the next chapter, but, basically, since the 1980s the United States has relied heavily on Pakistan's support, influence, and intelligence in Afghanistan, with complicated and not entirely happy results. Pakistan, which has a huge Pashtun population, never liked the troublesome Northern Alliance warlords, and always threw its influence behind the Afghan Pashtuns—which included backing the Taliban in the civil war. When we pushed the Taliban and Al Qaeda out of Afghanistan in 2001–02, many crossed the border into western Pakistan, where they were welcomed by the largely Pashtun locals. And it was from there, pretty much everyone agreed, that the resurgence of Taliban and Al Qaeda fighters in Afghanistan was coming.

"We have one enemy, and that is Pakistan," General Haider said to me. "Because they created Al Qaeda and terrorism and the Taliban. And they are hiding them." But the Coalition, he complained, "are listening to Pakistan. And Pakistan is leading them, giving them wrong information, and giving them wrong advice. And if they keep doing this, asking Pakistan for advice and information, they are going to lose this war, and be defeated. Pakistan is playing everyone. Playing the West, playing Afghanistan, playing everyone."

I was not surprised that General Haider was dismissive of the ANA as a fighting force.

"It's not what we expected, and we are quite disappointed," he said. "They are not trained properly. They are not well equipped. They don't have the proper ammunition and guns. My soldiers . . . could carry mines and bombs and explosives on their backs for five hours, and they would put them under the Russian tanks, and they would have waited for another five hours until the Russian tanks exploded. . . . When the ANA is trained to that level, then I will be happy. But this ANA is not going to be that effective. It's just going to run away. It's good for show, it's good pictures, but it's not good for action. They're wearing military clothes, and they have their sunglasses on, they have helmets on, and they have guns, and their pickup trucks will drive really quite fast. It's good for show. But for real stuff? No. The Coalition should give the ANA a test and see if they can handle it, without asking for backup from the Coalition or NATO. I think they're not going to be able to handle it."

As for the Northern Alliance, General Haider told me in no uncertain terms, "We are not going to sit quiet. We are going to fight them until they are finished. . . . The mujahideen are big. They are everywhere. . . . They are very watchful of the situation. They have open eyes and ears, and are seeing what's going on. They are waiting for the orders from their leadership. There are still some leaders. And when they have been ordered they will march."

To get the Taliban's side of the story, I spoke with Mullah Abdul Salam Zaeef in Kabul. Under the Taliban regime in the late 1990s, he was Afghanistan's ambassador to Pakistan. When 9/11 happened, it was Zaeef the Taliban put on international TV, condemning the attacks, but adding that the Taliban did not believe Osama bin Laden was responsible, and would not hand him over without evidence of his guilt. It was because of that refusal that the United States invaded Afghanistan.

In January 2002, Pakistan arrested Zaeef and handed him over— "sold" him was how he put it—to the Americans. The United States held him for three years and ten months, much of it in the Guantánamo Bay detention center, about which he has written a book that is, of course, highly critical. He returned to Kabul on his release.

I asked him, "Did you believe, one hundred percent, in everything the Taliban stood for while they were in power?"

"It's very difficult to find a country where everyone has the same ideology," he said through Naji. "I agreed with the good stuff that the Taliban regime were doing, and they did great stuff."

First, he said, they united all the tribes, factions, and classes into a nation under one rule and one law, Sharia. Also, by cracking down on crime, they made it "a pretty safe place for Afghans to live. . . . The country was secure. There was law and order. Police were able to arrest thieves and criminals and prosecute them. You could go anywhere you wanted without fear of kidnapping or being ambushed. . . . Security is the most important thing in a country. Because if you have security you can do education, you can do business, you can work, you can live. I was a minister, and I was going to Kandahar, because that is my birthplace. And I was driving without any bodyguards, without any security, just me and my kids. Driving in the middle of the night from Kabul to Kandahar, you would not have fear that you were going be stopped by any-one. . . . But now, if a minister wants to go to the local market he can-not do that." At least, not without a bodyguard.

Under the Taliban, he said, Afghanistan was an independent nation, free of meddling from both neighbors and foreign powers like the United States. Today, he said, the Karzai government is weak, corrupt, and totally dependent on and run by outsiders.

"During the Taliban, the neighboring countries had respect for Afghanistan," Mullah Zaeef went on. "They were not intervening in Afghan internal affairs. But it's not the case now. Iran is interfering, and Pakistan is interfering a lot in Afghan politics and security. In every area, whatever they want they can do. Under the Taliban, it wasn't like this. Yes, you can say we had some foreigners—Arabs and others from other Islamic countries. But those people were under our control. They could not arrest anyone, they could not kill an Afghan. They were stay-ing as guests here. But [they had] no authority. . . . But now it is not the case, you know? There's lots of foreign troops, and whatever they want they can do."

On the downside, he was willing to admit that the Taliban "didn't have time" to clear up all the corruption in government, and lacked the resources to provide adequate government services, such as schools and electricity.

Wait—was he saying the only reason women couldn't get an educa-tion under the Taliban was that they couldn't afford to run the schools?

"The Taliban were not against women's education, but they did not have the resources to provide a safe and secure environment for a woman to go to school according to the Sharia," he insisted. "The an-nual budget of the Taliban was $18 million. This was not enough to ac-commodate good schools for women."

But my understanding was that women were educated only for those roles the Taliban said were appropriate. They needed female doctors, for instance, to treat women, because they were not allowed to see male doctors.

"They were allowed to get education through primary school and high school," he hedged. "But the Taliban did not have the budget or the resources to provide them higher education."

Uh-huh. That's funny, because the Taliban did have the resources to *destroy* more than 175 schools after they lost control of the country. Classy guys. Now that Zaeef and his crowd were out of power, at least women could walk down the street by themselves in Kabul, and choose whether to cover their faces, without fear of Taliban religious police beating them. Shop owners had cricket and soccer games on the TV again. Everyone in the city seemed to have a radio, and they were all enjoying music again.

I wondered what Zaeef thought of all these new freedoms that Afghans were enjoying. "Are they good things or bad things?" I asked.

"It's not appropriate for people to waste their money on these things, given that they are not a priority for Afghanistan," Mullah Zaeef said. "Now, one in ten people have enough food to eat and drink, but the other nine don't have food to eat. They are hungry, and they don't have the facility to send their kids to school to be educated. I'm not getting into if they should be allowed or should not be allowed. I'm saying that it is not appropriate for Afghans to waste their money on these things. I'll give an example. If I buy a TV and just relax, watching it, and my neighbor has no food to eat, this is not justice. This is not according to Islam. This is a very bad thing to do."

Mullah Zaeef said he was not really in touch with the new generation of Taliban who had appeared during the years of his detention. When I asked if he thought the Pakistani government was supporting them, he replied that the *last* thing the Pakistani government wanted was for the Taliban to take over Afghanistan again. Pakistan had sold out the Taliban to the United States, he said, and helped it kill or capture many Taliban (like himself), and the Taliban would never forget that.

The *people* of Pakistan, he said, were another matter.

"Pakistan is a Muslim nation, very good people," he continued. "They have sympathy for the cause of their own brothers in the Taliban. So they will do their best to look after them, to pray for them. But the leadership, the policymakers, the intelligence service, the army— they are mainly against the Taliban and they do not want Taliban to take power again, because if the Taliban take power again the first thing they will do is take revenge on Pakistan."

I'd heard that former members of Pakistan's intelligence service, the ISI, were helping to train Taliban fighters.

Mullah Zaeef scoffed. Afghans don't need anyone to show them how to fight, he said. "I can use any weapon. I can use any gun and ammunition. There is no one in Afghanistan who doesn't know how to use weapons. The Taliban don't need training. They are well trained. . . . This is in their blood."

I wanted to hear about his experiences at Guantánamo. I asked him first what he had been charged with.

"That question should be referred to the government of the United States," he said. "Why they arrested me, and why they put me in prison without any crime, and why they oppressed me. When they interrogated me, I told them they shouldn't be behaving the way they are behaving. . . . What is my crime? I haven't done anything wrong to anyone. I just wanted to bring good for the people. . . . You should ask them why they arrested me in the first place, and then released me without any charge. Why, most important, they are keeping hundreds of other innocent people the same way they kept me. The oppression and the torture and other appalling conditions."

"Were you tortured while you were there?"

"Several times. They tortured us so many times I cannot even give you an account. And some of the things they did to me and the others I cannot really speak about, because they were so degrading, so I am decent enough not to tell you. It was very shameful what they did. And illegal."

And although he tried to write about it in his book, *A Picture of Guantánamo*, he said, it was just too difficult.

"Well, I tried to write everything, but I couldn't because my pen was shaking," he said. "It was shameful stuff that happened here. . . . Imagine yourself being a prisoner in Guantánamo. You're sleeping in a toilet, you're eating in a toilet, you're praying in a toilet. It's a cage, one and a half meters. Imagine that. You're worshipping your God in a toilet."

"Were inmates beaten?" I asked.

"Sometimes they were beating you. Sometimes they were abusing you. Sometimes they were swearing at you. Sometimes they were abusing your religion, and swearing at your religion and your God and your book."

I asked him how he thought Guantánamo and Abu Ghraib affected Muslims' views of America and Americans.

"Because of what they are doing, because of U.S. policy, ninety-five percent of the Muslims hate Americans," he said. "Unfortunately, it's not the government or the military—they even hate ordinary Americans for what they are doing."

I told him I thought his statistics were 38 percent accurate 52 percent of the time, and that that wasn't what I'd heard from Muslims in my travels. They'd usually been careful to distinguish between American policy and the American people, saying that they believed the American people were inherently good people with strong ideals.

"Yes," he countered, "but the American people had the choice, and they elected Bush. Twice. And Muslims around the world blame them for what he has done to them."

Since his release in 2005, Mullah Zaeef said, he'd spoken to many, many Afghans from all walks of life, and he "didn't find a single person who says America is good, Americans are good, and American policy is good for our country. Even the people of this current government hate the Americans and the American foreign policy."

Well, when you're running with an Osama kind of crowd, I'm sure that's all you hear.

I knew Osama wasn't there anymore, but I couldn't leave Afghanistan without visiting Tora Bora, his last stronghold in the country during the invasion in December 2001. It's on the Afghan slopes of the tall, snow-peaked White Mountains, which form the border with Pakistan, not too far east of Kabul and Jalalabad, where I set out. The Khyber Pass isn't too far away, either.

The road from Jalalabad to Tora Bora passed through landscape that was very different from what I'd seen down in southern Afghanistan. It reminded me of the Alps—high, sharp peaks of white to my left as we headed south, cradling green valleys of decent-looking farmland and fruit groves. As we climbed closer to Tora Bora, we entered forests of pine trees. Then, as we continued to ascend, there were fewer trees and more rocks. And more rocks and more rocks, piled on top of one another, all the way up to the blue sky. I wondered how many of those rocks the American B-52s had pounded out of bigger rocks when they were bombing the hell out of this area.

As pretty as they are, those mountains along the Afghanistan-Pakistan border can be dangerous. Webs of mule trails and footpaths scramble through the high passes and down on either side of the border. On the other side of those mountains, the Taliban and Al Qaeda were training their fighters, then sending them over. The roads winding up the slopes get awfully lonely and, as many a journalist and soldier told me, are a "nice place for an ambush."

So we called ahead to the governor of Nangarhar Province, Gul Agha Sherzai, who said that he would send a group of ANPs to travel with us. "But it is safe, don't worry," he assured us.

The ANP troops were packed like sardines into their little pickup trucks, and as the road corkscrewed up into the vicinity of Osama's complex the officers started dropping the soldiers off one at a time, stringing them out like Christmas lights along the trail, two every five hundred meters or so. Yeah, this place is safe, so long as you travel with a small army, leave behind troops to make sure no one plants an IED on the road while you're gone, and get back to a safe area before nightfall. As long as you do all that . . . it's safe.

Eventually we dismounted as well, and climbed a slope of tumbled brown boulders the rest of the way up to Osama's old hideout. Using equipment from his family's construction firm, he had bored a large system of tunnels roughly a thousand feet into the mountain's core. Nothing fancy, but reportedly room enough for up to a thousand fighters, dug into an almost inaccessible spot. Most of these tunnels were blown to bits by the bunker-buster bombs that were dropped by the United States in 2001, but some smaller caves were still intact.

I saw a few of the entrances, low holes in the rocks. I stood at one that looked like . . . a cave. Just a cave, anywhere.

Still, it wasn't just a cave, any more than Hitler's bunker was just a sub-basement. This was Osama's cave, or one of them, anyway. There probably wasn't a soul in the world who hadn't seen the pictures or videos. This was one of the most historic sites in modern times. So historic, in fact, that the governor of the province wants to build a theme park here. I'm not kidding. Osama Land, right here in the middle of Tora Bora, complete with roller coasters and water slides and fried dough. Mmm, fried dough. Hey, the guy's got vision, but Osama ain't Mickey Mouse, and the idea of people coming from miles around to ride the Bunker Buster, the Magic Carpet, or the Infidel Express is a little out there.

But still, to see a decrepit, bombed-out Soviet-era tank sitting in front of Osama's old blown-up digs was chilling. The paths leading up the steep faces to the hidden bunkers were still intact, and every so often I'd find a rusty, spent AK cartridge on the ground.

Suddenly a gunshot rang out. We all hit the dirt. The ANP soldiers locked and loaded their weapons. From over the hill we heard someone yell. It was one of their guys whom they'd sent ahead to scare off any potential threats. He had just seen a deer, and got a shot off at it. I wondered how many more ANP soldiers had been ordered to fan out over this "safe" area.

One guy pulled me aside as the sun started to set and told me that we really needed to be moving. "You don't want be here when it's dark," he said.

Whatever was still around Tora Bora, whether it was real scary people or just spooks from scarier times, these guys were afraid. And me, all I could think was that wherever Osama was—in the mountains farther north, or across them over in Pakistan, or even the outlandish places I'd heard, like on the beach or in Langley, Virginia—he sure wasn't here anymore. Elvis had left Tora Bora. I had to keep looking.

CHAPTER 16

TALIBANISTAN

‒ ‒ ‒ ‒ ‒ ‒ ‒

We will not let Pakistan and its people stand alone. We will protect
Pakistan. But General Musharraf has disappointed us. He says that
the majority supports him; I say that they oppose him. He is standing
in the enemy ranks. . . . He will receive his punishment from God and
the Pakistani people.

Osama bin Laden, November 2001

While standing in the middle of Camp Wolverine, deep in the mountains of southern Afghanistan, I received a call on the satellite phone about my attempts to get permission to enter Pakistan. For more than seven months I had tried to get a visa to get into the country, and request after request had been denied.

Then an insider in Pakistan called and told me why I was continually being rejected. First, the person said, "They are very afraid that something may happen to you while you are there." Apparently, the last thing they wanted was another high-profile Daniel Pearl–style murder, which would generate volumes of negative PR. Second, "They are very worried about what you will find."

I wasn't so crazy about the first part, either, but that second reason was pretty intriguing. Afraid of what I might find? That only made me want to go there more! So, while in Afghanistan, we hired a local to do everything possible to get us into the country.

We'd considered just crossing the border in a bus or hiking into the Tribal Areas illegally, but if you get caught, either by the police or, worse, by the ISI, you could wind up going to jail for a *very* long time. That's the *good* side of what could happen if you're caught. The bad side is that you could just disappear. Years later, someone finds your body or your head lying at the bottom of a giant ravine. I'd heard too many horror stories already, and the last thing I wanted to do was take a risk like that.

Then our new fixer called on the satellite phone. He said he had a friend at the Pakistani Embassy in Kabul whom he talked to about getting us in. His friend brought up our names on the computer, and mine had a big red flag next to it—*denied*. He begged the official, said we were just journalists, what harm would it do. The official agreed, if we paid him $2,000. The average Afghan doesn't make that much in a year. How could we say no?

So, thanks to a resourceful fixer and a well-placed bribe, we would soon be on our way to what I'd heard was one of the most violent, hostile, and unstable countries in the world: Pakistan. Lucky me. But I had to go, first because the Man might be hiding there, and second because even if he wasn't, he had a lot of friends and supporters there. In fact, you could call this leg of my trip:

STAGE 11: ENTER THE HEART OF DARKNESS

Peshawar means "City on the Frontier." And boy is it. The capital of Pakistan's North-West Frontier Province (NWFP), it sits just across the Khyber Pass from Afghanistan, in a wilderness of mountains folded upon mountains. Heading west out of the city, you pass crowded souks and buses stacked sky high with not only luggage on the roof but usually passengers holding on tight to the bags, until you finally enter the Federally Administered Tribal Areas—basically an autonomous area run by local warlords, with very little interference from the national government in Islamabad. It stretches five hundred miles along the border from the provinces of Southern and Northern Waziristan to Bajaur in the north. This is Pakistan's Wild West, and Peshawar is its Tombstone, the magnet for all the outlaws and bad guys in the region— tribal bandits, arms dealers, drug smugglers.

It has also been a magnet for war refugees. During the Soviet-Afghan War in the 1980s, more than six million Afghans fled their country—the largest refugee group in the world—pouring into Iran and Pakistan. Some returned home in the 1990s, but the civil war kept many away. A 2005 census showed that three million Afghan refugees were still in Pakistan, over half of them in the NWFP.

War refugees of another type were also drawn to Peshawar and the surrounding countryside. After the U.S.-led invasion of Afghanistan in 2001 pushed Taliban and Al Qaeda fighters across the border, many of them ended up in the NWFP. Both Taliban leader Mullah Omar and Osama himself were rumored to have spent at least some time in Peshawar. If they did, they must have felt right at home. Peshawar and its surrounds are deeply traditional and pretty conservative, though not as conservative as I'd found parts of Afghanistan to be. But hey, this was still the "big city." Just as you would in America, I expected to find the most conservative elements out in the quiet countryside, where their ideals and opinions remain largely unaffected by outside forces.

Almost all of the men I saw wore long beards and the traditional Pakistani dress, the *shalwar kameez*, which consists of very roomy and baggy drawstring pants and a long, knee-length shirt that matches them. (Coincidentally, Shalwar Kameez is my rap name.) I instantly thought they were the greatest invention since pajamas, and then decided that whoever invented pajamas must have spent time in Pakistan.

All the people were hustling to work, running through the streets just as they do in New York City. In fact, the city bustled with an energy that instantly reminded me of home: people yelling in the streets, selling food, clothes, tools, books, and anything else you can imagine. Outside the city, I was told, it's common to see the men carrying a rifle or an AK-47, and they hold them casually, as if they were born with weapons in their hands. Which automatically made me think of my birthplace, West Virginia, where I had learned to shoot years before when I was given my first rifle, at the age of twelve. Everyone I knew there seemed to own and know how to use a gun. I had more in common with these folks than I'd thought. Wherever you go, the country is still the country and a redneck is still a redneck.

Women walk the streets freely in Peshawar. Some wear full-length black burkas, cloaking them from head to toe, with not even a fingertip showing; others wear bright-colored fabrics that are intricately wrapped around them, with matching head scarves that cover only their hair. The latter were a far cry from the full-length, ribbed blue accordion burkas—"Blue Ghost" burkas—I'd seen everywhere in Afghanistan. I was shocked, especially since I'd heard so much on the news about how scary and oppressive Pakistan was.

In Afghanistan, at least for me, it had been a bizarre sight to see these women going around in outfits that made them "invisible." Not only could you not see them; they were treated as though they didn't exist. Outside the home, women were rarely acknowledged in conversation or pleasantries or anything that could remotely be deemed courteous. If they asked for something at the market, they got it swiftly, with no eye contact from the grocer, and then they were on their way, with no further interaction. And while you may see a woman with her face uncovered in Kabul, you would never see that in the conservative countryside. I could only imagine that the same was true in Pakistan.

Many mullahs in Peshawar's mosques preach extreme fundamentalism—and many of them have positions in the provincial government. The madrassas in and around Peshawar are filled to bursting with young men, at least some of whom are indoctrinated in the ideals of the Taliban and global jihad, then sent off to fight the infidels in Afghanistan, Iraq, and farther afield—if they should decide that this is their calling. Osama has given his personal blessing to this endeavor. In 2001, an international conference of fundamentalists called Deobandi (basically, the South Asian equivalent of the Wahhabis and Salafis) drew *half a million* believers to Peshawar. Many attendees were teachers or students in Pakistani madrassas. Highlights of the event were taped addresses from Mullah Omar, Muammar Qaddafi, and Osama, who told the crowd, "For it is a duty, as you well know, to stand up for the truth and show the way to the waiting throngs who crane their necks to see you. Teach them that there is no pride or victory except in jihad for the sake of God. . . . Teach them that there is no Islam without a spirit of kinship, no kinship without authority, and no authority without listening and obeying."

So, figuring they might be good places to meet someone who could tell me where to look for Osama, I visited two madrassas near Peshawar: Madrassa Darul Uloom Haqqania and Madrassa Jamia Noumania. With its plain, whitewashed study halls, dormitories, and mosque, Haqqania reminded me of a poorly funded community college. In fact, Western media often refer to the school as "the University of Jihad," and say that many of its students over the years have gone off to be Taliban fighters or leaders. Its most famous former student, after all, is none other than Mullah Omar, the founder of the Taliban.

I watched some boys kicking around a soccer ball in a courtyard with a scraggly lawn, and a couple others playing badminton. No one was learning how to pack explosives into an IED or fieldstrip an M-4, but maybe those activities are saved for a field trip.

Before we arrived, our local fixer turned to me and said, "Do not tell them you are an American."

"Why not?" I asked. I mean, that's the whole reason I was there, to help them also see that I'm human, that I'm a real person just like them. Our fixer told me that it was not the students he was concerned about but someone on the outside that they may notify.

"Anyone who may be sympathetic to the cause will call ahead to somebody on the outside, and when we leave the madrassa you may be shot or kidnapped, or worse."

"So what should I do?"

"Tell them you are Swiss," he said.

Amil ul-Haq, who led me around, told me that his grandfather founded the school in 1947. There were only eight students then. Now there were three thousand, with another thousand on a waiting list. They were all Pakistani, he said, because the government had cracked down on the madrassas' admitting foreign students. Later, I would be told by countless locals that this was untrue, and that Pakistani madrassas were now bursting with Afghan refugees who were there to learn and then wanted to go fight the "American oppressors." I didn't meet any of these Afghans, mainly because we were watched closely the entire time we were in the madrassa. They allowed us to talk only to people they approved, and they never let me or Daniel, the cameraman, out of their sight. Steve Martin's advice in *The Jerk* had never been more diligently observed: "Don't trust whitey."

The school had graduated about fifteen thousand students since it opened more than fifty years ago.

"That's a lot of terrorists," I said.

Amil, to his credit, laughed. In fact, he said that, along with memorizing the Koran, students study Greek philosophy, general sciences, and learn Urdu, Arabic, and Farsi. They get up at five to pray, have breakfast, then memorize the Koran until eleven. After a break, they start studying again at two.

It's an eight-year course of study. I had thought most of them went on to become mullahs and imams, but Amil told me that in addition to becoming clerics they enter all walks of life—politics, teaching, business, the military. Some graduates continue their education at Oxford or Cambridge.

Saifullah was in his fifth year of study. I asked him why he was at the madrassa.

"I want to know about Islam and I want to please my God, Almighty Allah, and I want to serve the community," he said.

Did he plan to become a religious teacher?

"I don't know what I will do in the future, but I will certainly abide by the Sharia law, and try to spread religion everywhere—even to you," he told me, smiling.

I told him that in the West all we hear about madrassas is that they're cranking out jihadists.

"Yeah, they think that we are like red Indians," he said with a nod. If we knew anything about Islam, he added, we'd know it's a religion of peace. "Those who are doing the violence are really damaging the religion and defaming Islam."

I went into a four-story dormitory, with 150 rooms, seven students to a room. Cozy. It looked like a college dorm anywhere, with stickers on the doors and graffiti on the walls. It even had a resident smart-ass, a funny kid who asked me the name of the movie I was making.

"We don't have a name yet," I told him. "Maybe if you have a good one you can help me."

"Call it *Stop Negative Propaganda*," he suggested.

I told him I wanted to do something that was different from what we're always seeing and hearing on the news.

Oh well, he said, "it's all George Bush TV anyway." And in Pakistan, he noted, it was all President Musharraf TV—all media in Pakistan is state-run. "Mush, Bush, same, same," he said with a shrug. "They are brothers."

Madrassa Jamia Noumania, on the other hand, was small, like a private academy run out of a home. I met Hassan, the administrator, and a mullah who pretty much looked like every stereotypical image of a jihadist I'd ever seen on the news. It occurred to me that if this guy tried to get on a plane in the States he'd be detained for hours.

In Hassan's loose definition, *jihad* means "defending Islam against its enemies"—and when I asked him how important jihad is to Islam, he replied that it is "the main principle." When I asked if any of his students have gone off to fight jihad, he replied that "when the time comes we will all wage jihad." Some would do it by preaching, he said, "and those who are really young and have energy can go physically to wage jihad."

Then we got into it over 9/11. He said that everyone knew it was done by "the Jews in the Pentagon and the Bush administration." Why else would they have done it on Saturday, the Jewish Sabbath, when none of them would be in the buildings? The four thousand Jews who worked at the World Trade Center were absent that day.

"Actually, it was a Tuesday," I said. "And lots of Jews were killed."

He shrugged that off.

He had his own theories about why the United States invaded Afghanistan, too. It was because Mullah Omar was such a successful and popular leader, and Bush feared that this kind of good, Muslim leadership would spread to other countries, causing a clash of American and Islamic interests.

Since he had another madrassa in Bajaur, I asked the mullah if he knew where I could find Osama. He laughed and said we all read about imaginary animals in books, but who knew where this particular one was hiding? Maybe he was in India, maybe in Pakistan, maybe in Afghanistan.

"We don't have any idea," he said.

"So you don't think he's in the Tribal Areas?"

"No no no no."

In a classroom that was just an empty cube of concrete, students sat cross-legged on the floor with copies of the Koran open in front of them on low wooden benches. Rocking back and forth as they chanted, their individual voices were lost in a babble of different passages. They looked remarkably like Jewish students reciting from the Talmud, and reminded me of the Jews I had seen at the Wailing Wall in Jerusalem during Sukkoth. One was a kid, but the rest were in their teens and twenties. Their days were gruelingly long. They got up at four o'clock in the morning, and read the Koran, prayed, or studied until eleven. After a break, they started again at one and kept at it until ten in the evening.

They paused in their reading of the Koran so that I could sit and talk with them for a minute. They were all very shy around the painfully white, blond Westerner, but without the slightest hint of hostility. One boy smiled nervously every time I met his eye. He told me, in halting English, "I was sort of afraid of you, that you are American."

"You're afraid?" I said, acting the Swiss journalist. "Have there been Americans here?"

They all shook their heads.

"Why not?"

"They are afraid to come here," he said.

This killed me. Here I was, sitting with these kids who are just as afraid of us as we are of them, lying about who I was and further perpetuating the problem.

Amjad, who was eighteen, had been at the madrassa for only three days. "I am here just to know the purpose of my life," he told me. "We don't have any idea what is the purpose of the human being, so here we read the Koran and we get education in the purpose of human beings, why we were created, so we know about our God, our prophet." He intended to become a mullah "to disseminate the same knowledge to others." He figured he'd be studying for eight or nine years.

I told him that one of the things we hear in the West a lot is that madrassas are places where hatred is taught. Hatred of the West, hatred of people who think differently, of other religions.

He said there's no hatred in Islam, adding, "The other people are opposing us, we are not opposing them." He included America among "the other people," and said, "America is the enemy of Islam." He thought that more Muslim teachers should go to the West and teach people, to clear up the misunderstandings.

Jamil, who was also eighteen, said he thought Westerners "are not on the right path, because they are not on the path of Islam. That's why they are facing problems."

One guy joked that he was going to give me a turban, so that I could go and fight.

"You gonna put me on jihad?" I laughed. "I'm already on a jihad. Jihad means to struggle, right? I'm struggling to understand."

He approved. Jihad is the best way to get into heaven, he said. "Jihad will continue until the Day of Judgment."

I don't know. Except for that mullah, I met no one at either of these madrassas who looked or spoke as if he could be a fanatic jihadist. I know looks can be deceiving, and maybe they were on their best behavior talking to the filmmaker, or they'd locked all the crazies in a room until I was gone. But still, these young guys just seemed like what they were supposed to be, religious students, maybe naïve, certainly young. But they didn't seem to hate Westerners; they just thought we were . . . misguided. I felt hopeful that someday we could reach out to the students in the madrassas we were told to be so scared of, to sit and actually share ideas and have conversations with them. Then again, I remembered what Dr. Post had told me—that terrorists were frightening precisely *because* they seemed completely normal, except for their ideological zeal.

On the surface Pakistan is a democracy, but it's the kind of democracy that's a heavily militarized feudal state where the generals have more power than the politicians. Military coups are more the norm than free elections. Presidents serve at the pleasure of the generals, and have often been generals themselves—like the current president, General Pervez Musharraf, who took power in a bloodless coup in 1999. There's a rash of political parties, mostly either tribal or Islamist in orientation, but they have little power. Along with coups, other bad business, like vote rigging, corruption scandals, and assassinations, have been regular occurrences in Pakistani politics.

A few months after I visited the madrassas, students gathered in Islamabad, the capital, to stage a huge demonstration in the streets near Lal Masjid, the Red Mosque in the center of town. The *khateeb* (administrator) of the mosque, Maulana Abdul Aziz, organized them in a Taliban-style movement to clean up Pakistan's sinful and Western ways. Male students went around the markets confiscating videos and DVDs they said were "pornographic." They made a pile of them in the street and burned them in a giant bonfire. Female students in black burkas lined the nearby rooftops and cheered them on, like at a bizarre pep rally. I watched it on TV. It was amazing. I couldn't help thinking of the Nazis burning piles of "degenerate" books by Jewish authors. The terrible, disgusting movies the students burned included *Home Alone 4* and *Free Willy*—not a porn movie about a guy who offers his willy for free but the original whale flick.

Darn, I was sorry I'd missed it. I would have cheered, too, when they threw *Home Alone 4* on the fire. If they'd given me advance notice, I could have sent them some other things to burn. The entire *Saved by the Bell* DVD collection, for example. I mean, Screech is just plain evil. And why stop with Willy? I think *Bambi* should be burned, too. The bit with the hunters killing Bambi's mom scarred me for life. I blame all my problems on Disney. Not to mention Snow White and her seven dwarfs. What were *they* up to? Nothing Allah would approve of, I betcha.

The Taliban wannabes weren't just burning bad movies, though. They were closing brothels and threatening barbers who shaved beards. Aziz had set up his own Sharia court right in Islamabad, and warned President Musharraf that if the government tried to stop him or the students there'd be suicide bombings. Incredible.

A few weeks after that, two thousand lawyers, along with members of various political parties, marched in the streets to protest Musharraf's firing of a Supreme Court judge, probably because the judge opposed his desire to hold on to both the presidency and his general's rank. There were some high-level political people marching, including Abida Hussein, who was Pakistan's ambassador to the United States in the early nineties.

"Musharraf is a liar," she declared. "He looks straight into the camera and lies to the people of Pakistan. He has zero credibility. . . . Musharraf is a primitive. He's incompetent, he's dishonest, and he has taken the whole world for a ride."

So Musharraf was getting it from both ends: from the radical Islamists, who would like Pakistan to become a rigid theocracy; and from lovers of freedom, who want the country to be a true democracy.

I met with Zafarullah Khan of the nonprofit Centre for Civic Education Pakistan, to see if he could help me understand the politics of this country that most people said had become Osama's home away from home away from home (if he really had left his home away from home, Afghanistan). Was Pakistan a democracy, a military dictatorship, or something in between? I wanted to know. And what did it all mean for Osama and his supporters?

"For the last sixty years, can you imagine, we have never voted out a single government," Zafarullah said to me. "At best, we can elect. I, as a citizen of Pakistan, have never been empowered to vote out somebody who has betrayed or shattered my dreams."

Zafarullah advocates for a full, open democracy in Pakistan. He has been jailed three times for his views.

So much for full, open democracy. The United States says it brings democracy to "friendly" nations like Pakistan, I noted. But Pakistan's democracy sounded pretty watered-down to me.

"You can't import or export democracy," Zafarullah said, echoing what I'd heard from many others on my trip. "At best, you can support democracy where people are struggling for that. And there is no one international, standard definition of democracy. Democracy varies. . . . But democracy is, in my opinion, a mind-set where you are free to choose your rulers, you can hold them accountable at the polling booth, there are systems where taxpayers' money could also be audited and accounted for, there should be some element of transparency. Some channels to voice my grievances, my views, my concerns." Not much of which exists in Pakistan.

With the spread of fundamentalism in Pakistan, Zafarullah said, the country was increasingly run by what he called a "mullah-military alliance." There were Islamist political parties that he felt were legitimate, but he didn't like the fact that they advocated "Islamic democracy." Democracy is democracy, he insisted—don't add qualifiers to it. Then there were the jihadists and the Taliban, who had no interest in democracy at all.

The United States is partly to blame for this situation, he said. Before the Soviet-Afghan War, religion in the region was more tolerant and pluralistic. During the war, we helped build and fund an entire industry for training and arming hard-line mujahideen and jihadists. When the Soviets were kicked out, he told me, "all these people became freelancers. They know only one art, and that art is to kill. So maybe ideally what should have happened was a transition of Afghanistan from an economy of war to an economy of peace." Instead, the country has just gone from one war to another.

When I asked Zafarullah if he thought the West could win the battle of hearts and minds against the Taliban and Osama and the jihadists, he said no, not as long as it's "coming as one component of a war ma-chine, as propaganda. Soldiers distributing toffees and all that."

If we bring real economic and humanitarian assistance, not just guns and tanks, he said, maybe we'll win people over.

Pakistan is supposed to be one of our allies in the War on Terror, yet it is constantly accused of being a terrorist factory. On the list of Amer-ica's allies in the GWOT, few have played a more confusing role. At the same time that Pakistan was making a grand show of helping its Amer-ican friends fight the Taliban and Al Qaeda, it was said to be a prime breeding ground for the Taliban—and, since 2001, the home base and central staging area for Al Qaeda's global jihad. I'd heard from numer-ous people that Pakistan was playing a dangerous game, trying to have it both ways—the moral equivalent of a mullet haircut.

In the 1980s, the CIA and Pakistan's Inter-Services Intelligence (the ISI, whose reputation for being badass nearly rivals both the Israeli Mossad and Suge Knight) worked together to help the Afghan rebels kick the Soviets out. After the defeat of the Soviets, the United States basically abandoned the Afghans to their fate. But Pakistan didn't. Not long after the Taliban appeared in 1994, Pakistan's military and the ISI began to give them weapons, money, and other forms of support in their civil war with the Northern Alliance. The Taliban became, in ef-fect, Pakistan's proxy army in Afghanistan. Why? Because, I was told, many of the Taliban had been radicalized in madrassas and mosques in Pakistan. And an Afghanistan run by the Taliban would likely be a friendlier neighbor to Pakistan than one in which unruly Northern Al-liance warlords were in control.

After the U.S. invasion of Afghanistan in 2001, President Musharraf found himself wedged between an enormous rock and a *very* hard place. The United States pressured him to help us round up all the Taliban and Al Qaeda fighters who had fled across the border into the Tribal Areas, and Musharraf had to show that he was complying with his U.S. backers' demands. But he had to move with extreme care so as not to alienate the Taliban-friendly ISI or the Pakistani people. The winds of fundamentalism blew very strongly through Pakistan. If Musharraf cracked down too hard, his own people could turn against him.

Pakistan arrested hundreds of alleged Taliban and Al Qaeda operatives, including Mullah Zaeef, whom I'd interviewed in Kabul. They
handed some over to the United States, and detained the rest in Pakistani prisons. In December 2003, there were two failed assassination
attempts against Musharraf in retaliation. Musharraf also sent troops
into Waziristan, where they got their asses handed to them in intense
fighting with the Taliban and the Taliban-loyal locals. In September
2006, he threw in the towel and negotiated a truce with Waziristan,
pulling his troops out. In effect, this left the area an autonomous state,
now run by the victorious Taliban—"Talibanistan," one observer called
it. That same month, Pakistan further shocked its U.S. ally by releasing
some 2,500 prisoners it had detained as suspected Taliban and Al Qaeda
members.

Not much had changed when I arrived in Pakistan two months later.
The Pakistani government, desperate to show that it wasn't *completely*
flubbing its role as America's partner in the GWOT, did offer to build
an Israeli-style security fence and lay mines along the western border,
to stem the free flow of Taliban and Al Qaeda fighters back and forth.
Given that the border runs along fifteen hundred miles of some the
steepest mountains in the world, no one took the idea seriously.

For me, General Hamid Gul embodied Pakistan's tricky role in regional affairs. He was the head of the ISI back during the Soviet-
Afghan War. In those days he was our ally, but by the time I met him he
had turned vehemently anti-American. At seventy, he was friendly and
courteous, speaking English with a wonderful Pakistani lilt. At the
same time, he ranted more like a teenage jihadist than any of the students I met at the madrassas.

I asked General Gul if he now thought it was a mistake that Pakistan
aligned itself with the United States back in the days when he ran the
ISI.

"I think it was necessary," he said. "*Now* aligning ourselves with the
Americans is a mistake. Because at that time it was in our interest. Now
Americans are at a cross-purpose with Pakistani objectives. And so they
are bullying us into cooperation. Threatening us to be bombed to the
Stone Age. What nonsense is this? They're disgracing us, aren't they?"

When I asked him how he felt about what was happening in
Afghanistan and Iraq, he said, "Well, there are two sentiments which

come up. One is, it's damn good that the entire Western part is getting a drubbing. And when the American ship sinks, all those sitting on that ship will go with it. So this will be the end of the Western domination. . . . And the second, it's awful, because it is going to disturb the world order which has existed, and has provided a certain modicum of security and harmony. [When] that gets disturbed, Muslims will suffer the most, this region will suffer the most. And perhaps the entire humanity will suffer. Already it is suffering more than ever before."

General Gul was certain that "the Americans are going to be defeated. And they will pull out. . . . Technology will not be defeated. Like the Russians—technology wasn't defeated. It was not the Russian tanks that were defeated, it was the Russian willpower that was defeated. The political will. The political will of America is the target of Al Qaeda or the Taliban or the people who are fighting in Iraq. So once their political will breaks . . . It's already become very feeble, it's come to a breaking point. When it goes, that's it."

General Gul scoffed when I asked him if Pakistan's policy of backing jihadists had blown back on it.

"What is jihad?" he demanded. "It is spirit, the spirit to resist, to stand up against oppression, against tyranny, against foreign occupation. That's what jihad is all about. It's a good thing. Jihad is a very good spirit. It's spirit that every young man must possess in himself." He said that among Pakistanis support for the jihadists was "very deep, because the political parties have failed them, the military establishment has failed to protect their frontiers against American onslaught. . . . In the eyes of the common man, the jihadi is a wonderful man. A man who is sincere, honest, pure, clean. He may look very simple, he may not have many words to offer, no big ideas, but there he is—he can lay down his life for a cause, and he's convinced that the cause is right. Otherwise you don't lay down your life."

Whoa. After that, I wasn't surprised to hear that General Gul was yet another 9/11 conspiracy theorist. He did not believe Osama bin Laden was involved in the attacks. He believed the Jews were behind it. Specifically, he was convinced that Mossad had actually recruited and trained the hijackers, not Al Qaeda.

Yes, even in Pakistan they drink the Kool-Aid.

General Gul seemed so bitter and angry, I had to ask him if he saw any hope for the future at all.

"Victory for us," he said. "That means if Afghans win, if Iraqis win, it's victory for all of us. And that's coming soon, sooner than we had all calculated."

Wow. After meeting General Gul, it seemed to me that maybe we should be less worried about the people running the madrassas in Pakistan and more concerned about the people running the government. The truth is, I heard more anti-Americanism and jihadist zeal from this grandfatherly man than from anyone else in Pakistan.

How some of America's former friends in Pakistan had become our bitter enemies was the topic of conversation over a candlelight dinner one night at the home of Kaiser and Faiza Hameed. They lived with two grown daughters in a big, suburban-style house in Islamabad. (They also had a son who was going to college in England.) I met them through Khurram Khan, a handsome young guy who looked like a movie star but actually ran the Kaghan Memorial Trust, which provides relief and aid to the millions of poor Pakistanis in the northern Kaghan Valley, devastated by a massive earthquake in 2005.

The Hameeds and Khurram belong to a part of Pakistani society that we rarely hear about, or from—the professional middle class. Nixon might have called them the Silent Minority. Well-educated and well-off, extremely articulate and worldly, they struggle to enjoy a good life in the midst of Pakistan's political and social turmoil. They're politically moderate and religiously tolerant, but they also sympathize with the anger and frustration they say can lead to violent extremism. And, like a lot of other people I spoke to, they were very critical of America's role in the region.

"I really get very upset and annoyed when people talk about 'Islamic extremism,'" Khurram told me. "There's no such thing. The term has no meaning. Islam isn't an extreme religion, it's a moderate religion. Talk about *Muslim* extremism, yes. The Islamic world, unfortunately right now, is in decline. We are in the Dark Ages. Like the Christian world went through its Dark Ages. Severe ignorance, violence, whatever. The religion has nothing to do with it, and this is what people need to understand. Now you've got societies around the world which are Muslim, which because of their colonial past, because they lost a lot out in the bigger game, whatever, they are in their worst moments right now. The governments maybe aren't functioning, and the economies aren't functioning, and the prosperity of the world isn't filtering down to the grass roots. And millions and millions of people who are extremely poor. And they are struggling day to day, trying to pay the bills, get food on the table for their children. . . . And so discontent is at the core of it, and discontent comes from the Muslim world being where it is right now. Islam should not be blamed. It's a socioeconomic problem."

Kaiser agreed. "After 9/11, the whole thing sort of blew up in our faces," he said. "And instead of trying to understand why it happened, you go around bombing the world—the Islamic world. You have to understand why it happened, and get down to the root causes of it. Try to redress those, not just that Islam is bad. Islam is one of the most liberal and easiest religions to follow. It's a very liberal religion, a very enlightening religion. But if it falls into the wrong hands, then any religion can become extremely violent. . . . We believe in the same God. We believe in the same messages. It's only the interpretation. Islamic interpretation has become a little wild. That needs to be redressed."

"What's led it to that, in your opinion?" I asked.

"I think the global politics," Kaiser said. "Because the modern-day jihad was created when the Soviets took over Afghanistan. That's where radical Islam took over. . . . The Americans financed jihad through various agencies. They were then freedom fighters. Suddenly the tables turned, and now they become terrorists. For nine to ten years, you armed them, you financed them, you built them. You trained them. Who is Osama bin Laden, whose creation was that? Or, for that matter, Saddam Hussein? Now you have a constant jihad."

Khurram agreed. He said the great powers have always treated Pakistan like a pawn in their geopolitical games.

"We get drawn into all of these games and we are used and we are taken in a certain direction, and then when the objective is achieved we are dropped," he said. "And it's happened several times in our history. In the seventies, when I was small, and in the early eighties, I remember very clearly, our people used to be very fond of the Americans—I guess the Second World War hangover, America being heroes all over the world. The public really loved them. And then we became their allies in the eighties, and that should have strengthened that bond. And then something really weird happened—the Americans won, and Americans not only didn't need us anymore but they suddenly turned on us. And the public, I think, was pretty hurt, and I think a lot of them were angry. It's like somebody you care about basically snubs you and insults you."

"But does that explain why there seem to be so many radicals and extremists in Pakistan now?" I asked.

"There are always radical elements in any society," he said. "There are radical elements in *your* society. They are always a very small minority, and they are normally on the fringe; nobody listens to them. Which is the situation that is here. Until the eighties, our religious elements were always fringe, and in the elections, I think, they never won more than two or three percent of the vote—never until the last election, where they won two provinces. That was post-9/11. . . . They were a fringe element, but when the economy was shattered, when our institutions were failing, people were suffering, and then you have a lot of dissatisfied young men, decent men from decent families, but they don't see any hope and they have soft minds and they are impressionable. And then these radical elements have the perfect recruiting grounds."

Khurram repeated his idea that the problems were political and social, not religious. "I mean, we need to understand that everything that is happening in the world does not have to do with Islam, and I would say it has nothing to do with Christianity," he said. "It's not a religious war as far as I'm concerned. This is a political war, it's a war for power. . . . I don't think any sane person in the world would actually say that suicide bombing is the right thing to do, but just try to understand why somebody would get to that mental level. Life is very precious, you know. Why would they put their life on the line? What would get them so frustrated? They are so frustrated because they've been lied to and they've been misled their whole lives by these big powers."

"Everywhere I've been in Afghanistan and Pakistan, people told me that suicide bombing is really new to this region," I told them.

"We never had this phenomenon," Khurram said. "And we ourselves are scared at what's happening. We've never seen this kind of thing. I tell people in the USA how I grew up in Peshawar, and Peshawar used to have bomb blasts literally every week, during the Soviet war—in shops, in markets, in cinemas, everything. And we lived with it. It didn't change our way of life. We adjusted. But after 9/11 I remember very clearly, I was going to my office—I was in Islamabad then—and I was at this traffic light, and there's this big American Embassy and a car parked next to me. I started feeling nervous, like, this is a target and I'm right next to it. It had changed so much, 9/11 changed so much. I was, like, shit, this is the first time I'm actually feeling scared."

"And what about the Taliban and Al Qaeda?" I asked. "Don't a lot of the Taliban come from Pakistan? And don't a lot of people in Pakistan, and even in the government, support the Taliban and Al Qaeda?"

"It's just unfortunate that Pakistan has been so badly targeted," Kaiser said. "Because of, supposedly, the terrorist training, or whatever. But if you look back into history, you then have a different point of view. We didn't set up the camps. We didn't finance them initially. It was the jihad that the Americans were fighting, and we fought on their behalf. Against what was then the Russian Empire. So overnight if you cut off these camps, their bread and butter is totally cut off. What do these people do who've been trained, who've been looked after? They're basically like orphans. Their families can't support them. So they get a life outside that structure. They are on the loose now. We are trying to cut it off, but it will take some time."

Unfortunately, it seemed to me that time was one of many resources Pakistan was sorely lacking.

CHAPTER 17

INTO THE WILD

— — — — — — — —

Your security is in your own hands.

Osama bin Laden, October 2004

My time was getting short, too. Li'l SpongeBob was almost due to bust out of the joint. I had promised Alex and myself that I'd be home for that. No way I was gonna miss it. If I was gonna find the Man, I had to do it now.

Since pretty much everybody told me that if he was in Pakistan he was probably in the mountainous areas along Pakistan's western border, that's where I'd search. Everybody had also told me it'd be really dangerous, but I'd come this far.

Just then, a madrassa in the Federally Administered Tribal Area of Bajaur was blown to bits, supposedly by a Pakistani air strike, killing eighty students. People there believed that it was done by the United States, and that Musharraf claimed responsibility to shield himself from backlash for allowing U.S. fighter planes to conduct an air strike in the Tribal Areas. Reports that the madrassa was an Al Qaeda training camp also received mixed reviews throughout the country.

The attack amplified everyone's opinion about my going into the North-West Frontier Province or the Federally Administered Tribal Areas.

"You will be killed, immediately," my fixer told me, "especially now."

"Someone will target you as soon as you get out of the car," another translator added. "You won't have a chance."

"I know why you want to go," a local journalist chimed in, "but they aren't even letting locals into that area now. I am a Pakistani, and they won't let me near the bomb site. If an Al Qaeda or Taliban fighter saw you walking around, you would become a symbol to them, and they probably wouldn't kill you right away. They would most likely use you for PR, torture you a bit before cutting off your head for the whole world to see."

I had to decide. I'd traveled thousands of miles, through all those countries, meeting hundreds of people. I'd learned so much about Osama and the impact of his ideas in the world. It was really hard to think about giving up now when I was so close. I wanted to meet him. I wanted to ask him how he justified all those innocent men, women, and children being murdered around the world for the sake of what he considered to be true Islam. I'd met so many other Muslims who were disgusted by these acts. I wanted him to explain himself. He was a family man. He surrounded himself with wives and children. He had sons the same age as those students I met at the madrassas. How did he rationalize the fact that some of those students might be persuaded to become suicide bombers for his cause, and go off to massacre other innocent fathers, mothers, and children? I wanted some answers.

During the 2001 invasion, when we had him cornered in Tora Bora, why didn't we do what it would take to capture him? Why did we hold back our troops and let the Northern Alliance fighters go in there after him—only to have him slip through their fingers? Back in the late 1990s, when the CIA had him in their crosshairs several times, why did the Clinton White House refuse permission to take him out?

Not to go all conspiracy-theory, but it did raise the remote possibility that our government might be playing some kind of game by keeping this guy alive—using him, as I'd heard from more than one person on my travels, as a "scarecrow," to keep us all in a state of fear and to justify some highly questionable foreign policy. Or maybe they *had* killed him, and decided it was better to just let him fade away. Or maybe they really didn't know where he was.

Who knows. One man in Kabul had told me I'd never find Osama because he was "invisible." Like a ghost, a myth, a figment of our imagination. He was everywhere and nowhere, like Keyser Söze in *The Usual Suspects*, a man who had become a living myth.

And yet wasn't I on this trip to confront that myth, that ghost, and the fears you and I have been trained to feel about him? Wasn't that the whole point?

Oh man, I was filled with questions, confusion, and fear. It seemed that my options were (a) give up and go home, or (b) get kidnapped and killed. I hate choices like that. I have enough trouble choosing between asparagus and broccoli, Cherry Garcia and Chunky Monkey, Bennifer and Brangelina.

In the end, I decided that I, at least, had to go and have a look. Maybe everyone was exaggerating the dangers. I had to find out for myself.

From Peshawar we drove west, until we reached the border of the Khyber Agency. It's the Federally Administered Tribal Area that includes the Khyber Pass through the mountains to Afghanistan. It's real Talibanistan, and as likely a place as any for the Man to be hanging.

The border crossing turned out to be just a couple of bedraggled cinder-block shacks on either side of the road, with a pair of bored-looking guards lounging around, their automatic weapons casually slung over their shoulders. A steady flow of trucks, cars, and bicycles passed in both directions. The guards weren't stopping any vehicles to check IDs or, you know, take a peek in the back of any truck for weapons or explosives.

It looked easy enough. I decided to cross the border on foot. It just seemed appropriate. One small step for a man, one giant leap into the unknown for me. We pulled the car over a few hundred feet from the crossing and I got out.

And right on cue, I swear to Allah, there was an explosion somewhere across the line. Not in the distance but nearby, and *very* loud. Like a huge clap of thunder, only it wasn't thunder. It made me jump inside my skin, and my heart began to race. And then there was another explosion, and another and another and another. They sounded like grenades or mortars, followed by the crackle of automatic weapons.

Nice welcoming committee. What was I walking into?

Nothing else changed. The guards didn't stir, the trucks and cars kept passing me. I guess if you live in that area you get used to the sounds of explosions and machine guns.

But not me. My heart pounded as loud as those explosions as I trudged reluctantly up the side of the road toward the border line. Every step brought me closer to the boom-boom and rat-a-tat. What the hell was I doing? You're supposed to run away from those kinds of noises, not stroll toward them.

About ten feet from the line I stood under a big green sign, the kind you'd see along any highway. It said:

WELCOME TO KHYBER AGENCY

Well, that seemed friendly enough. But right next to it was a smaller sign that said:

ATTENTION
ENTRY OF FOREIGNERS IS PROHIBITED
BEYOND THIS POINT
BY ORDER OF
THE PAKISTANI GOVERNMENT

I could have kept going. Those guards sure wouldn't give a damn. But as I stood there, listening to the gunfire and explosions up ahead, I suddenly began remembering everything people told me over the course of this joruney. There were voices swimming through my head as I stood there on the edge of the deep end of the pool.

First, there was Reza Aslan, way back in New York, who told me over a plate of hummus that "fundamentalism is a *reactionary* ideology, that it needs something to rebel against," and that the United States has "legitimized the vision of the world that this small group of lunatics have . . . by the way we've conducted ourselves in the War on Terror." I didn't believe what he was saying until I started seeing what he was talking about outside my country. It was a sentiment that was reiterated by Steve Coll, who told me in D.C. that since September 11, we've "expected pure military force to be the answer to too many questions," and that "you can't win the War on Terror with an army alone." That was becoming perfectly clear to me.

In London, Muslim MP Shahid Malik said that "condemning these people isn't enough," and went on to say that he and his fellow Muslims around the world have a responsibility "to *confront* them. . . . We've got to create zero tolerance." After all, it's their religion that is getting hijacked.

But as former PIRA leader turned MP Martin McGuinness pointed out while I was in Northern Ireland, "people who are not prepared to talk or to resolve conflict through peaceful and democratic means are absolutely doomed to failure."

And Judge Brugière in France first brought up the cold reality that "if Osama bin Laden is captured or killed, unfortunately, that event will not have any specific impact on the revolution," underscoring that it wasn't about Osama bin Laden per se, but about the lives of the people to whom his message appealed.

I remembered Habib in the high-rise concrete apartment building, in the poor outskirts of Paris, who awoke some mornings wondering if he was in an insane asylum, where, he said, crime or religion were the only salvation.

And Saad Ibrihim in Egypt, who was jailed and tortured by the Mubarek regime, pointed out that "people are not born radical. . . . [But] if you block channels of fair and equal participation, people become radicalized. They become outraged and angry."

I also couldn't forget the Muslim Brotherhood member arrested and jailed for years, who asked, "Who could imagine that the United States, the mother of democracy and freedom, supports regimes like these tyrannical Arabic ones . . . regimes that kill people, practice corruption, and steal the wealth throughout the region? . . . This is not the face of America." And it was not a face I liked seeing being reflected back at me in a mirror.

I remembered the ghetto of Sidi Moumon in Morocco, where the young suicide bombers came from, and where journalist Aboubakr Jamai told me the people "are completely forgotten by the state in general. No electricity, no sewer system, no running water." And I wondered what providing things like that would do for people in a place so desperate. Then I thought of the meal I'd shared in that shantytown, in that tiny little house, with Ahmed and his family, where he told me that he just wanted "to be happy in my life and have a very good family. . . . And sleep without any problem."

I recalled the advice of Nadia Yassine, who said, "All we have left for a peaceful future and world is one possibility—it is civilian societies. . . . We have to reach out to each other. And ignore official political lines." It's what I'd been trying to do on this trip.

Then I thought back to all the people living in fear in Israel and in the Palestinian territories. The young boys in the refugee camp who idolize Osama bin Laden, who see him as a hero. And the boy who said that when he says "America's name, it gives me stomach and chest pains" because "their [American's] lives are to be against Islam."

And I will never forget the face of Aliyah, the Iraqi mother I spoke to in the camp, one of the millions of Iraqis who have fled the country since the U.S. invasion in 2003, who felt lost, who felt she had nothing, neither in Jordan nor in Iraq. How will she and her family see America in the years to come? What will become of *her* sons? Will they become martyrs like their uncles? Or will they strive for peace? Some would say that's impossible, but the time I spent under the olive trees with Elik, the former IDF soldier whose own sister had been killed by a suicide bomber, reminded me otherwise. He said, "As an Israeli who has a responsibility for what's happening here, I must come here and tell them that I am willing to work for peace." A sentiment that was reiterated by the Palestinian tour guide Ali Jiddah when he said "give my people hope."

On my trip it seemed like that's what a lot of people were looking for.

I thought of the talk I'd had with Vice Premier Shimon Peres (who would go on to become president of Israel) in which he reminded me, "We all the time have handled the situation through strategies and diplomacy. They are useless. What introduces the new age is a modern economy." The sooner we can pick up the countries that are so far behind economically, the sooner people won't be looking to lash out.

Then the night I spent in the desert of Saudi Arabia came rushing back. I thought of all the people I'd met in that country who were incredibly honest about the existence of terrorists in their homeland and what should be done from within.

And then there was Afghanistan, a place that had suffered through so much in the last thirty years and was again caught in the middle of a siege with no end in sight. I remembered all the weathered locals who looked as if they'd already lived three lifetimes. Colonel Steve Williams sat in his plywood office drinking Dr. Pepper, saying that the key to defeating the Taliban and ending the fighting was to focus on the "center of gravity," the people. He said when you provide the basics—clean drinking water, schools for their kids, medical clinics, roads, electricity—you make it harder for counterinsurgencies to gain momentum.

And at that moment, I heard the words of an Iraq war veteran named Joe B., whom I'd spoken to months earlier when I was home in West Virginia. He had recently returned from his second tour in Iraq and had since retired from the military. He told me that America has a great responsibility and a tremendous amount of power in the world, today, and that "each day, we have the ability to either help or to hurt."

And here I stood. Staring at that sign, the road beside me running up to where Osama could be. Somewhere up the Khyber Pass. Somewhere in those mountains. Somewhere that still felt a million miles away.

"He's just one man," a local Pakistani in Peshawar had told me a few days earlier.

"Osama bin Laden is nothing, sir. You have to focus on the root causes," his friend added.

After traveling thousands of miles to get to this one point, the sum of my entire trip finally fell into place. We can't fight a War on Terror without fighting the things that cause normal, rational people to sympathize with terrorists. That's the only way ahead in this struggle.

This whole quest began because nineteen normal, sane young men were mesmerized by what Dr. Post called "the destructive, charismatic leadership of Osama bin Laden," and were convinced that committing suicide on 9/11 was a noble, sacred act. I'd heard so much about others committing suicide for Osama and his ideals at every stage of my trip. And I did not want to join their ranks. Getting blown away for the sake of meeting Osama bin Laden had never been part of the plan. I had promised Alex I'd come home in one piece. I was about to become a father. That was more important to me than anything else.

I then remembered something else Colonel Williams at KAF said to me when I asked him for some fatherly advice. I asked him what was the most important thing I could do as a father, and he said *be there*. Be there for your children.

"Enjoy them while you have them," he said. "The biggest thing I miss is that my boys grew up so fast, and because I've been in the military their entire life, and gone a lot, I missed a lot of things. So enjoy your children. Try to teach them right from wrong, teach them how to trust people and what not to trust, and hope they grow up to be good human beings, because it's a role of the dice sometimes. But enjoy them, that's the biggest thing."

I remembered Colonel Leppert at Fort Apache saying pretty much the same thing: "Don't sacrifice your family for your career. If anything, sacrifice your career for your family." And Avi, the bomb-squad guy in Tel Aviv, telling me, "Quality time with your kid. That's the most important."

I thought of all the beautiful families I'd met on my journey. Some extremely poor, like Ahmed's in Sidi Moumen and the people at the refugee camp. Others better off, like the Maxes in Jerusalem and the Hameeds in Islamabad. I remembered how the love, warmth, care, and commitment I'd felt in those households—rich and poor—had been so strong it had moved me to tears more than once.

I wanted that more than I wanted to meet Osama. As much as I would love to cross that border, go deep into those mountains, and knock on OBL's door, I felt that those bombs and guns were telling me it was time for me to finally exercise some good judgment. I had come so far, realized so much, but with a baby on the way, I had so much farther to go. I closed my eyes for a second and thought of home and how much I missed Alex, and how much I loved the beautiful little baby that was in her tummy. How I couldn't wait to see them both.

And that was when I decided.

"This is far enough," I said to myself. "Screw Osama. I'm going home."

And I turned and walked back down the road to the car.

That was that. I hadn't found Osama bin Laden—but then again, no one else had, either. I didn't feel so bad.

On my flight back to New York, I thought again about what Othman had said to me in Saudi Arabia, about Osama living in the hearts of Muslims everywhere. I still didn't fully agree, but it made me feel better about not actually meeting the Man face-to-face. I knew now I never had to. The place to look for Osama—or at least the spirit that created him—wasn't in some cave in Afghanistan or the mountains of Pakistan, but in the hearts and actions of the people everywhere whose lives he's had such a huge impact on. Even though I never got to look him in the eye, I saw reflections of him in hundreds of faces, and occasionally saw him glaring at me through the eyes of people along the way. One way or another, I'd found Osama everywhere I'd gone—in London and Paris, in Cairo and Casablanca, in the Baqa'a refugee camp, Throatcutter's village, Jeddah, and the madrassas of Peshawar.

It also occurred to me, now that I'd spent months looking for him all over the place, that if I wanted to find Osama I never even had to leave home. Yes, I could have found Osama without ever leaving Kansas, Toto. Because he was right there all around me, in every newspaper and magazine, all over the TV and the Internet; he was there whenever a cop waited at the subway entrance to check my backpack, and whenever I saw an "Arab-looking" guy on the street and felt an involuntary flicker of suspicion; he lived in the way the U.S. government had turned itself inside out and our lives upside down in reaction to him. He *was* everywhere.

Not that I regretted a second of this trip. It had been such a blessing and an eye-opener for me just to be able to experience so many cultures and meet so many people. Since September 11—heck, since the beginning of time—one of the biggest fears we've had to face is our fear of the Other, the Outsider, the Stranger. And since 9/11 the Other looked like almost everybody I saw or met on this trip once I left Europe. The Other was that dark-skinned, Arab-looking man with the black beard, or the shaved head, wearing a *kufi* (skullcap). The Other was that woman wearing a veil over her head. From Egypt to Pakistan, I didn't see or meet a soul who couldn't have been stopped and interrogated coming into JFK, and gotten suspicious, fearful looks anywhere they went in the United States. (Months later, MP Shahid Malik would be detained at JFK, and he doesn't even have a beard!)

For me, the tables were turned on this trip. Now I was the Outsider, the Stranger, the one who stood out in every crowd. The one who couldn't speak the language, who didn't know the customs, who drew suspicious stares every time I stepped out of a car. I was the Other everyone looked at and wondered, "Who is he? Why is he here? What does he want?" It's a pretty frightening experience to be that person, the one people are afraid of, because in their minds I represented the invader, the enemy of their culture, who want to destroy their way of life.

And sometimes it was just pretty funny. Like in Pakistan, when we were driving through a village and I looked out and said, "Dude, I'm the palest guy in the village."

Then—I'm not making this up—an albino rode by on a bicycle.

"All right," I said, "I'm the *second*-palest guy in this village."

See, Allah does have a sense of humor.

And yet, as different as I was everywhere I went, I could never get over how warmly I was greeted and how generously I was welcomed into people's lives and homes. People who had nothing, almost literally nothing, begging me to share it with them. And how very careful they were, everywhere, to distinguish between the American people and the policies of the American government that they didn't agree with. I met people everywhere who expressed tremendous love and respect for America and Americans, and great anger and hurt over what our government has done. They believe we have turned the world against us, and have become the last country that should be preaching "democracy" or "peace."

Everywhere I went, whether it was a shantytown like Sidi Moumen or the wilderness of western Pakistan, people were connected to the rest of the world through satellite TV, the Internet, cell phones. Everywhere. It was incredible. And it means we have these extraordinary opportunities to reach out to one another—to communicate, to educate. There's no excuse for ignorance anymore—whether it's us holding on to our ignorant stereotypes of Muslims or not taking responsibility for our role in the world's problems or Muslims insisting on believing conspiracy theories and not taking responsibility for the problems within their own communities. Everyone waving the finger at somebody else, and nobody willing to clean up his own house. There's no excuse for that anymore. We're all on this *Titanic* together.

We Americans, as the world's superpower, have both the ability and the obligation to start changing that. That isn't restricted to people at the top; it needs to start at the bottom, with folks like you and me. We should be the ones who reach out, who try to understand the Other. All those Others we're told are bad people, violent people, hateful people—I met a lot of them on this trip, and the vast majority didn't fit any of those stereotypes. They're people like us. They want the same things for themselves and their families that we do. They want peace, they want security, they want respect, they want to be able to give their children a good, decent life, an education . . . a home. Just like us. Remember what the kid said to me at the madrassa in Pakistan? "We're afraid of you." The sooner we make the effort to reach out to them, the sooner we can turn the *Titanic* around before it hits the iceberg.

Another thing this trip taught me for sure: the United States is in no position to be marching around the world, ordering everyone to love democracy and imitate our idea of what society should be. If they want democracy, great—but they have to work for it and fight for it and create it themselves, their own version. Democracy has to be a choice in order to be successful. And, given an equitable playing field, a good example, and the support to succeed, democracy can flourish.

Can democracy and Islam coexist? Sure, they can. But they have to stop qualifying it. Democracy is democracy. Period. Turkey's an Islamic state, and Turkey has a functioning elected government. It could happen in Egypt, Morocco, Jordan, even Saudi Arabia. It's just going to take time.

And it's going to take America's leaders in government trying to understand what regular people in all the nations of the world—especially those experiencing heart-wrenching conflict—hope for. We need to pursue policies that support the organic growth of democracy. Because, in the long term, that's what will make America prosperous, respected, safe, and maybe even beloved again. The more we try to call for democracy while supporting repressive regimes, the more resistance, anger, and violence we will see in the world. How many times did I hear people say that on my trip?

If we're really going to try to make the world a better place for our children and all the children everywhere, we have to reexamine where we're putting our efforts, our money, our armies, everything. And we individual Americans, as citizens of "the world's greatest democracy," have to do it. It's our responsibility as citizens and voters to make our country a more positive influence on the world stage. We need to beome problem-*solving* citizens of the global community, and we need to elect leaders who are open and willing to make these tough decisions.

Then maybe we won't have to live in a culture of fear, always looking over our shoulders, wondering what bad thing is going to happen next. That'll be a great day. Hopefully, it will come soon.

When my plane landed at JFK, a rush of relief overtook me. I was so close to home. After traveling more than thirty thousand miles, the end was in sight.

I went through customs, and when the official looked at my picture and then at my bearded face, he said, "Where have you been?"

"Where haven't I been?" I responded, and then rattled through my itinerary for the last few months. He flipped the pages in the passport, looking at all the stamps, the visas, the dates, the signatures.

"That's quite a trip," he said.

"Tell me about it."

He slammed the stamp on the inkpad and then in my passport.

"Welcome home, Mr. Spurlock," he said, as he handed it to me. I wanted to kiss the ground I was so excited.

I grabbed my bags and loaded them into the van waiting outside. When my friend Rob dropped me off three months prior, I was a straight-and-narrow, clean-shaven kid. When he saw this bearded, swarthy character emerge from the gate, he couldn't help laughing.

"Look at you, ya terrorist. You need anything?"

I gave him a big hug.

"I need to go home," I said, and we pushed the cart outside, packed the van, and headed to Brooklyn.

I hadn't seen Alex in almost two months, and my whole body had butterflies. It was eight in the morning, and after more than twenty-four hours of straight travel all I wanted was to be in her arms. I ran inside, throwing my bags in the doorway, and jumped into bed with her. She started crying, and I couldn't let go of her. She felt so good, I had to keep opening my own eyes just to be sure it was happening. I was home, I was really home. Safe and sound . . . finally.

I put my head on her stomach and spoke to little Spongey, who would be in our arms in less than two weeks.

"I love you, little baby. You hear that? It's your daddy and I'm home and I love you and I won't leave again."

"You promise?" Alex asked me.

I held her tight.

"I promise."

On the morning of December 8, Alex went into labor. Not panting, "hoo ha, hoo ha, hoo ha" labor but definitely signs that the alien inside wanted out. We spent the day walking in the park, watching movies, eating good food, and timing the contractions. She would grab my hand, the sign that one had just started, and then I would look at my watch, seeing how long it lasted and how close it was to the previous one.

This went on for thirty-two hours, until noon on Friday, December 9, when she went into active labor. We'd decided to have the baby at home, against the advice of both our parents, my sister-in-law, and every other person we knew who was a doctor or knew a doctor or watched doctor shows on TV.

We'd rented a birthing tub, and I had put it together a few days earlier in the basement. (As well as rigging new lamps and dimmers so we could film the birth, in hi-def no less. What do you expect? I'm a filmmaker and, yes, my wife is a saint for putting up with me. We've already agreed on that.) We climbed into the tub together and spent the next four hours in it while she pushed and rested, pushed and rested, pushed and rested.

With the help of our midwife, doula, and homeopath, Alex worked through the entire process like a trooper. Then, at 3:30, the midwife said, "Morgan, put your hand between her legs. You can feel the baby's head." I reached down with my right hand and touched the top of the little head that was trying to come out. I lost it. Tears poured from my eyes and I kissed Alex. I held her close as she pushed for the next forty minutes, encouraging her, loving her, helping in the only way I could. She had decided against any drugs or medication, opting to experience the birth as millions of women had for centuries. "We've numbed ourselves to the experience of creating life, and I want to know how that feels," she always said. Well, now, *boy* was she feeling it. She was in the zone, on another plane, and doing something that I was amazed by.

At 4:10 P.M., as I held Alex, our baby was pulled from the water and placed in our arms.

"It's a boy," the midwife said.

A boy. A son. Our son. I wiped the tears from my cheeks and kissed Alex, and he opened his eyes and looked at us. I had thought for months that we would have a girl, but now, here in my arms was my son, Laken James.

As I sat there looking at him, I felt my world change. My life as I had known it was over. Not in a bad way, but in a way that instantly showed me that this little man in my arms was now the most important thing on the planet. He was my life. I suddenly didn't matter.

And I resolved that day to do many things for him:

To make him proud and to make him happy. To love him every day and to teach him love. To offer him every opportunity possible and not to spoil him.

To teach him to work hard and to play every day, and that the two can be the same thing. To expose him to as many people and cultures as I possibly can and always to be there for him, whatever he needs: a shoulder to cry on, an arm to lean on, a friend to listen, or a hand to pull him up. And most of all . . . to keep him safe.

These are the things that people all over the world told me they wanted for their children, and it never hit me how similar all our wishes were until I looked into my son's eyes and saw the beginning of his life.

I want him to know these people. Not to see them as "the Other," but as people he shares this world with, people who have ideas that he can learn from and share experiences and ideas that will alter his worldview. I don't want him to be afraid of what's out there or of what might happen.

And if he can start to see the world through eyes of acceptance, then maybe another child can, and another, and another.

Maybe one day, if we're lucky, all these children can teach us something, and open our eyes and our hearts and our minds to peace.

Insha'Allah.

Im Yirtzeh Hashem.

God willing.

ACKNOWLEDGMENTS

There are so many people to thank for making this book and journey possible. First, I'd like to again acknowledge my wife, her support and her patience, especially because after she had the baby, I spent the first eight weeks of Laken's life banging out the majority of what you just read, taking breaks to make food for Alex, stare at this amazing little creation, and dispose of the creations he made in his pants. Next to her, the most important person I want to thank is my editor, Jennifer Hershey, for always supporting me, my voice, and my vision. Her input, guidance, and ability to find the story were irreplaceable. As was her patience, especially because I kept missing deadlines. And you wouldn't even be holding this if it wasn't for all those tenacious geniuses at Random House who stood by me even when most people thought this idea was nuts. I want to thank my agent, Elyse Cheney (who was also having a baby at the same time as Alex), who called me to find out how the book was coming mere days after she had had her daughter! With dedication like that, believe me, her advice is always worth taking.

And I want to thank Adam and Stephen Dell. (Who would have thought that drinks at Bungalow 8 would turn into this?!) Thanks for lighting the fuse behind my search. Everyone at Sloss Law and Cinetic, especially John Sloss and Paul Brennan, you guys are my heroes. To the whole gang at Wild Bunch, thanks for letting me make the movie and write this book. Vincente and Agnes, I would work with you guys any day. I want to tip my hat and my heart to all the folks at the Gersh Agency: David Gersh, Bob Gersh, Kara Baker, Jen Konawal, and Richard Arlook (I'm gonna miss you, man). I want to kiss Arianna Bocco on the mouth for opening the door to make this whole thing happen.

I want to thank my family at Warrior Poets and the whole WITW Is OBL production team: Jeremy Chilnick, Elizabeth Hamilton, Stacey Offman, Sarah Timewell, Jamin Mendelsohn, Daniel Marracino, Fish, Pallie G, Julie Bob, Freedom, Gavin, Jen, Katrina, Alyssa, Nick, and The Mangler. My assistant, Sarah Nevada Smith—thanks for telling me when to go home and for helping me keep my head on straight. My researcher and AP, Karen Pelland—thanks again for helping pull all the pieces of the puzzle together, even when we had no idea what the puzzle was gonna look like! John Strausbaugh, Jim Armstrong, and Jonathan Drubner—thanks for always helping me find more "smart and funny" in what I'm doing.

I especially want to acknowledge war correspondent and Brit journalist James Brabazon and our right-hand security man, AJ, for keeping me alive in all the hairy places we went! I owe you guys one. I also couldn't have done this without all the fixers who watched over us and helped set up interviews in all the countries we traveled to. These guys have become targets now, they get kidnapped and killed for commiserating with the "enemy," so they are truly heroic.

And most importantly, for all the men and women of the U.S. military I met overseas—thank you for your service and for doing what you do without question. I hope you get to come home soon.

And lastly, the man this book wouldn't have been possible without, Osama bin Laden—let me know where you are and I'll send you a copy.

BIBLIOGRAPHY

Abdelhadi, Magdi. "Accused Morocco Islamist Speaks Out." BBC News, September 30, 2005.

Abrashi, Fisnik, and Jason Straziuso. "Afghanistan Five Years Later: Poverty, Violence, Misery." Associated Press, October 7, 2006.

Agence France-Presse. "Iran Sheltering bin Laden Sons and Al-Qaeda Members." October 26, 2005.

Ahmed-Ullah, Noreen S., and Kim Barker. "Schooled in Jihad." *Chicago Tribune*, November 28, 2004.

Al Jazeera. "French 'Had bin Laden in Sights.' " December 19, 2006.

Allam, Abeer. "Egyptian Mobile Phone Provider Treads Where Others Dare Not." *The New York Times*, February 13, 2006.

Ambah, Faiza Saleh. "The Would-Be Terrorist's Explosive Tell-All Tale." *The Washington Post*, July 24, 2006.

Amnesty International. "Afghanistan: Refugees from Afghanistan: The World's Largest Single Refugee Group." November 1, 1999.

Applebaum, Anne. "Finding Things to Fear." *The Washington Post*, September 24, 2003.

Aslan, Reza. *No god but God*. New York: Random House, 2005.

Assad, Samar. "A History of Israeli-Palestinian Prisoner Exchanges." *CounterPunch*, July 14–17, 2006.

Asser, Martin. "Mubarak's Quarter of a Century." BBC News, October 13, 2006.

Associated Press. "Fierce Debate Over Veils in Egypt." October 31, 2006.

Associated Press. "Reserves, National Guard Feel Strain." December 16, 2006.

Bard, Mitchell G. "Myths & Facts Online: Jerusalem." Jewish Virtual Library, www.jewishvirtuallibrary.org/jsource/myths/mf20.html#k.

BBC News. "Full Text: 'Bin Laden's Message.' " November 12, 2002.

———. "Saudi Police 'Stopped' Fire Rescue." March 15, 2002.

Berger, Robert. "Abbas Mulls Next Move as Unity Talks with Hamas Collapse." Voice of America, December 1, 2006.

Birsel, Robert. "Pakistan's Afghan Border Fence Plan 'Impractical.' " Reuters, December 27, 2006.

Boof, Kola. "His Prerogative." *Harper's*, September 2006.

Bowcott, Owen. "Gerry Adams to Meet Hamas Leaders." *The Guardian*, September 4, 2006.

Carter, Jimmy. *Palestine: Peace Not Apartheid*. New York: Simon & Schuster, 2006.

Center for Policing Terrorism. "Analysis: May 16, 2003, Suicide Bombings in Casablanca, Morocco." See http://209.85.165.104/search?q=cache:N4ThVn8uyioJ:www.centerforpolicingterrorism.net/pdf_secure.php%3Fpdffilename%3DCasablancav2+morocco+bombings+may+16&hl=en&ct=clnk&cd=1&gl=us.

Clarke, Liam, and Kathryn Johnston. *Martin McGuinness: From Guns to Government*. Edinburgh and London: Mainstream, 2001.

Clarke, Richard A., et al. *Defeating the Jihadists: A Blueprint for Action*. New York and Washington, D.C.: Century Foundation Press, 2004.

CNN. "Al Qaeda Threatens More UK, U.S. Attacks." August 4, 2005.

———. "Al Qaeda Threat Over Pope Speech." September 18, 2006.

Coll, Steve. *Ghost Wars*. New York: Penguin, 2004.

———. "Young Osama." *The New Yorker*, December 12, 2005.

Cornwell, Rupert. "Bush: God Told Me to Invade Iraq." *The Independent*, October 7, 2005.

Cyphers, Luke, and Bruce Feldman. "The Good Son." *ESPN Magazine*, September 16, 2002.

Daily Times (Pakistan). "Americans Bombed the Bajaur Madrassa." November 27, 2006.

———. "No Law at Guantánamo Bay Prison, Says Zaeef." September 17, 2005.

Eggen, Dan. "FBI Agents Still Lacking Arabic Skills." *The Washington Post*, October 11, 2006.

El-Hennawy, Noah. "Abdel Monem Abou El-Fotouh." *Egypt Today*, March 2006.

Fallows, James. "Declaring Victory." *The Atlantic Monthly*, September 2006.

Farah, Douglas, and Dana Priest. "Bin Laden Son Plays Key Role in Al Qaeda." *The Washington Post*, October 14, 2003.

Ford, Peter. "Deep Roots of Paris Riots." *The Christian Science Monitor*, November 4, 2005.

Furedi, Frank. *Politics of Fear*. London: Continuum, 2005.

Gall, Carlotta. "Pakistan Premier Wants Afghan Refugees to Return Home." *The New York Times*, January 5, 2007.

Glassner, Barry. *The Culture of Fear*. New York: Basic Books, 1999.

Glazov, Jamie. "Eurabia." FrontPageMagazine.com, September 21, 2004.

Glover, Julian. "British Believe Bush Is More Dangerous Than Kim Jong-Il." *The Guardian*, November 3, 2006.

Goldberg, Jeffrey. "Inside Jihad U." *The New York Times*, June 25, 2000.

Griffin, Christopher. "An Imperiled Mission?" *Armed Forces Journal*, April 2006.

Haider, Kamran. "Thousands Protest Over Move to Sack Pakistani Judge." Reuters, April 3, 2007.

Hamm, Mark S. "Crimes Committed by Terrorist Groups: Theory, Research and Prevention." Report commissioned by the U.S. Department of Justice, September 2005.

Harrigan, Steve. "Swedes Reach Muslim Breaking Point." Fox News, November 26, 2004.

Harter, Pascale. "Morocco's Shock at Madrid Bomb 'Link.' " BBC News, March 17, 2004.

Hederson, Dan, and Dan McGinn. "IRA Challenged for 'Holding on to Weapons.' " *The Independent*, February 1, 2006.

Human Rights Watch. "The Silent Treatment: Fleeing Iraq, Surviving in Jordan." November 28, 2006.

Khan, M. Ilyas. "Will Pakistan's Fence Plan Work?" BBC News, January 4, 2007.

Klausen, Jytte. "Counterterrorism and the Integration of Islam in Europe." *Watch on the West*, vol. 7, no. 7, July 2006.

Lang, Thomas. "Aboubakr Jamai on Fighting Moroccan Government Censorship." *CJR Daily*, May 20, 2005.

Laurence, Jonathan. "Islam in France," The Brookings Institution, December 2001.

Lawrence, Bruce, ed. *Messages to the World: The Statements of Osama bin Laden.* New York and London: Verso, 2005.

Lipton, Eric. "Come One, Come All, Join the Terror Target List." *The New York Times*, July 12, 2006.

Lipton, Eric, and Matthew L. Wald. "Liquid Explosives Still Tough to Detect." *The New York Times*, August 10, 2006.

Lipsky, Seth. "A Fair Sheik?" *The Wall Street Journal*, October 24, 2001.

Looney, Robert. "Can Saudi Arabia Reform Its Economy in Time to Head Off Disaster?" *Strategic Insights*, January 2004.

Loyd, Anthony, and Tahir Luddin. "The Face of Afghanistan Five Years After Fall of the Taleban." *The Times* (London), November 11, 2006.

MacLeod, Scott. "Aboubakr Jamai." *Time Europe*, May 14, 2006.

Mannes, Aaron. "Inadequate Response." *National Review*, July 7, 2005.

Mascolo, George, and Erich Follath. "Meet the bin Ladens." *Der Spiegel*, June 6, 2005.

McGrory, Daniel. "The Day When Osama Bin Laden Applied for Asylum—in Britain." *The Times* (London), September 29, 2005.

McMahon, Janey. "For Security Reasons." *Washington Report on Middle East Affairs*, September 1998.

McNaught, Anita. "The King and the Sheikh's Daughter." BBC News, March 28, 2002.

Migdalovitz, Carol. "Morocco: Current Issues." CRS Report for Congress, January 11, 2005.

Musharbash, Yassin. "The Future of Terrorism." *Der Spiegel*, August 12, 2005.

Page, Jeremy. "Pakistani Hardliners 'Cleanse' Capital Taleban-Style." *The Times* (London), April 7, 2007.

Pelham, Lipka. "Finding Holes in West Bank Barrier." BBC News, November 30, 2006.

Pew Research Center for the People & the Press. "A Year After Iraq War." March 16, 2004, http://people-press.org/reports/display.php3?ReportID=206.

Post, Jerrold M., ed. *The Al-Qaeda Training Manual*. USAF Counterproliferation Center, Maxwell Air Force Base (Ala.), 2005.

Powell, Bill. "The Enemy Within." *Time Europe*, October 23, 2005.

Prados, Alfred B., and Christopher M. Blanchard. "Saudi Arabia: Terrorist Financing Issues." Congressional Research Service Report for Congress, updated December 8, 2004.

Rachidi, Ilhem. "Pushing Islam to the Extremes." *Asia Times*, July 1, 2005.

Rashid, Ahmed. "US Support for Northern Alliance Rankles Pakistan." The Eisenhower Institute, October 22, 2001.

Reporters Without Borders. "Managing Editor Resigns to Spare His Newspaper Impossible Damages Payment." January 18, 2007.

Ridolfo, Kathleen. "Al-Zarqawi Brings Al-Qaeda's Jihad to Jordan." Radio Free Europe, November 10, 2005.

Roggio, Bill. "Talibanistan: The Establishment of the Islamic Emirate of Waziristan." *The Fourth Rail*, September 5, 2006.

Rovers, Ronald. "The Silencing of Theo van Gogh." Salon.com, November 24, 2004.

Sahar, Pakhtun. "Refugees: Afghan Camps in Pakistan to Close in July." Inter Press Service News, June 6, 2006.

Scheuer, Michael. *Through Our Enemies' Eyes*. Dulles, Va.: Potomac Books, 2002.

———. *Imperial Hubris*. Dulles, Va.: Potomac Books, 2004.

Schweid, Barry. "Aid to Palestinian Projects to Continue." Associated Press, December 22, 2006.

Sharp, Jeremy. "U.S. Foreign Assistance to the Middle East: Historical Background, Recent Trends, and the FY2006 Request." Congressional Research Service, June 13, 2005.

Siegel, Marc. *False Alarm*. Hoboken, N.J.: John Wiley, 2005.

Simpson, Mark. "Martin McGuinness: Sinn Féin." BBC News, March 15, 2001.

Singel, Ryan. "One Million Ways to Die." *Wired News*, September 11, 2006.

Smucker, Philip. "How bin Laden Got Away." *The Christian Science Monitor*, March 4, 2002.

Stalinksky, Steven. "Arab Press Says Jews Perpetrated 9/11 Attacks." *The New York Sun*, August 30, 2006.

Suskind, Ron. *The One Percent Doctrine*. New York: Simon & Schuster, 2006.

U.S. Department of State. "International Religious Freedom Report 2006: Netherlands."

———. "International Religious Freedom Report 2006: Spain."

———. "Saudi Arabia: Country Reports on Human Rights Practices—2003."

U.S. News & World Report. "Sultans' Heir, 'His Majetski.' " May 9, 2005.

Waldman, Amy. "Seething Unease Shaped British Bombers' Newfound Zeal." *The New York Times*, July 31, 2005.

Waller, J. Michael. Testimony before the U.S. Senate Subcommittee on Terrorism, Technology and Homeland Security. October 14, 2003.

Walsh, Declan. "After the Fighting, a Battle for Hope." *The Guardian*, September 25, 2006.

Walsh, John. "Egypt's Muslim Brotherhood." *Harvard International Review*, Winter 2003.

Weisman, Jonathan. "War Costs Approach $10 Billion a Month." *San Francisco Chronicle*, April 20, 2006.

Wilkinson, Isambard. "US Outraged as Pakistan Frees Taliban Fighters." *The Telegraph*, September 15, 2006.

Wilson, Scott. "Hamas Sweeps Palestinian Elections." *The Washington Post*, January 27, 2006.

Wright, Lawrence. *The Looming Tower*. New York: Knopf, 2006.

———. "The Master Plan." *The New Yorker*, September 11, 2006.

NOTES

CHAPTER 1

4 **Americans actually live longer:** Marc Siegel, *False Alarm*, p. 15.

5 **the average American civilian's chances:** Anne Applebaum, "Finding Things to Fear," *The Washington Post*, September 24, 2003.

5 **In that same period, in round numbers:** Ryan Singel, "One Million Ways to Die," *Wired News*, September 11, 2006.

6 **"culture of fear":** Barry Glassner, *The Culture of Fear* (New York: Basic Books, 1999); Frank Furedi, *Politics of Fear* (London: Continuum, 2005).

7 **On the list of 77,069 potential terrorism sites:** Eric Lipton, "Come One, Come All, Join the Terror Target List," *The New York Times*, July 12, 2006.

7 **"largely for show":** James Fallows, "Declaring Victory," *The Atlantic Monthly*, September 2006.

7 **banana:** Eric Lipton and Matthew L. Wald, "Liquid Explosives Still Tough to Detect," *The New York Times*, August 10, 2006.

11 **$10 billion a month:** Jonathan Weisman, "War Costs Approach $10 Billion a Month," *San Francisco Chronicle*, April 20, 2006.

11 **Bush . . . visit to Kabul:** Christopher Griffin, "An Imperiled Mission?," *Armed Forces Journal*, April 2006.

CHAPTER 2

13 *No god but God:* Reza Aslan, *No god but God* (New York: Random House, 2005).

17 **Born in 1957, Osama grew up:** George Mascolo and Erich Follath, "Meet the bin Ladens," *Der Spiegel*, June 6, 2005.

18 **an elite local high school:** Steve Coll, "Young Osama," *The New Yorker*, December 12, 2005.

18 **"Jihad and the rifle alone":** Aslan, *No god but God*, 86.

22 **Sheikh Muhammad Al-Gamei'a:** Seth Lipsky, "A Fair Sheik?," *The Wall Street Journal*, October 24, 2001; Steven Stalinksky, "Arab Press Says Jews Perpetrated 9/11 Attacks," *The New York Sun*, August 30, 2006.

23 **videotaped message:** "Full Transcript of bin Ladin's Speech," Al Jazeera, November 2, 2004.

CHAPTER 3

27 **Steve Coll:** *Ghost Wars* (New York: Penguin, 2004).

28 **a secret list of these funders:** Mascolo and Follath, "Meet the bin Ladens."

32 **Mike Scheuer:** *Through Our Enemies' Eyes* (Dulles, Va.: Potomac Books, 2002); *Imperial Hubris* (Dulles, Va.: Potomac Books, 2004).

33 **the FBI has struggled:** Dan Eggen, "FBI Agents Still Lacking Arabic Skills," *The Washington Post*, October 11, 2006.

35 *The Al-Qaeda Training Manual:* Jerrold M. Post, ed., USAF Counter-proliferation Center, Maxwell Air Force Base (Ala.), 2005.

35 **"The confrontation that Islam calls for":** *The Al-Qaeda Training Manual*, p. 18.

39 **In 1989, FBI agents surveilled:** Mark S. Hamm, "Crimes Committed by Terrorist Groups: Theory, Research and Prevention," report commissioned by the U.S. Department of Justice, September 2005.

39 **a farm in Pennsylvania:** Luke Cyphers and Bruce Feldman, "The Good Son," *ESPN Magazine*, September 16, 2002.

40 **AKE Group:** www.akegroup.com.

CHAPTER 4

45 **Advice and Reform Committee:** Aaron Mannes, "Inadequate Response," *National Review*, July 7, 2005.

45 **he applied for asylum in England:** Daniel McGrory, "The Day When Osama bin Laden Applied for Asylum—in Britain," *The Times* (London), September 29, 2005.

45 **Reza argues:** Aslan, *No god but God*, 255–56.

46 **After the bombings, Zawahiri said:** "Al Qaeda Threatens More UK, U.S. Attacks," CNN, August 4, 2005.

46 **"The Enemy Within" and "Generation Jihad":** Bill Powell, "The Enemy Within," *Time Europe*, October 23, 2005.

47 **November 2006 poll:** Julian Glover, "British Believe Bush Is More Dangerous Than Kim Jong-Il," *The Guardian*, November 3, 2006.

48 **poverty rate among . . . Muslim children:** Bill Powell, "The Enemy Within," *Time Europe*, October 23, 2005.

51 **Two of the 7/7 suicide bombers:** Amy Waldman, "Seething Unease Shaped British Bombers' Newfound Zeal," *The New York Times*, July 31, 2005.

53 **a biography of him:** Liam Clarke and Kathryn Johnston, *Martin McGuinness: From Guns to Government* (Edinburgh and London: Mainstream, 2001), 172–74.

53 **"Britain's Number One Terrorist":** Mark Simpson, "Martin McGuinness: Sinn Féin," BBC News, March 15, 2001.

55 **Good Friday Agreement:** The full text can be found at http://cain.ulst .ac.uk/events/aia/aiadoc.htm.

55 **PIRA had . . . decommissioned:** Dan Hederson and Dan McGinn, "IRA Challenged for 'Holding on to Weapons,' " *The Independent,* February 1, 2006.

55 **"proxy bomb":** Clarke and Johnston, *Martin McGuinness,* 186.

57 **Adams . . . Palestinian Authority:** Owen Bowcott, "Gerry Adams to Meet Hamas Leaders," *The Guardian,* September 4, 2006.

CHAPTER 5

59 **Why are your governments:** "Full Text: 'Bin Laden's Message,' " BBC News, November 12, 2002.

60 **an estimated fifteen million Muslims:** Jytte Klausen, "Counterterrorism and the Integration of Islam in Europe," *Watch on the West,* vol. 7, no. 7, July 2006.

60 **Eurabia:** Jamie Glazov, "Eurabia," FrontPageMagazine.com, September 21, 2004.

60 **Muslims in . . . France:** Jonathan Laurence, "Islam in France," Brookings Institution, December 2001.

60 **Muslims in Spain:** U.S. Department of State, "International Religious Freedom Report 2006: Spain."

60 **Muslims came to Germany:** http://www.germanculture.com.ua/library/ facts/ bl_immigration1.htm.

61 **Muslims . . . the Dutch:** U.S. Department of State, "International Religious Freedom Report 2006: Netherlands."

61 **Malmö:** Steve Harrigan, "Swedes Reach Muslim Breaking Point," Fox News, November 26, 2004.

61 **Theo van Gogh:** Ronald Rovers, "The Silencing of Theo van Gogh," Salon.com, November 24, 2004.

64 **Unemployment runs around 20 percent:** Peter Ford, "Deep Roots of Paris Riots," *The Christian Science Monitor,* November 4, 2005.

CHAPTER 6

80 **Muslim Brotherhood:** John Walsh, "Egypt's Muslim Brotherhood," *Harvard International Review,* Winter 2003.

81 **as a student ... helped found Al-Gama'a al-Islamiyya:** Noah El-Hennawy, "Abdel Monem Abou El-Fotouh," *Egypt Today*, March 2006.

82 **Egypt and Israel get 93 percent:** Jeremy Sharp, "U.S. Foreign Assistance to the Middle East: Historical Background, Recent Trends, and the FY2006 Request," Congressional Research Service, June 13, 2005.

82 **Mubarak:** Martin Asser, "Mubarak's Quarter of a Century," BBC News, October 13, 2006.

87 **"To kill the American":** Bruce Lawrence, ed., *Messages to the World: The Statements of Osama bin Laden* (London: Verso, 2005), 61.

87 **"I have only a few words":** Ibid., 105.

89 **God told *him* to invade Iraq:** Rupert Cornwell, "Bush: God Told Me to Invade Iraq," *The Independent*, October 7, 2005.

91 ***niqab* ... banned:** "Fierce Debate Over Veils in Egypt," Associated Press, October 31, 2006.

CHAPTER 7

98 **King Mohammed VI:** "Sultans' Heir, 'His Majetski,'" *U.S. News & World Report*, May 9, 2005.

98 **"Speedy Mohammed":** Anita McNaught, "The King and the Sheikh's Daughter," BBC News, March 28, 2002.

99 **The young men who dispersed from Sidi Moumen:** "Analysis: May 16, 2003 Suicide Bombings in Casablanca, Morocco," Center for Policing Terrorism.

99 **Salafiya Jihadiya:** Richard A. Clarke et al., *Defeating the Jihadists: A Blueprint for Action*, chapter 3.

100 **Pierre Richard Robert:** J. Michael Waller, testimony before the U.S. Senate Subcommittee on Terrorism, Technology, and Homeland Security, October 14, 2003.

100 **Some of the perps:** Pascale Harter, "Morocco's Shock at Madrid Bomb 'Link,'" BBC News, March 17, 2004.

100 **Zacarias Moussaoui ... assassin of Theo van Gogh:** Carol Migdalovitz, "Morocco: Current Issues," CRS Report for Congress, January 11, 2005.

100 **In an audiotaped message of February 2003:** Lawrence, *Messages to the World*, 183.

100 **Kola Boof:** Kola Boof, "His Prerogative," *Harper's*, September 2006.

101 **more than two thousand people:** Ilhem Rachidi, "Pushing Islam to the Extremes," *Asia Times*, July 1, 2005.

101 **Aboubakr Jamai:** Thomas Lang, "Aboubakr Jamai on Fighting Moroccan Government Censorship," *CJR Daily*, May 20, 2005; Scott MacLeod, "Aboubakr Jamai," *Time Europe*, May 14, 2006.

105 **Aboubakr . . . forced to resign:** "Managing Editor Resigns to Spare His Newspaper Impossible Damages Payment," Reporters Without Borders, January 18, 2007.

107 **Nadia Yassine:** McNaught, "The King and the Sheikh's Daughter"; Magdi Abdelhadi, "Accused Morocco Islamist Speaks Out," BBC News, September 30, 2005.

CHAPTER 8

111 **Jordanian regime is an infidel regime:** Lawrence, *Messages to the World*, 258.

112 **Abu Musab al-Zarqawi . . . claimed responsibility:** Kathleen Ridolfo, "Al-Zarqawi Brings Al-Qaeda's Jihad to Jordan," Radio Free Europe, November 10, 2005.

113 **"Ben and Izzy":** www.benandizzy.com.

116 **Benedict XVI . . . lecture:** Catholic World News, www.cwnews.com/news/viewstory.cfm?recnum=46474.

117 **Hundreds of thousands protested:** "Al Qaeda Threat Over Pope Speech," CNN, September 18, 2006.

121 **"the mother of all causes":** Lawrence, *Messages to the World*, 17.

122 **people of Palestinian heritage live in Jordan:** UNRWA (United Nations Relief and Works Agency for Palestine Refugees in the Near East) figures as of March 31, 2005, www.un.org/unrwa/refugees/jordan.html.

130 *one million . . .* **seeking asylum:** Human Rights Watch, "The Silent Treatment: Fleeing Iraq, Surviving in Jordan," November 28, 2006, www.hrw.org/reports/2006/jordan1106/2.htm#_Toc151445620.

135 **Fouad Hussein:** Lawrence Wright, "The Master Plan," *The New Yorker*, September 11, 2006.

137 **Al Qaeda . . . seven phases:** Yassin Musharbash, "The Future of Terrorism," *Der Spiegel*, August 12, 2005.

CHAPTER 9

140 **We are in a strong and brutal battle:** Lawrence, *Messages to the World*, 126.

140 **Our terrorism against America:** Ibid., 152.

142 **Rabbis for Human Rights:** www.rhr.israel.net/projects/oliveharvest_english.shtml.

143 **Between September 2000 and the spring of 2006:** Jimmy Carter, *Palestine: Peace Not Apartheid* (New York: Simon & Schuster), chapter 17.

145 **Hamas had won a landslide:** Scott Wilson, "Hamas Sweeps Palestinian Elections," *The Washington Post*, January 27, 2006.

145 **In 2006 . . . to Israel:** Barry Schweid, "Aid to Palestinian Projects to Continue," Associated Press, December 22, 2006.

145 **Tensions between Abbas and his Hamas:** Robert Berger, "Abbas Mulls Next Move as Unity Talks with Hamas Collapse," Voice of America, December 1, 2006.

150 **"land grab":** Lipka Pelham, "Finding Holes in West Bank Barrier," BBC News, November 30, 2006.

150 **Jimmy Carter:** Carter, *Palestine*, 185.

CHAPTER 10

156 **attacks in Israel:** www.mfa.gov.il/MFA/Terrorism-%20Obstacle%20to%20Peace/Palestinian%20terror%20since%202000/Suicide%20and%20Other%20Bombing%20Attacks%20in%20Israel%20Since

162 **Ali Jiddah:** Janey McMahon, "For Security Reasons," *Washington Report on Middle East Affairs*, September 1998.

163 **Jews, who had been the largest group:** Mitchell G. Bard, "Myths & Facts Online: Jerusalem," Jewish Virtual Library, www.jewishvirtuallibrary.org/jsource/myths/mf20.html#k.

164 **1985 . . . exchange of prisoner:** Samar Assad, "A History of Israeli-Palestinian Prisoner Exchanges," *CounterPunch*, July 14–17, 2006.

172 **Israel arrested sixty-four Hamas MPs:** Carter, *Palestine*, 197–98.

CHAPTER 11

175 **The greatest disaster to befall:** Lawrence, *Messages to the World*, 25.

178 **Women's rights:** "Saudi Arabia: Country Reports on Human Rights Practices—2003," U.S. Department of State.

178 **I look at the statistics in the United States:** National Coalition Against Domestic Violence, www.ncadv.org.

179 **fifteen students . . . died:** "Saudi Police 'Stopped' Fire Rescue," BBC News, March 15, 2002.

180 **"throats must be slit and skulls must be shattered":** Middle East Research Institute TV Monitor Project, http://memritv.org/Search.asp?ACT=S9&P1=445.

180 **unemployment rate:** Robert Looney, "Can Saudi Arabia Reform Its Economy in Time to Head Off Disaster?," *Strategic Insights*, January 2004.

181 **"It is proven, O King":** www.answers.com/topic/open-letter-to-king-fahd-from-bin-laden.

181 **Al Qaeda operative Yusef al-Ayeri:** Ron Suskind, *The One Percent Doctrine*, pp. 146, 217–18, 235–36.

181 **Prince Turki al-Faisal:** Coll, *Ghost Wars,* chapter 4 and pp. 400–402.
197 **Abdullah Thabit:** Faiza Saleh Ambah, "The Would-Be Terrorist's Explosive Tell-All Tale," *The Washington Post,* July 24, 2006.

CHAPTER 12

203 **I miss my country greatly:** Lawrence, *Messages to the World,* 258.
208 **"a land in which I could breathe":** Ibid., 50.
208 **"the ruler and rightful commander":** Ibid., 91.
208 **"the Zionist-Crusaders alliance and their collaborators":** PBS, www.pbs.org/newshour/terrorism/international/fatwa_1996.html.
208 **"to kill the Americans and their allies":** Lawrence, *Messages to the World,* 61.
208 **John Miller interviewed Osama:** PBS, www.pbs.org/wgbh/pages/frontline/shows/binladen/who/interview.html.
209 **The CIA developed several plans:** Coll, *Ghost Wars,* chapter 21.
210 **roughly forty thousand U.S. and NATO:** Fisnik Abrashi and Jason Straziuso, "Afghanistan Five Years Later: Poverty, Violence, Misery," Associated Press, October 7, 2006.
210 **Taliban . . . poppy production:** Ibid.

CHAPTER 13

223 **Operation Medusa:** Declan Walsh, "After the Fighting, a Battle for Hope," *The Guardian,* September 25, 2006.

CHAPTER 14

232 **What is unfolding now in Afghanistan:** Lawrence, *Messages to the World,* 143.
238 **National Guard . . . active duty overseas:** "Reserves, National Guard Feel Strain," Associated Press, December 16, 2006.
239 **stop-loss:** Iraq and Afghanistan Veterans of America (IAVA), www.iava.org/index.php?option=content&task=view&id=47&Itemid=66.
243 **Osama . . . multiple wives:** Lawrence Wright, *The Looming Tower,* 72–82.
243 **Abdullah [bin Laden]:** Steve Coll, "Young Osama," *The New Yorker,* December 12, 2005.
243 **the extended bin Laden and Zawahiri families:** Wright, *The Looming Tower,* 250–55.
244 **In Kandahar, he once took over a former movie theater:** Ibid., 333–34.

244 **Saad [bin Laden]:** Douglas Farah and Dana Priest, "Bin Laden Son Plays Key Role in Al Qaeda," *The Washington Post*, October 14, 2003; "Iran Sheltering Bin Laden Sons and Al-Qaeda Members," Agence France-Presse, October 26, 2005.

CHAPTER 15

247 **General Gul Haider:** Anthony Loyd and Tahir Luddin, "The Face of Afghanistan Five Years After Fall of the Taleban," *The Times* (London), November 11, 2006.

249 **since the 1980s:** Ahmed Rashid, "US Support for Northern Alliance Rankles Pakistan," The Eisenhower Institute, October 22, 2001.

250 **Mullah Abdul Salam Zaeef:** "No Law at Guantánamo Bay Prison, Says Zaeef," *Daily Times* (Pakistan), September 17, 2005.

CHAPTER 16

257 **We will not let Pakistan:** Lawrence, *Messages to the World*, 143.

258 **magnet for war refugees:** "Afghanistan: Refugees from Afghanistan: The World's Largest Single Refugee Group," Amnesty International, November 1, 1999.

260 **"For it is a duty, as you well know":** Lawrence, *Messages to the World*, 97.

260 **Madrassa Darul Uloom Haqqania:** Jeffrey Goldberg, "Inside Jihad U.," *The New York Times*, June 25, 2000; Noreen S. Ahmed-Ullah and Kim Barker, "Schooled in Jihad," *Chicago Tribune*, November 28, 2004.

265 **students gathered in Islamabad:** Jeremy Page, "Pakistani Hardliners 'Cleanse' Capital Taleban-Style," *The Times* (London), April 7, 2007.

266 **two thousand lawyers:** Kamran Haider, "Thousands Protest Over Move to Sack Pakistani Judge," Reuters, April 3, 2007.

268 **Not long after the Taliban appeared:** Coll, *Ghost Wars*, chapter 16.

269 **"Talibanistan":** Bill Roggio, "Talibanistan: The Establishment of the Islamic Emirate of Waziristan," *The Fourth Rail*, September 5, 2006.

269 **releasing some 2,500 prisoners:** Isambard Wilkinson, "US Outraged as Pakistan Frees Taliban Fighters," *The Telegraph*, September 15, 2006.

269 **Israeli-style security fence:** Robert Birsel, "Pakistan's Afghan Border Fence Plan 'Impractical,' " Reuters, December 27, 2006; M. Ilyas Khan, "Will Pakistan's Fence Plan Work?," BBC News, January 4, 2007.

CHAPTER 17

275 **Your security:** "Bin Laden: 'Your Security Is in Your Own Hands,' " CNN.com, October 29, 2004.

275 **madrassa . . . blown to bits:** "Americans Bombed the Bajaur Madrassa," *Daily Times* (Pakistan), November 27, 2006.

Morgan Spurlock is an award-winning writer, producer, and director. A graduate of NYU's Tisch School of the Arts, Spurlock directed and starred in *Super Size Me*, one of the highest-grossing documentaries of all time. That movie earned him an Oscar nomination in the Best Documentary Feature category, Best Director at the Sundance and Edinburgh film festivals, Best Documentary from the New York Film Critics Circle Online, and Best Documentary nominations from the National Board of Review and The Broadcast Film Critics Association. Spurlock has also produced documentary films such as *What Would Jesus Buy?* and the acclaimed television show *30 Days*, which airs on FX. He is the author of one previous book, *Don't Eat This Book: Fast Food and the Supersizing of America*. He lives in New York with his wife, Alex.

ABOUT THE TYPE

The text of this book was set in Janson, a misnamed typeface designed in about 1690 by Nicholas Kis, a Hungarian in Amsterdam. In 1919 the matrices became the property of the Stempel Foundry in Frankfurt. It is an old-style book face of excellent clarity and sharpness. Janson serifs are concave and splayed; the contrast between thick and thin strokes is marked.